SURVIVE AND THRIVE IN ACADEMIA

A pocket mentor for the early career academic learning to strategically navigate the demands of an academic role, this book is a friendly and constructive companion providing hands-on advice about how to balance teaching responsibilities alongside other duties. More than just a 'how to', the text is a timely commentary on changes in higher education. Discussing contemporary developments and offering guidance on how to negotiate this evolving climate, the book uniquely captures the political, social, economic and cultural forces at play, taking into account the issues which influence and shape an academic's career trajectory.

Organised around the three main tasks within a conventional academic post – teaching, research and administration – the book includes tips, pauses for thought, author reflections and sources for further reading, and provides insight to help the reader reflect on what they are doing, why, and where to go next in their career. Crucially, it shows that in order to survive and flourish, the early career academic needs to take a strategic view as to their function, purpose and contribution both inside and beyond the intellectual establishment.

From establishing a research niche to getting stuck into administration *Survive and Thrive in Academia* empowers the early career academic, helping them to build their academic reputation both internally and externally and maintain a sense of personal fulfilment and accomplishment within an increasingly commercialised higher education environment.

Kate Woodthorpe is Senior Lecturer in Sociology at the University of Bath, UK and is a Fellow of the Higher Education Academy.

SURVIVE AND THRIVE IN ACADEMIA

The New Academic's Pocket Mentor

Kate Woodthorpe

LONDON AND NEW YORK

First published 2018
by Routledge
2 Park Square, Milton Park, Abingdon, Oxon OX14 4RN

and by Routledge
711 Third Avenue, New York, NY 10017

Routledge is an imprint of the Taylor & Francis Group, an informa business

© 2018 Kate Woodthorpe

The right of Kate Woodthorpe to be identified as author of this work has been asserted by her in accordance with sections 77 and 78 of the Copyright, Designs and Patents Act 1988.

All rights reserved. No part of this book may be reprinted or reproduced or utilised in any form or by any electronic, mechanical, or other means, now known or hereafter invented, including photocopying and recording, or in any information storage or retrieval system, without permission in writing from the publishers.

Trademark notice: Product or corporate names may be trademarks or registered trademarks, and are used only for identification and explanation without intent to infringe.

British Library Cataloguing-in-Publication Data
A catalogue record for this book is available from the British Library

Library of Congress Cataloging-in-Publication Data
A catalog record has been requested for this book

ISBN: 978-1-138-04865-2 (hbk)
ISBN: 978-1-138-04866-9 (pbk)
ISBN: 978-1-315-17005-3 (ebk)

Typeset in Interstate
by Apex CoVantage, LLC

For all those embarking on their academic career.
Remember to enjoy the journey.

CONTENTS

Foreword — ix
Acknowledgements — xiii

1 The university workplace — 1

SECTION 1 TEACHING — 25

2 The context in which you teach — 27
3 Finding your feet — 51
4 Behind the scenes of teaching — 81

SECTION 2 RESEARCH — 107

5 Establishing your niche — 109
6 Building critical mass — 136
7 Beyond the ivory towers — 159

SECTION 3 ADMINISTRATION, MANAGEMENT AND LEADERSHIP — 175

8 Getting stuck in — 177

| 9 | **Leadership beyond your institution** | 198 |
| 10 | **Your journey ahead** | 213 |

| *Index* | 235 |

FOREWORD

As an early career academic embarking on your research or teaching post, first lectureship, or as someone hoping to become an early career academic, it is all too easy to feel overwhelmed as you join, or prepare to join, the lower ranks of the academic hierarchy. You may arrive at this juncture with a wealth of experience gained from a different sector, or having just finished an intensive period of doctoral study. Whatever your origins, what lies in wait for you is a varied and at times contrary role that requires navigation as you take the step up or sideways from being a student, a practitioner, or a professional in another field.

Joining higher education as an academic is certainly a very exciting time, one that is full of potential. Although the organisation, funding and priorities of contemporary universities has changed exponentially over the last few years, the academic role – for now – retains an amount of autonomy and self-determination that is hard to find elsewhere. This level of self-rule is most visibly reflected in research and teaching employment contracts, where there are often no specified contracted hours of work: you work until the job is done. Sometimes throughout the academic year such flexibility will mean times of overload and stress, at others it will mean you are given considerable freedom over how you spend your time, and where. Unlike many other forms of employment, including those within a university, as an academic you do not clock in and out, and even if you are required to specify the days you are working 'in the office' or at home (as some institutions expect) you do not have a set lunch break, nor are you expected to sit at your desk to 'prove' you are working.

Such liberty is wonderful but without clear boundaries it can be accompanied with the risk of exhaustion and, if not addressed, burnout. As an academic you are expected to manage your own time, your own responsibilities, and your short, medium and long-term goals. You are simultaneously working for an institution while also building up and trading on your academic 'name'. Success and failure is in the higher education sector is typically highly individualised and as a result you can find yourself carrying responsibilities alone, with no one able or willing to step in when you are overloaded, struggling or suddenly experiencing a diverting urgent priority. You are simply expected to use those prioritising and time management skills – simultaneously a privilege and a burden – to get the work completed to a satisfactory level, and on time. From the very outset you are expected to know *what* to prioritise and *how* to do so, with little preparation.

This pocket mentoring guide is intended to be a friendly and constructive companion as you learn how to navigate your academic life. Some parts of it will resonate with you more strongly than others depending on your life experience, your role and your employer. As you start reading my hope is that you have supportive colleagues and an excellent line manager that you can turn to in tough times, to help you cope and importantly to *learn* to cope with the demands of the job. Some people reading this book will be in such an environment, and may find descriptions later in the book of atomised working at odds with their own experience. If that is the case, celebrate and learn from how your department or faculty is working well. Who or what enabled that? What is the culture of the working environment? What are your colleagues saying about job fulfilment, satisfaction, workloads and so on?

Alternatively, you may be in an environment where a 'sink or swim' mentality and culture is rife. You may have been told to 'publish or perish', seen colleagues fail probation, or witnessed disillusioned, cynical and burned out senior colleagues leave for pastures new, sometimes telling you and others how awful the institution you have just joined is. To them, and to those of you working in those environments, it is for you to say thank you for the opportunity to learn and let's make the most of this chance so that I can (1) maintain my integrity and (2) make sure that I am on an upward trajectory that does not confine me to this institution.

Whether you are in a well or poorly functioning department, faculty or university, I hope this book is useful. Its aim is to act as a supportive comrade throughout the early phase of your academic career as you encounter institutional culture and expectations, learn how to balance the differing demands of the role, and build up your academic reputation both internally and externally. It is organised around the three main tasks within a conventional academic post: teaching, research and administration, and includes tips, pauses for thought and author reflections so that you have the opportunity to stop, reflect, plan, and learn.

Depending on your contract of employment, some parts of the book may be more relevant to you than others, so use it as you see fit and according to need. Read it from start to finish, or pick out chapters and sections as you feel they are appropriate. Please, do not regard or treat the book as another weighty task to complete – the last thing I want is for this book to add to your workload! Instead, regard it as a handy mentor, providing insight that may help you reflect on what you are doing and why, and where you are going in your career. Use the tips sections embedded within chapters to act. Use the pause for thought sections for reflection on the context(s) in which you work, your goals and ambitions, how you approach your role and what you can learn from others. Use the author reflection sections to learn what may, or may not, work. Use the sources at the end of each chapter to explore further reading.

At its heart, the book aims to empower you and endow you with a better understanding of how the higher education sector works, and what that means for the everyday work of the early career academic.

December 2017

ACKNOWLEDGEMENTS

I have been very fortunate over the years to have received words of wisdom from many colleagues for which I am profoundly grateful. A special note of thanks must go to Jenny Hockey, Carol Komaromy, Jane Seymour, Tess Ridge, Ian Butler, Louise Brown, Joe Devine, Tony Walter, Sarah Moore, Tina Skinner, Liam Foster, Christine Valentine, Jaime Waters, Allan Kellehear, Lucy Easthope, Kathy Almack, Paula Smith, Caron Staley and Lesley McKay.

Thanks to my departmental colleagues now and over the last decade for being genuinely nice people to work with, and for providing a supportive environment in the early, formative years of my career.

A big thank you to Hannah Rumble for being a friend and excellent colleague, and for proofing part of this book. Special thanks too to Ruth Penfold-Mounce and Stuart Coles, for providing insight on parts of this book.

Thanks to Sarah Tuckwell and the team at Routledge for their editorial support.

Thanks to my parents for always believing in me and instilling in me the confidence to go for a PhD and academic post in the first place.

And finally, thank you to my husband and children, who keep my feet on the ground and remind me every day of what is truly important in life. I have days when I love my job, and I have days when I don't. Throughout it all, my family are my constant and I am so very lucky to have them.

1 The university workplace

So, how did you get to this point? What is the appeal of working in academia? And how do you fit into the sector? In this introductory chapter, my objective is to provide important context on the social, economic and political changes that shape and shift the purpose, organisation, and function of the contemporary university institution. The chapter aims to provide perspective, and an opportunity to (re)set the scene for you, the early career academic, enabling you to identify and position *yourself* within the enormous juggernaut that is the global higher education (HE) sector.

In order to do so, the chapter provides an overview of the shifts that have occurred in HE in the last few decades. Following on from this it identifies some of the very real implications of these shifts for the everyday work of the early career academic, thereby setting the tone for what follows. As part of its scene setting function, the chapter introduces the rest of the book at its end.

Current trends

As you will observe in other parts of this book, I do not wish to repeat or rehash the already very well written texts on key areas of academic life, such as how to lecture. In the same vein, I do not intend in this opening chapter to document the origins of the modern university, nor focus on the neoliberal rationalisation of HE. These have been articulately accounted for elsewhere and I have provided references to useful texts at the end of this chapter if you wish to engage with this material. No, for this chapter and the rest of the book, I want to provide a contemporary focus on what life in academia is like *now* for an early career academic and how you can survive and thrive in this environment. However, in order to do so I need to explain briefly in

2 The university workplace

this chapter some of the changes that have occurred since the start of the twenty-first century.

Various terms are used to describe change that has taken place and continues apace in academia and universities, for example: massification, corporatisation, vocationalisation, commercialisation, privatisation, quantification, metricisation, monetisation and so on. Much of these phrases have been, and continue to be used, to summarise the expansion of HE both in the UK and around the world.

Included in this expansion of HE is a diversification of degree subjects, a growth in the number of undergraduate students, and changes the way in which knowledge production within HE institutions is framed, valued and assessed internally and externally. In what follows in this chapter, the intention is not to expand, intellectualise or particularly critique these terms, as this has been done eloquently elsewhere. Rather, the aim is to set the scene for the context(s) in which you can find yourself working as an early career academic, and some of the very real consequences for your role(s) and responsibilities. In other words, its purpose is to establish the social, cultural, economic and political background in which you are employed, and upon which the remainder of the book is based.

Marketisation

One of the most popular ways of examining HE today, marketisation refers to the infusion of market forces into universities. Underpinned by neoliberalism, these market forces have been shaped by changes in funding structures and sources, positioning universities and their staff in competition with one another for resources, and students as consumers of their educational 'product'. Brown (2011a: 1-2) neatly summarises two opposing views of marketisation in HE as follows:

Table 1.1

Proponents	Opponents
- Increased resources	- Increased stratification of institutions and the groups they serve
- Institutions more responsive to meeting student needs	- Loss of institutional diversity
- Greater flexibility, innovation and receptivity to change	- Ever more divided academic community
- Incentives to raise standards	- Detrimental to quality
- Incentives to attend to costs and make best use of resources	- Less autonomy
- Offers best value for society	- Reinforces the marketisation of society

In order to better understand how market forces can shape the organisation of HE, drawing on Jongbloed's (2003) model of freedoms to identify an HE market, Brown (2011b) outlines the eight conditions required for a market to operate, separated into providers and consumers as follows:

Table 1.2

Providers	Consumers
1. Freedom of entry for new providers	5. Freedom to choose provider
2. Freedom of suppliers to specify the product	6. Freedom to choose degree
3. Freedom to choose and deploy resources	7. Freedom of information to make above choices
4. Freedom to set prices	8. Cost-covering prices paid directly (tuition fees and living costs)

If this model of an HE market were to operate, Brown posits, there would be little – if any – role for the state or academics in establishing the quality and quantity of HE provision. With little market regulation, in this vision students would exercise consumer choice and institutions would thrive or wither on their ability to attract and retain those students.

Yet in HE, Brown notes that as "no major developed system currently fulfils these criteria [it] takes us into 'market failure'" (2011b: 9). The factors that indicate some form of market failure in HE, he suggests, are monopolies of power, information asymmetry, and imbalance in the benefits and costs of some products – that is, those products that are regarded as 'public goods' (good that are a net benefit to society) but may be unattractive to the provider because of their prohibitive cost. An example of this within HE is costly degrees and research that requires expensive facilities (for example, science and engineering subjects that require extensive and often pricey laboratory and test centre space), but which may be of great technological and economic benefit in terms of what the student(s) and researcher(s) studying them may potentially contribute to society.

Problems with markets can lead to state intervention, which in turn can create a 'non-market' whereby prices and numbers are closely regulated; there are high barriers to entry; there is limited information about quality; and where quality is determined via self-regulation by the state and the academy. Brown (2011b) warns however, that non-markets too can fail, owing to "the absence of mechanisms for reconciling calculations by decision makers of their private and organizational costs and benefits with the

4 The university workplace

costs and benefits to society as a whole" (p. 13). In terms of where this leaves HE, it is neither fully at the whim of market forces, nor does it operate as a non-market. In the UK this means it is in flux in terms of an institution's autonomy, its ability to respond to market forces, and the conditions imposed on it by the state.

> **Pause for thought**
>
> What are the current state interventions or political debates that are shaping HE at the time of reading? Regulation? Managing competition? The scrapping, capping or introduction of tuition fees? The funnelling of funds to specific areas of research?

Such flux, at worst, can translate into lack of clarity of vision and mission at an institutional level. It can also lead to a permeation of corporate values and discourse within HE, which you will find orbiting around you as you commence your career. These are, as Brown (2011c, p. 50) argues, potentially the biggest challenge to HE and those working in it.

> The biggest threat to liberal higher education appears to come from the increasing interpretation of the values and practices of business and commerce. These are already blurring the boundaries of the academy and pose a potentially serious threat to its long standing and generally beneficial (for both sides) relationship with society.

Commercial values and practice are having a profound effect on the functioning, funding and organisation of universities, and are increasingly politicised as questions are raised about the role of the state in overseeing university priorities, budgets, student fees and research agendas. Demands are made that universities provide 'value for money' and that academics contribute something of 'value' to the economy and society more broadly. But what constitutes 'value' is habitually poorly defined and open to debate. For example, value in HE could be regarded according to:

- The teaching and contact hours a student receives on their degree;
- The balance between teaching quality and research outputs;
- The utility or blue-skies potential of research;
- The economic need of a particular degree programme;

- The societal worth of a particular degree programme (which may not have much economic need!);
- The fostering of independence and resilience in the next generation;
- The engagement with different publics to influence and affect change.

With the creep of commercial values and practice into universities, perceptions of 'value' in HE are increasingly conceptualised according to economic and corporate imperatives (O'Leary, 2017). As a result universities are expected to demonstrate their economic contribution to society, measured in, for example, the number of graduate students in employment six months after graduating and their starting salaries. This position overlooks or downright neglects important founding principles such as the role of HE in fostering resilience and fortitude, independence, and the development of transferable and soft skills, such as written and spoken communication (see chapter 9).

Corporatisation

Corporatisation is a regularly used phrase to describe the corporate imperatives that have permeated HE and university expansion within the last couple of decades. These imperatives have shifted emphasis onto discernible results that can be used to explain and account for monetary investment and productivity pound per pound – whether that investment comes from students, the taxpayer or commercial interests. Through this process of corporatisation the funding and regulation of HE has become a policy concern in order to ensure best 'value' for money (Hazelkorn, 2016) that is assessed according to visible and often commercial criteria for success.

> Increasingly, the public is calling for 'relevance' and 'accountability', and the modernist scholar is being asked to provide compelling material justifications for his or her scholarship, especially in times of severe economic downturn. And as funding is tied to programs that produce tangible and immediate results, the traditional idea of the university is giving way to the results-orientated mandate which sees the modern university being run by CEOs or those trained in their methods, and which hears the language of business in discussions of departmental budgets while witnessing the replacement of non-instrumental decision-making practices with rational business models.
>
> (Côté and Allahar, 2011: 17)

Although this instrumentalism is not confined solely to the management of universities, and will be considered again in chapter 2 in relation to new millennial students, it is important to reflect on what these tangible and immediate results might look like, and the pressures they can create. In terms of a university's 'outputs', quantifiable and measurable indicators of success can include:

- The number of applicants per student place;
- The retention of students in year one;
- The proportion of top-rated degree classifications;
- The student evaluation of teaching quality and facilities;
- The number and ranking of academic peer reviewed publications;
- The monetary value of research income.

All of these indicators can be, and are, used to determine the 'quality' of an institution, made manifest in and perpetuated by national and international league tables. As Côté and Allahar go on to note, with this idea of quality,

> the factory or customer service industry comes to mind and suggests such things as quality control, client satisfaction, and product inspectors. University campuses, on the other hand, do not lend themselves quite so easily to quality considerations and their measurements, for scholarship and learning do not always have clear quantifiable ends in mind.
> (Côté and Allahar, 2011, p. 18)

Herein lies one of the key tensions at the heart of contemporary HE: a misalignment between indicators of quality based on corporate models of productivity and measurement, and the purpose and principle of the individual and societal value of learning, which cannot always be anticipated in advance nor quantified.

> **Pause for thought**
>
> How does your current/prospective employer/institution identify measures of success? Are there 'key performance indicators' or targets for research and teaching? If not, what are the institution's specified goals? How are these articulated by senior management?

Quantification

'Metricisation' (Burrows, 2012) and the quantifying of quality has become the norm within HE, both in teaching and research. While the mechanisms through which quality is assessed will be dealt with in more detail in subsequent chapters, for now it is important to note that an intense and continued assessment of perceived quality in teaching and research is both time-consuming and inhibiting, and fosters a competitive working environment. Your teaching evaluations and peer reviewed journal outputs (to name but two of the tasks that are measured) come under ever increasing scrutiny and are measured against your colleagues, creating an atmosphere where anything less than a stellar evaluation or output can equate to 'improvement required'. Such evaluation removes the context in which teaching is provided and received, and research produced, and moves individuals and departments away from collaboration and cooperation towards an environment of comparison and competition (Watermayer and Olssen, 2016).

A consequence of a fixation and prioritisation of measurement and metrics is that early career academics (and more senior ones) can become risk-averse, as they engage in teaching and research that they know will be either well-received or at least *less* problematically received. For example, teaching continues using long-established methods and on what are perceived to be student-friendly, 'popular' topics so that students do not complain and/or evaluate the teacher and institution poorly. Research areas become less ambitious, less innovative and, as Back (2016) notes, increasingly specialised as academics seek to limit the risk of their research funding bids and peer reviewed papers being unsuccessful.

This move towards risk-averse academic practice is in direct contrast to some of *the* central pursuits of the academic. These include:

- To innovate, to create new knowledge and fresh perspectives;
- To foster individuality and resilience in the next generation of students, encouraging them to take risks in their learning of and about the world around them;
- To support others in the development of ideas, and
- To provide an independent outlook on, and solutions to, the historical, political, economic, social and technological developments of the day.

Given this divergence in purpose and practice it is little wonder that as you commence your academic career you may well hear more seasoned academics talk about the conflict and inner turmoil they experience as they feel the pressure to ensure that their research and teaching conforms to the metrics of quality of the day.

The rise of league tables

The intensification of measurement of teaching and research quality has led to, and been led by, an increased reliance and value placed on league tables (such as, in the UK, the *Times/Sunday Times* league table and the competing *Guardian* league table) as a way of positioning institutions in rank order. So readily accepted are league tables as a way of determining 'the best' and 'the poorest' universities that there is very little public critique of either their composition or their usefulness, with most attention paid to those at the top and little recognition of the complexity of HE and changing geography (Hazelkorn, 2016). As Collini puts it:

> [league tables] are readily cited for publicity and propaganda, yet the truth is that *they are practically worthless*. On many matters the data are not available in strictly comparable form, and the use of subjective and inadequate opinion surveys, such as the 'student satisfaction' survey, provides little information that is both reliable and useful.
> (Collini, 2012: 17, emphasis added)

Collini goes on to sum up the consequence of this eloquently which I cannot hope to paraphrase it better, so is quoted in full here:

> The significance attributed to these largely vacuous exercises indicates the conjunction of two forces which bear directly on the discussion of the role of universities. The first is the glib assumption that universities are locked in combat with each other in some form of worldwide competition, itself a transposition of larger assertions about the centrality of national economic competitiveness. The language here betrays a kind of mercantilism of the intellect, a fear that the stock of national treasure will be diminished rather than augmented by the success of enterprises elsewhere. It is remarkable how quickly and easily this language has become naturalised in the past two or three decades, even though it is damaging to the intrinsically cooperative nature of all science and scholarship. The second force is the growing distrust of reasoned argument, now often seen as either a cloak for special interests

or a form of elitist arrogance, and the substitution in its place of any kind of indicator that can plausibly be reduced to numerical terms.

(p. 17)

The artificial competition created by such a commercial approach to academics and students has led to a national and international 'market' for research and education, stifling cooperation, collegiality and collaboration – unless there is a net benefit to the collaborator. Moreover, as Collini notes, competition and rankings perpetuate a sense that success and outputs within universities can be reduced to numbers and statistics, whether they are:

- The quality of papers based on a rating;
- Research income;
- Staff student ratios;
- Employment after graduation.

Such quantification belies the vitality of what goes into teaching and research; it conceals efforts that cannot be quantified; and it negates the way in which education and research is utilised beyond the yearly figures.

The extent to which an institution embraces any or all of these imperatives can often be found in its mission statement or overarching strategies that set out the longer-term priorities of the university.

> **Tip**
>
> Whether you are searching for a job or currently employed, it is worthwhile researching the stated mission of the institution you (want to) work for. What does the mission statement indicate is valued within that institution? Are there any other institutions that have a mission statement that resonates with you?

Where does this then leave the modern university and how you work within it? Right now, it leaves institutions in something of an identity crisis as they try to cover as many bases as possible: as education providers; as employee trainers; as intellectual powerhouses; as economic and technological innovators; as entrepreneurs; as knowledge brokers; and as policy guiders. It further leaves them with a case of 'Champions League syndrome' (Collini, 2012: 18) where the 'best' universities are regarded as 'competing' with others around the world which, as Collini posits, needs to be treated with caution, if not downright scepticism.

You, and every other early career academic, are in effect a tiny cog within this global and increasingly corporatised HE machine. When put in this context, while there are some parts of the job that you can and *should* affect, there are momentous forces that are outside your control that can dictate the direction and focus of your employer and subsequently your employment within it.

Although this sounds like a rather defeatist position, it is not to say that you cannot professionally try to influence that direction and focus, nor personally celebrate or rage against it. You may choose to get involved in your local trade union and campaign vigorously against these changes in HE. You may embark on a career journey in academic leadership that means that you have a say over the direction of an institution or the sector overall. You may opt to 'knuckle down' and disengage from the political and economic pressures that determine and shape the provision of education and status of academic research. Whatever you choose to do, what is important is that you can put your contribution to academia and HE *in perspective* and concentrate on the areas that *can* be shaped, influenced and controlled at any given time. It is about you exploring your own priorities and boundaries, about learning when to 'stick your head over the parapet' and when to let events wash over you. Indeed, these are the principle aims of this book:

- To (re)claim the areas of your work that can be influenced;
- To focus on sources of fulfilment within the role and the areas to which you are accountable, and
- To identify personal strengths, priorities and areas for development.

In this way the book is unashamedly focused on you, the individual. It could be critiqued for an emphasis on personal satisfaction rather than critique of and resistance towards the forces that shape the environment in which the early career academic works. If you wish to find that type of critique then there are some fantastic resources out there, some of which are listed at the end of this chapter. Rather, this book is intended to be a *tool* to enable you to navigate these contexts, to help you consider which battles to fight, and to enable you to feel confident and secure in your journey, purpose and contribution to HE and society more broadly. It is driven by my own personal commitment to supporting colleagues, sharing the ethos of Berg and Seeber (2016: ix) who maintain that "those of us in tenured positions, given the protection we enjoy, have an obligation to try to improve in our own ways the working climate for all of us".

Given the remit of this book, where do these economic and political contexts leave the early career academic? And what are the consequences? What is your purpose, function, and how does this shape your 'job' and professional role, both within the university and externally? And how does this book seek to help you navigate these contexts?

Some of the major influencers and shapers of the early career academic's experience

In the early years of your academic career there will be a number of influential features of the HE workplace that will shape your experience:

Performance management

A key impact of changes to HE has been the intensification of performance management, as the output of staff within the institution comes under increasing pressure and scrutiny to demonstrate 'value for money'. As a result, academics at all levels are expected to perform excellently in all facets of their role: research, teaching and administration. Publishing in highly ranked journals (see chapter 5); bringing in research funding (see chapter 6); providing teaching that is robust and highly rated by students (see chapter 4); while also ensuring that a tight ship is being run (see chapter 8) - with ever widening goalposts in all these areas - means that the academic role has extended exponentially over the last two decades. Moreover, such changes mean that working in a university as an academic is now comparable to any other large organisation, with your performance increasingly under surveillance via measurement techniques that are both internal via appraisals and external via the measurement of research and teaching quality (Collini, 2012). In the UK these external assessors of quality are currently called the Teaching Excellence Framework (see chapter 4) and the Research Excellence Framework (see chapter 5).

A move towards performance management nullifies, at least in part, the long held idea that academics are not working 'in the real world', as they are subject to the same neoliberal forces and expectations regarding productivity and utility. What is different is that knowledge production and utilisation can be very difficult to quantify. This has not however prevented ideas and intellectual contribution(s) to society being ever more appraised as a representation of the societal worth and added value of academia, as noted earlier in this chapter.

Such a shift towards quantification and measurement of intellectual work has monumental consequences for the early career academic in terms of how your work is valued, regarded, prioritised, promoted and used, all of which can be detrimental or fantastically rewarding depending on your discipline, topic area, and the popular social, political and economic issues of the moment. If your discipline or specialist area is 'on the up' (for example, at the time of writing if you are working on issues related to on climate change, migration, land sustainability, ageing, and any other 'hot' topic right now) then you are in a much stronger position than a colleague working in a smaller field or specialist area that is not quite as 'hot'.

At the same time, being in a 'hot' field or one that is regarded as 'important' does not automatically equate to accomplishment and success. It can mean that finding your niche can be difficult, particularly when it comes to convincing research funders that your work is novel, or at least different to the litany of work being produced by your peers who are potentially much more established and have track records of achievement.

In such a capricious environment regarding what is 'important' to society, in the early days of your career, when trying to build up a record of success, you can find yourself compromised in how your intellectual pursuits develop. Do you, for example, attach yourself and your work to the latest social, political, economic and technological trends or do you pursue your own interests regardless? Indeed, is that second option even possible? Do you want to be an academic superstar in a relatively small field, or a relatively small star in a large one? When do you need to make that decision, if ever? And even if you make that decision who or what might pull the rug from under you at any moment? Are there any risks to being in a large or small field?

> **Pause for thought**
>
> What type of academic do you want to be – do you want to be a superstar big fish in a small pond, or a little fish in a big pond? Does being a good citizen of a department appeal to you? Why? This will be covered in more detail in chapter 5 when thinking about research priorities and networking.

> **Author reflection**
>
> I write this based on my experience of being a sociologist who specialises in death and dying. Sociology as a discipline is nowhere near as large as, for example, Psychology. As a result there are less journals in which to publish,[1] fewer colleagues to cite your work and so on. On top of this, my area is often regarded as 'niche' – even though death is one of the very few universal truths of life. There are a handful of journals that specialise on the topic, and the academic community is very small. It is thus possible to 'rise to the top' faster perhaps than colleagues working in more populated disciplines and/or specialist areas, but there is less room for collaboration, sharing good practice and publishing; and there is almost always the need to make the case for *why* death requires attention when it is an 'unfamiliar' topic for most peer reviewers of the large disciplinary journals.

One outcome of a move towards performance management is that, for example, two peer reviewed papers in highly ranked journals can be 'worth' more to an employing institution than a lot of work that you can find yourself doing to (for example) promote your discipline and degrees; to build networks and to support the students that come to you for help, such as talks to secondary school students to encourage their path into HE; to write provocative articles in trade journals that challenge the status quo in industry and encourage dialogue; or the sensitive handling of a personal matter behind closed doors that is impacting on a student's ability to do their study. All of these are pursuits that you may end up doing and which can take a disproportionate amount of your time and energy compared to what is going to be 'measured' via performance management tools.

Bureaucracy

Coupled with the intensification of performance management is its accompanying bureaucratic imperatives. This bureaucracy can constitute, for example, accounting for time spent on tasks, auditing what is being provided,

---

1 According to InCites Journal Citation Reports for 2016, there were 412 journals for Sociology and 824 for Psychology when all sub-sets of Psychology were included.

the peer/student evaluation of teaching, evidencing perceived indicators of success, and so on. This takes considerable energy and time, and is often hidden from public view beyond minutes of meetings – usually produced to ensure paper trails should anything go amiss rather than to demonstrate 'performance'. As a result, the intellectual pursuits of academics can become "largely external to the objectives of the bureaucratic regimes that dominate universities, and academics who careers were built on intellectual labor turn out to be deskilled workers in organizational settings indifferent to their concerns" (Nehring, 2016).

Certainly, the bureaucratisation of universities and HE has changed (some might say distorted) expectations about the early career academic's role and, potentially, priorities. An example of the impact of this has been that passing probation and seeking promotion to more senior academic posts has become increasingly bureaucratised, with expectations about the criteria against which applications are judged.

There are limitations and benefits to this intensification of bureaucracy. On the one hand, these expectations have grown in number and there is often a sense of the goal-posts continually extending out of reach. On the other hand, explicit criteria of probation and promotion can be helpful in that there is clarity as to what is valued by an institution and the mix of evidence required to support a case. Such bureaucratisation masks challenges and inequity within the system however: research evidence suggests that women shoulder more of the academic 'service' positions during their career (see Guarino and Borden, 2017) and that having a family can make a difference to academic career advancement (Ahmad, 2017; Mason et al., 2013).

In bureaucratic terms, meeting the criteria for probation or promotion thus does not necessarily reflect or account for your (1) day to day work or (2) your potential. A lot of an early career academic's work cannot be made visible or quantified, nor be convincingly used to explain why that paper never got published, or why that research bid was never submitted. For example, how can the early career academic whose dynamism and cheerful demeanour is popular with students articulate that they were unable to complete a task valued by the institution (for example, writing and submitting a research bid) because they were bombarded by student requests for support and assistance at the time of assessment, which coincided with the funder's deadline? Does this mean that they are expected to turn away students requesting help to focus on the quantifiable outputs required by their institution? And if so, how can they do this in a manner that does not detrimentally impact on the students' evaluation of their teaching – which in turn will be used in probation and promotion to determine the quality of their teaching?

These are the types of quandaries in which early career academics can find themselves as they navigate the competing demands of their role, namely the visibility and institutionally valued/measured parts of their job, and the invisible and potentially distracting tasks they take on behind closed doors, which cannot easily be publicised or quantified – and which are taken on to sometimes protect other performance indicators.

> **Pause for thought**
>
> How is performance measured at your institution? If you mapped out your average day or week, how much time do you spend on the activities that will be used to assess/measure your performance? How much time is spent on less visible, or even invisible, activities?

Moreover, and importantly, the distribution of who takes on these invisible roles within an institution is not necessarily equal (see earlier) and depends on the rigour and conscientiousness of the individual(s) involved (see chapter 8). It also depends on the personality of the individual. Some will find it easier than others to (for example) tell students that they cannot assist with their assessment, whereas others will feel compelled to extend their availability to all their students at great personal cost. As one senior colleague once told me, the choice for the early career academic can be whether they want to 'be an academic star or a good citizen of the department'. Thus how you navigate these, at times, highly pressured and competing demands depends on your institution and your personal priorities and values – which, I hope, this book will help you review and (re)establish.

Job security

For some early career academics probation and promotion may seem like a distant and unattainable dream. With a growing number of academics on fixed term, temporary or zero hours contracts (Chakrabortty and Weale, 2016), job security is a growing issue within the organisation of universities. You may be one of these people, an 'academic nomad' of HE, moving between institutions and even subject areas as you seek continuous employment. A move towards short-term and insecure employment has led to a populace of academics who cannot settle into a department, an institution, a geographic area, a community or a family, as they need to be focused on securing the next contract, or that elusive permanent position. Such a fluid and unstable employment experience does not correspond with institutional investment in their ideas, in their research, in their teaching progress, or in the development of their administrative and management experience and skills. Instead, individuals in this position become expendable research and teaching providers, plugging gaps in departments and institutions as and when needed, and can lead to a potentially demoralised and under-valued population of academics who struggle to achieve their full potential. It further creates much wastage of ideas and energy within the academic workforce as, for example, the fixed-term researcher leaves a project before their end date as they move onto their next contract elsewhere. As a result, the researcher cannot complete the publications from the project, the employer needs to go through a process of recruitment to hire a researcher unfamiliar with the project and on an even shorter fixed-term contract in order to complete the work, and, ultimately, the potential achievements of the project are compromised.

> **Tip**
>
> It is worthwhile having a basic understanding of the make-up of academic staff at your institution. What proportion are on permanent or temporary contracts? Has there been any impact on the organisation of workloads and so on?

Disciplinary value

A move towards performance management, bureaucratisation and job insecurity has further consequences for the early career academic depending on the academic discipline and intellectual areas of pursuit, as different disciplines have different 'outputs' both in terms of volume and frequency. Continual change within the schooling education system and an ever-changing job market for graduates, along with the emphasis on measurement, leads to an instrumental and commercial approach to university activities and outputs at almost every level and in almost every context. For example, research projects are measured depending on their 'impact' (see chapter 7) and utility in industry, policy and commerce. Teaching, both in terms of pedagogy and disciplines, is shaped and determined according to the 'student market' and the likelihood of recruitment, and the perceived needs of the graduate market.

Within this environment you can find yourself riding high on a wave of populism in terms of your topic area and discipline; conversely, however, you may find yourself in a tenuous position if your area of study or discipline is determined by policy-makers, by students, by their parents, or by the graduate market to be impractical, vacuous, self-indulgent or simply 'not needed'. Derogatory terms such as 'Mickey Mouse degrees' are often used in the media to describe topics and disciplines that are regarded by some to be superfluous to the economic needs of society, or not necessitating a qualification. Such an approach to subject areas reeks of anti-intellectualism and suggests that the sole purpose of universities is to power the machine of the economy, acting as an employee-producer for business or research incubator to boost commercial interests.

The difficulty here is that, as Côté and Allahar (2011) note, "the public *per se* is not necessarily equipped with the specialized skills and knowledge to dictate the terms of that pursuit" (p. 12, original emphasis). Moreover, that same public or those determining the value and need for different disciplines may have objectives and priorities that do not necessarily align with, or equate to, 'the best interests' of the future of a population and/or society. Certainly, an increased emphasis on training and preparation for the job market within HE teaching has seen a growth in degrees with a vocational component/identity and a decline in humanities subjects (Jaschik, 2017) that are arguably perceived to insufficiently 'equip' students with the transferable skills for the job market. This move towards assessment of universities based on the utility of education has two effects: in the short to medium term it means that a university must produce research and graduates that are in demand by employers. At the same time, it turns a university into a supplier of services to an economy and population, rather than a place for innovation, challenge and critique.

Being driven by the immediate needs of the labour market has significant consequences for those working in HE. Dis-incentivising originality, the commercialisation of HE can undermine a key purpose of learning and scholarly exploration: the development of intellectual capacity, critique and development for the benefit of society. This 'public good' mission of a university may not correspond with what employers or even fee-paying students – with their individual agendas, priorities and concerns – want or need at that moment.

As an early career academic, you may therefore find yourself caught between these two competing purposes of a contemporary university, and the key is – for me – learn to traverse them both without compromising too much of your integrity, nor becoming disillusioned or burned out. The aim of this book is to give you the time and tools you may need to navigate these waters ahead.

The outline of this book

This book is about how you, the early career academic, can find your 'space' within the HE environment outlined in this chapter. As a mentoring companion its aim is to help you survive, thrive and flourish from the start of your academic career. The emphasis throughout is on personal integrity, fulfilment and strategy – embodied in the requirements of the academic role and pursuits that are not necessarily complementary, and which may require reflection and a (re)consideration of priorities. My hope is that the ideas presented throughout this book provide you with opportunity for considered thinking, so that you can (re)gain a sense of purpose, focus and motivation for your future direction, secure in the knowledge that your individual contribution and work is both valued and valuable. I cannot promise that the book will change your life, but I hope that it gives you the space and time to reflect and consolidate, through its reading and your undertaking of the reflective activities.

The book is organised around the three key components of an academic's role: teaching, research and administration. Each section and chapter has been purposely written so that they can be read together or independently depending on your employment contract, interests, where you want to focus, the issues you may be facing, and the time you have available. There are a number of themes that are relevant across all the sections but to avoid repetition and replication they have been located in different sections of the book. For example, although located in specific chapters, the themes of value for money (chapter 1), self-care (chapter 2), imposter syndrome (chapter 3), having a thick skin and saying 'no' (chapter 4), shaping your academic identity (chapter 5), the importance of building networks (in chapter 6), working out what drives you (in chapter 7) your existing skillset and skills to develop (in chapter 8), pacing yourself (in chapter 9) and documenting your work (in chapter 10) are pertinent for all three contexts of teaching, research, and administration and management. Given the need to locate specific topics within specific parts of the book, and if you are not going to read the text in its entirety, it may be worth therefore browsing the index to check for specific issues that you would like to consider and reflect on as you may not automatically come across these within the chapters you select to read.

Section 1 is focused on the teaching element(s) of the academic role. In order to understand how your teaching practice is organised and structured, and why you may face certain challenges, Chapter 2 focuses specifically on the characteristics of the current 18 to 21-year-old undergraduate student, their expectations, and how you can respond to these. Chapter 3 explores student groups that you may teach, including mature and part-time students, international students, postgraduate students and students with disabilities. It identifies the different ways in which you can teach, and how you can teach outside of your 'comfort zone' with confidence. Chapter 4 sets out some of the more nuanced parts of teaching, including how to negotiate teaching topics, and navigating student evaluations.

Research is the focus of Section 2. Chapter 5 considers how you find your niche within academia and how to establish your credentials. It examines publishing culture(s) and the political economy that shapes research activities. Arguing that working with others is critical in getting your academic career going, chapter 6 examines the importance of building critical mass through leading projects, PhD supervision and networking. Moving beyond HE, chapter 7 explores the expanding role of the academic outside of the academy, covering issues such as impact and public engagement, and how to work with and within other sectors.

Section 3 focuses on administration, management and leadership, both within and outside HE. Chapter 8 specifically examines HE administration and governance, including the ways in which you can get involved in administration and management as an early career academic, how to influence, and the pitfalls to avoid. Developing your leadership interests, abilities and skills outside HE is the theme of chapter 9, exploring the opportunities and risks associated with taking on commitments in other organisations and sectors, and the issue of academics' relevance. Concluding section 3 and the book overall, chapter 10 aims to consolidate what you have learnt throughout the book, with a focus on the future. It asks what you want to get out of your career, what may help you achieve it, and suggests ways for how you can set, review and achieve short, medium and long-term goals. If you are only going to read one or two chapters of this book, make sure to include this one.

Throughout the book, each chapter contains opportunities to reflect on your goals and priorities, to consider what you could learn to help contextualise your experience, and a small number of personal reflections from myself that provide examples of how to negotiate, learn and move on. At the end of each chapter are references to further reading that may be of interest.

In terms of my own journey to this point, and to get the mentoring component of the book underway, it seems appropriate at this juncture to tell you a bit about myself, and for you to spend a few moments reflecting on why you have ended up reading this book in the first place, and where you want to go.

> **Author reflection**
>
> Learning when to respond or to take a stand has come at considerable personal cost and is one of the main drivers for my writing of this book, in that I hope to encourage others to take the time to reflect, to consider their priorities and to make informed decisions about 'getting stuck in'.
>
> Early on in my career I got involved in a lot of departmental activities, responding to policy and practice changes, fighting causes without due attention to their relative importance, and lacking an oversight of the toll it was taking on my physical and mental health. As a result I found myself at times in a constant state of anxiety, convinced that I was going to let someone else down if I did not honour the commitments I had taken on, and would give myself 'Sunday afternoon off' as a way of managing. Indeed, for a period of time I thought that an afternoon off a week was normal! I had no work-life balance, and within 2-3 years of finishing my PhD and embarking on my academic career I was very close to burnout. With the benefit of experience and hindsight, I now take a much more strategic view towards my work commitments, and although I still make mistakes about when/when not to respond to requests, I hope and feel that I am (a bit) better at organising my time and deciding what to take on, and when.

> **Pause for thought**
>
> Before you commence reading other sections of the book, spend a few moments reflecting on how you got to this point right now. Why have you picked up this book to read and what do you want from it?

> How can you envisage it helping you as you embark on your academic career?
>
> What are your short, medium and long-term goals? Where do you want to be in a a year's time? Five years' time? Ten years' time? It pays to have some idea of what you expect, want and need out of the next decade when it comes to your academic career.
>
> As you work through activities in the book, such as this one, make notes as and when appropriate. In the final tip in chapter 10 you will be reminded to bring them together and review them in 12 months' time, to reflect on how your perspective and priorities have evolved.

At the outset it is important to recognise that this book is intentionally and explicitly *not* a text on how to teach, how to conduct research, how to use social media for academics, or any of the 'how to' texts you may come across as you embark on this career. Such 'how to' guides are widely available elsewhere, and the chapters include references to some of the best sources for additional information. This book is also not about how to morph from a doctoral student into an academic. Nor is it a book that seeks to dismantle current university structures, or critique the individualist framework that underpins much of HE (see Gill and Donaghue, 2016). Instead, it is one person's take on the context(s) in which you work as an early career academic, and aims to provide insights into parts of the role that you may be less aware of, along with some supportive advice and guidance about how to navigate the demands of the job so that you can enjoy its challenges as well as deliver what your employing institution requires and expects. I thus anticipate that some readers will inevitably find the book lacking in critique on (for example) gender and ethnic inequality within HE, or the market forces that shape how success is measured. To reiterate, this is not that type of book. For those readers keen to engage with a critique of HE I have provided some suggested texts at the end of this chapter.

In sum, this book aims to be a user-friendly and helpful series of chapters that can be drawn on at times of both peace and flux, in order to make sense of what is happening around you, and how you might respond or seek to influence it. It seeks to provide useful and practical suggestions on how to act with integrity and how you can help yourself by establishing and holding on to your core values and purpose. It can be read in one go, or in sections, or a chapter at a time, it is entirely up to you, depending on your needs.

Overall, I hope this companion guide provides valuable thinking space for you to establish and reflect on your own goals and aspirations as an early career academic; to find out what your little cog in the giant HE machine is, does and can do; and to offer the chance for you to think about where you want to be in 5-10 years' time, and what you can do to help yourself get there. The book draws on academic-specific publications on the nature of universities, management in HE and academic leadership, alongside resources on the psychology and practice of leadership, resilience, career planning and so on, to provide context, guidance and questions that can help you move forward. It is my anticipation that this book can be thumbed through regularly by its owner, passed on to others so that they too may be given the opportunity to think, and ultimately, ends up torn and tatty by use. It is by no means a definitive account of HE today, but I hope that it goes some way in helping you understand your place within it.

References

Ahmad, S. (2017) 'Family or Future in the Academy?', *Review of Educational Research*, 87 (101): 204-239.

Back, L. (2016) *Academic Diary: Or Why Higher Education Still Matters* (London: Goldsmiths Press).

Berg, M. and Seeber, B.K. (2016) *The Slow Professor: Challenging the Culture of Speed in the Academy* (Toronto: University of Toronto Press).

Brown, R. (2011a) 'Introduction', in Brown, R. (ed.) *Higher Education and the Market* (London: Routledge), pp. 1-5.

Brown, R. (2011b) 'Markets and Non-Markets' in Brown, R. (ed.) *Higher Education and the Market* (London: Routledge), pp. 6-19.

Brown, R. (2011c) 'The Impact of Markets', in Brown, R. (ed.) *Higher Education and the Market* (London: Routledge), pp. 20-52.

Burrows, R. (2012) 'Living with the h-index? Metric assemblages in the contemporary academy', *The Sociological Review*, 60 (2): 355-372.

Chakrabortty, A. and Weale, S. (2016) 'Universities accused of 'importing Sports Direct model' for lecturers' pay', The *Guardian*, 16 November, available online at www.theguardian.com/uk-news/2016/nov/16/universities-accused-of-importing-sports-direct-model-for-lecturers-pay [accessed 16/11/17]

Collini, S. (2012) *What are Universities For?* (London: Penguin).

Côté, J.E. and Allahar, A.L. (2011) *Lowering Higher Education: The Rise of Corporate Universities and the Fall of Liberal Education* (Toronto: University of Toronto Press).

Gill, R. and Donaghue, N. (2016) 'Resilience, apps and reluctant individualism: technologies of self in the neoliberal academy', *Women's Studies International Forum*, 54: 91-99.

Guarino, C.M. and Borden, V.M.H (2017) 'Faculty Service Loads and Gender: are women taking care of the academic family?', *Research in Higher Education*, 58 (6): 672-694.

Hazelkorn, E. (2016) 'Globalization and the Continuing Influence of Rankings – Positive and Perverse – on Higher Education', in Yudkevich, M., Altbach, P.G. and Rumbley, L.E. (eds) *The Global Academic Rankings Games: Changing Institutional Policy, Practice and Academic Life* (London: Routledge), pp. 269–294.

Jaschik, S. (2017) 'Humanities Majors Drop', *Inside Higher Ed*, 5 June, available online at www.insidehighered.com/news/2017/06/05/analysis-finds-significant-drop-humanities-majors-gains-liberal-arts-degrees [accessed 16/11/17]

Jongbloed, B. (2003) 'Marketization in Higher Education, Clark's Triangle and the Essential Ingredients of Markets', *Higher Education Quarterly*, 57 (2): 110–135.

Mason, M.A., Wolfinger, N.H. and Goulden, M. (2013) *Do Babies Matter? Gender and Family in the Ivory Tower* (New Brunswick, NJ: Rutgers University Press).

Nehring, D. (2016) 'The Deskilled Academic: Bureaucracy Defeats Scholarship', *Social Science Space*, blog published 9 February, available online at www.socialsciencespace.com/2016/02/the-deskilled-academic-bureaucracy-defeats-scholarship/ [accessed 16/11/17].

O'Leary, M. (2017) 'Monitoring and Measuring Teaching Excellence in Higher Education: from Contrived Competition to Collective Collaboration', in French, A., O'Leary, M. with Robson, S. and Wood, P. (eds) *Teaching Excellence in Higher Education: Challenges, Changes and the Teaching Excellence Framework* (Bingley: Emerald Publishing), pp. 75–108.

Watermayer, R. and Olssen, M. (2016) '"Excellence" and Exclusion: The Individual Costs of Institutional Competitiveness', *Minerva*, 54: 201–218.

Further reading

Barnett, R. (2013) *Imagining the University* (Abingdon: Routledge).
Brown, R. (ed.) (2011) *Higher Education and the Market* (Abingdon: Routledge).
Brown, R. with Carasso, H. (2013) *Everything for Sale? The Marketization of UK Higher Education* (Abingdon: Routledge).
Collini, S. (2017) *Speaking of Universities* (London: Verso).
Cronin, B. and Sugimoto, C.R. (2014) *Beyond Bibliometrics: Harnessing Multidimensional Indicators of Scholarly Impact* (Cambridge, MA: MIT Press).
Furedi, F. (2016) *What's Happened to University?* (Abingdon: Routledge).
Gingras, Y. (2016) *Bibliometrics and Research Evaluation: Uses and Abuses* (Cambridge, MA: MIT Press).
Giroux, H.A. (2014) *Neoliberalism's War on Higher Education* (Chicago, IL: Haymarket Books).
McGettigan, A. (2013) *The Great University Gamble: Money, Markets and the Future of Higher Education* (London: Pluto Press).
Molesworth, M. (ed.) (2010) *The Marketisation of Higher Education and the Student as Consumer* (Abingdon: Routledge).
Olssen, M. and Peters, M.A. (2005) 'Neoliberalism, Higher Education and the Knowledge Economy: From the Free Market to Knowledge Capitalism', *Journal of Education Policy*, 20: 313–345.
Soto Antony, J., Cauce, A.M. and Shalala, D.E. (eds) (2017) *Challenges in Higher Education Leadership* (Abingdon: Routledge).
Vostal, F. (2014) 'Academic life in the fast lane: the experience of time and speed in British academia', *Time & Society*, 24 (1): 71–95.

Yudkevich, M., Altbach, P.G. and Rumbley, L.E. (eds) (2016) *The Global Academic Rankings Games: Changing Institutional Policy, Practice and Academic Life* (London: Routledge).

Useful journals

Compass: Journal of Learning and Teaching
Higher Education Quarterly
Higher Education Research and Development
Higher Education Review
Journal of Academic Development
Journal of Education Policy
Journal of Higher Education
Journal of Higher Education Policy and Management
Learning and Teaching: The International Journal of Higher Education in the Social Sciences
Quality in Higher Education
Review of Higher Education
Studies of Higher Education

Section 1
Teaching

The first of the three sections into which this book is organised, this section focuses on teaching as a key part of the early career academic's role. Having established some of the major trends that are shaping HE in chapter 1, this section explores the environment in which you teach and how you can find your feet when it comes to teaching in the early part of your academic career. You may have just finished your doctorate, during which time you did or did not take on teaching; you may be venturing into a teaching post following a period of research; or you may find yourself teaching with very little experience having moved into HE from a different sector. However you came to this point, starting teaching as an academic is a considerable challenge in terms of what it involves and how you negotiate its accompanying demands. Moreover, it can be quite an emotionally charged experience as you encounter the highs and lows of working with ever-demanding students. Be prepared, as a teaching academic sometimes you will feel like a fish fighting to swim upstream, yet at other times you will feel fantastic.

One thing is for sure, this section does not seek to provide bulletproof answers as to 'how to teach'. There are many, many excellent texts on pedagogy (the art of teaching – a word which you will likely hear a lot during the course of your career). Rather, this section intends to provide you with food for thought about the teaching environment of HE today, the extent to which you value teaching as part of your career going forward, how you teach, how you can establish credibility when teaching, and what good teaching looks like to you.

The following three chapters explore the contexts in which you teach, the types of students you will come across and why they behave in the way they do, how to manage student expectations, and how to deal with evaluations of your teaching. The section is intended to provide insight into current HE teaching practice and tips for how to make best use of the experience to develop your teaching skills.

2 The context in which you teach

This chapter focuses on the most likely group of students you will teach, undergraduate students, and the impact of their cultural and technological background on their expectations and your teaching practice. Reflecting on the last 20 years of social and economic change, the first part of the chapter explores the characteristics of the average 18 to 21-year-old undergraduate, and the knock-on impact on their expectations of attending university. In providing you with important context regarding teaching practice in HE, the chapter examines the key characteristics of the undergraduate student population today and the consequences for student expectations regarding HE and those who provide/facilitate it.

The second part of the chapter outlines a small number of ways in which you can navigate and manage student expectations within this environment. While the chapter does not seek to provide the 'answers' to working with this student population, building on chapter 1 it intends to provide important context for some of the demands and pressures faced by those teaching in universities today. The following chapter, chapter 4, focuses on diversity within student groups, and addresses some of the 'how to' questions you may have about getting started with your own teaching.

Undergraduate students: who are they?

If you are working for a typical HE provider today it is most likely that you will be teaching students aged 25 and under. Born after 1990, this population is variously referred to as 'Generation Z', the 'new millennials' (as opposed to the 'old millennials' who were born between 1977 and 1989, who are also termed 'Generation Y'), 'Generation Me' (Twenge, 2009) and the 'snowflake generation'. In part a consequence of the growth in the focus on the importance of the individual and the pursuit of individual dreams and goals, this generation of people have been characterised and defined as driven, ambitious and idealistic, along with being sensitive and easily offended. This is a population of people, it is often posited, that has been mollycoddled as children, hyper-scheduled, and lack resilience as a result of being guided and protected from the outside world by their 'helicopter parents'.

Unsurprisingly, many people who belong to this generation take issue with the negative associations and their supposed capacity to take offence, and point to the way in which their early lives have been framed and informed by a significant and world-changing transformation in communication and exposure to global events, information, ideas, and opinion (see Nicholson, 2016). It is, Tait (2017) argues, little wonder that such acquaintance with this volume of information, now readily on tap and accessible via handheld/portable devices, has led to a growing awareness and responsiveness within this generation to world events.

While debate continues about the derogatory nature of the labels attached to this population of young people, what seems to be accepted is that there is something palpably *different* about this generation. They have been born into a world dominated by information and communication technology and profound cultural shifts in the creation and dissemination of global events. Certainly, noting such a generational difference is not a new phenomenon; sociologists, historians, educationalists and psychologists have long pointed out that with every generation there are new challenges and older generations lament the passing of time and changes in expectation. In the context of this book however, there are substantial implications for providers of education and analysis to *this* generation. All those tasked with teaching this group of people, within and beyond HE, are having to keep pace with this technologically-savvy generation, their demands and expectations. In order to address some of these demands and expectations there are, I argue, several key characteristics of this generation that it may be useful to identify and name, in order to understand and contextualise their view of HE and their opinion of the early career academic, the education provider. The importance of this is paramount, as Hoffman et al. (2015) notes: recognising the context in which these students are entering university can help us all appreciate the source and instigators of some of the pressures that can be faced by you, the early career academic.

Characteristic 1: Valuing speed

In terms of *the* defining characteristic of the current undergraduate population this first characteristic of speed is perhaps, I suggest, the most influential. All others that follow are related to it in one way or another. It is within this context of speed that HE providers are now engaging with students, where they are open to constant challenge based on commercial imperatives, facing speculation regarding their purpose and social worth, and the broader social and economic contribution of HE (see chapter 1).

> **Pause for thought**
>
> What are your own expectations regarding speed? For example, how quickly do you expect an email response? Or for someone to reply to a text message?

Expediency has been identified as key to this generation (Tulgan, 2016) and, indeed, who can blame students born post-1990 for wanting and expecting things with haste? Growing up in a rapidly changing world dominated by technology, these are individuals who have very little recollection, if any, of a world pre-instant connection via mobile phone; of a world without immediate (or at least very quick) access to information via the world wide web; of a time before 24/7 rolling news and coverage of events from around the globe. They are a generation for whom it is *entirely normal* to be able to access swathes of current and historical information within seconds via a handheld device. They are a population that has grown up with an online world of relationships and instantaneous communication with others via social media. It is this capacity to connect with others via social media that, Tait (2017) argues, has led to such a heightened sensitivity and in particular, a compassion towards global events; social media is the 'snow machine' as she puts it, to their snowflake.

Certainly, the ability to associate instantly with individuals and organisations, regardless of geographical location, has shifted expectations about what constitutes information, and the speed with which it can be accessed. The sheer volume of information that is now available to this cohort of undergraduate students – regardless of quality – is staggering.

... as our world shrinks (or flattens), events great and small taking place on the other side of the world (or right next door) can affect our material well-being almost overnight. World institutions – nations, states, cities, neighborhoods, families, corporations, churches, charities, and schools – remain in a state of constant flux just to survive. Authority is questioned routinely. Research is quick and easy. Anyone can be published. *We try to filter through the endless tidal wave of information coming at us from an infinite number of sources all day, every day.* Nothing remains cutting-edge for very long.

(Tulgan 2016: 6, emphasis added)

For those born into this hyper-connected environment, Tulgan goes on to argue, the volume of information to which they have access is *not* overwhelming. It does not drown, overcome or intimidate them. Rather, this mass of available information is empowering and enabling, as new millennial users switch between websites and formats to source more and more detail; with carefully constructed algorithms pointing them where to go next. As Tulgan notes, "It makes them would-be experts on everything" (p. 7).

Characteristic 2: Shorter attention spans

Such immediate access to information does not lead this generation of students to feel sluggish however. They are not concerned about being out of touch or out of date, as they seek to keep pace with unremitting tidal waves of information. Instead, this ease of access feeds their appetite for more and more information, which leads to impatience and a desire to switch rapidly between different sources according to need (Tulgan, 2016). This capacity to move on and abandon has led to a growing trend towards the provision of customised information for this generation, as they travel between sources following personal interests, consuming information at a rate of knots. The speed of this consumption has had a profound impact on their experience of, and ability to, being able to focus.

Set against this backdrop, there are obvious implications for the education provider working with these would-be experts on everything; in how they teach, how they engage, their 'value added' and their very own expert knowledge. These will be covered in terms of managing student expectations later in this chapter. For now, however, it is important to note that this group of peoples' abilities to access, switch, change and move on within a moment means that, inevitably, their attention spans have decreased. Indeed, compared to the generations before them, it is possible that their attention spans have never truly been tested, at least in an educational setting. The typical undergraduate student (unless they are working within a particular academic discipline that requires specific skills) has, for example, little experience of time-intensive searching for books, journals, papers, or documents within the dusty and darkest recesses of a library. They may have little familiarity with three-hour or longer labs or lectures; writing coherent documents of length or trawling through weighty tomes. This is not to say that they are not capable of any of these things. Indeed, they may be the *most* capable, talented, exploratory and investigative generation that has ever lived owing to their capacity to access and filter volumes of information at such speed. They are, as Tulgan remarks, the ". . . info junkies compulsively poring through bits and bytes, mixing and matching the perspectives that appeal to them" (p. 9). Yet this speediness and a customised approach to processing information does not automatically correspond with sustained engagement or prolonged evaluation of the quality of said information, and this flitting from one source to another is thus one of the central challenges of working with undergraduate students today.

What is more, a customised approach to working with sources has shifted this generation's perception of what constitutes success. Born in a time with such easy access to information, it is no surprise to learn that these students can carry with them an expectation that filtering large volumes of information at speed is regarded as an indicator of accomplishment. The capacity to deal with a body of information *quickly* has, for some at least, become equated with an assessment of *quality*. Thus, their engagement with the information they are dealing may be superficial at best and disingenuous at worst (Hargittai et al., 2010).

This situation has been exacerbated by the way in today's students have been taught in their earlier education. Coming from a school culture that has emphasised home study and extra curricula attainment, while at the same time focusing on teaching for assessment success, this generation of students have grown up accustomed to a rapid turnover of standardised assessments and a drive for higher grades that has resulted in being increasingly taught to pass (Twenge, 2009). Rather than sustained engagement with undertaking a process of 'deep learning',[1] they have been trained to produce the 'right' piece of work to ensure the highest

---

1 Deep learning is an experience of learning, engaging, creating and acting that is often presented alongside a more superficial 'surface learning' experience. There are many, many texts available on pedagogy (the art of teaching) which cover these approaches to learning, some of which are listed at the end of this chapter.

mark possible (Fullan and Langworthy, 2014). It is little wonder therefore that these students arrive at university keen to know how to achieve the good mark and that consequently, poor grades can be a significant blow to their self-esteem (Hoffman et al., 2015).

> **Pause for thought**
>
> Have you ever encountered the consequences of the 'taught to pass' mentality that has permeated education? Have your colleagues? What does that mean for your own teaching and the role of HE more broadly?

Instead of having experienced sustained and risk-taking intellectual study, which may take time and runs the risk of resulting in a poor outcome which schools can ill-afford, and alongside the volume of information to which they now have relatively easy access, for this group of students their ability to concentrate for a sustained period of time has thus never truly been explored. They are the multi-taskers extraordinaire of the twenty-first century, flitting between information sources, tasks and interests as never before, with the touch of a button or the swipe of a screen. An implication of this for their learning and for those who teach them is that quickly moving on from something that does not engage them – or indeed, moving on if they wish to find out more – is *entirely normal* and, for them, to be expected. An example of this can be seen in every lecture theatre today where laptops are permitted; with multiple screens open the student can switch between their lecture content, social media, shopping sites, sites containing more information about the topic that they are studying, and so on, repeatedly throughout their lecture.

It is within this context that early career academics in HE can now find their teaching practice being interpreted, with queries raised about the value added when the students can find the information being taught readily online. Teaching academics therefore have to be providing something 'extra' to justify their existence and measurable contribution to these students' intellectual development. This questioning of the value of teaching and the need to provide something 'extra' has been exacerbated by two key changes over the last 20 years. First, the increasing commercialisation of education via the expansion of HE providers and the growth in fees seen in the UK and elsewhere, outlined in chapter 1; and second, by the move by publishers to provide complementary free-to-access teaching materials alongside their print offerings, and the open access to education online (see chapter 3). How to provide this added value in your own teaching is covered later on in this chapter.

Characteristic 3: Expectations regarding access and availability

The above point regarding the laptop is a useful starting point with which to discuss this third characteristic of the new millennials: their ease of access to information and to other people online. With the democratisation of technology and the spontaneous connection to their peers via social media has come a ubiquity that is now normal and readily accepted for a conversation, a dinner date, a coffee with a friend, or even a meeting with a tutor, to be interrupted by a phone call, a text, an email or a social media post. The emphasis on promptness seen in the first new millennial characteristic, coupled with an ever-present access point via a handheld device, has led to individuals living and responding both in the 'real world' and online at any one time. Online and offline life are synchronous, and require analogous attention.

> **Pause for thought**
>
> Have you or a colleague ever asked students to put their phones or laptops away during a lecture? What was their reaction? Have you ever been in a meeting that has been interrupted by the arrival of a message? How easy do *you* find it to put your phone away and not respond to online activity when you are doing something else?

Such synchronic existence is not unique to new millennials of course; just go into any café and you will see mobile phones on the table, being checked in the physical presence of others. But in the context of this chapter an important outcome of this simultaneous online and offline presence is that there has been seismic shift in expectations regarding availability and access to the academic. Without clear boundaries and expectations, you can find yourself on the receiving end of communications from your students on a 24/7 basis, with the expectation that you will similarly be engaged and responsive online, regardless of what you are doing offline. You may also find yourself on the receiving end of 'friend' requests via social media.

The ever-vigilant academic can exacerbate this pressure to be 'on' all the time by enabling notifications on their device, ensuring that they never miss a single bong, beep, or pop-up message telling them that a new missive has arrived. To combat such pressures, and the resulting increase in volume of requests at all times of day (I have had emails from students about assessments where they have openly acknowledged they are on the bus heading into the city for a night out – lucky them!), some institutions have created policies on how long a student can expect to wait before receiving a reply; for example, 48 or 72 hours for an email reply. There are benefits and problems with such an approach. On the one hand, institutionalisation of expected response times can help shield you from spiralling student expectations about instantaneous responses to their requests; yet on the other hand it could be seen to be another stick to wield if you do not conform to institutional diktats or are unable to respond in such a timeframe.

> **Tip**
>
> If you are in a very busy period of marking, for example, set an out-of-office bounce-back email that explains that you have a heavy workload at present and will respond to emails as you are able. This, at least, sets something of an expectation regarding how quickly you will reply.

A further challenge within this easy-to-access culture is inconsistency amongst colleagues as to how readily they will engage with students online. For example, you could reasonably take a day or two to respond to an email – thereby conforming to your institution's expectations regarding email replies, if one exists. Your office neighbour however may, again reasonably, choose to take a different approach and respond to student emails as quickly as possible, to get them dealt with. This may mean they are willing to respond in the evenings and at the weekends, which might be normally thought of as outside 'office hours'.

The context in which you teach

> **Pause for thought**
>
> What is your institution's policy on how quickly you are expected to respond to students via email? If not, how will you communicate expectations regarding contact and response to your students? Does your institution have a policy on engaging with students on social media? What is it?

It is within this context, that is, what constitutes normal 'office hours' and reasonable online availability, that academics can experience one of their greatest push-and-pulls. Usually able to exercise a high level of independence over their working hours and often their location of work, there are typically no 'set' or core hours of business. As a result, some academics can feel guilty whenever they are *not* working (Rockquemore, 2015). Pre-dating the advent and normalisation of 24/7 email and instant access via hand-held devices, this is clearly now a 'new' issue, nor isolated to working with this generation of students. This is clearly not a 'new' issue, nor isolated to working with this generation of students. Nearly two decades into the twenty-first century, what is different now however, is the commercial context in which HE is being provided, and the way in which this has impacted on the mind-set of those 'consuming' the education (see chapter 1).

> **Tip**
>
> Given the new millennial cohorts ease of technology use and in relation to access, you need to make sure that from the outset you have transparent, well publicised and, importantly, consistent expectations in place that make it clear to students as to your availability and how they can contact you/you will contact them. Make this available to students through all possible channels and stick to it, so that there can be no claims of favouritism or preferential treatment.

Characteristic 4: Transactional mind-sets

Exacerbated by the introduction of tuition fees in the UK, and underpinned by a market-driven economy that emphasises consumer choice and consumer power, this generation of students have reached legal adulthood well versed in their capacity to consume and contribute to the success or failure of products and services. This, coupled with the commercialisation of HE seen in chapter 1, means that they (and others) can see them as 'consumers' of HE, where the experience is:

> ... primarily judged on the extent to which it can be considered 'value for money' (or not). This question ... is almost entirely predicated on the idea that a university education increases individuals' employability and earning power, which further reinforces the idea of HE as a tiered marketplace with students located as consumers of a commodified educational product.
>
> (French, 2017: 14)

As consumers of an educational product, many students have come to regard their contribution to their education as a transaction where "they look at their own time, dedication, and best efforts as a kind of currency" (Tulgan, 2016: 96). In other words:

X input = Y output

This transactional approach to education has led to a tendency to focus on how, if they put in at least X input, they can expect *at least* Y output.

Author reflection

I have had this reflected back at me many times in my early career when a student who is disappointed with their assessment grade has come to see me and remarked along the lines of "I thought if I put so much time into it I would at least get Y mark". I have often wondered if they would challenge a more senior colleague in the same way – after asking around it transpires that yes, they do! It has thus become part of the job to explain to students that time and effort does not automatically equate to a particular outcome and to regard the critique of their work as an opportunity for learning.

It is in this transactional environment that early career academics are thus tasked with two (potentially contradictory) aims: first to educate, inspire, engage and encourage their fee-paying students, and second to penalise those whose performance is not up to scratch. While this critique can be interpreted as an opportunity for their intellectual and personal growth, it can also be received as a devastating blow to their ego and sense of self-worth. Many have written about the fragility of the new millennials' self-esteem (and which, as noted earlier, has been criticised for simplicity and crudeness), but it is not surprising when one considers that:

- They have come from a schooling system that has prioritised performance and attainment;
- They have grown up in a world where online activity is central to everyday life;
- They are surrounded by a language of rights (see later) and,
- They are used to a very hands-on parenting culture (see later).

As a result, this is a generation of people whose sense of self is deeply intertwined with their attainment. They enter into and engage with their university education with extremely high standards and expectations of themselves and their ability, with potentially little (tested) resilience and resource for dealing with criticism, failure and under-achievement. They are, often, perfectionists, resulting in how:

> Some university faculty describe the undergraduates entering prestigious institutions as falling into two types, neither of which is good: 'crispies' are burned out from too much work and too much perfectionism, and 'teacups' are perfect on the outside but easily broken if rattled.
>
> (Twenge, 2009: 403)

Although rather derogatory terms these 'crispies' and 'teacups' have, arguably, yet to learn and develop their *own* expectations of their own sense of attainment, and their responsibility for pursuing this. Trapped in a transactional mind-set of a set amount of input = a set amount of output, many have yet to fully engage with their individual responsibility for their learning, which can lead to their regarding of poor performance as the failure of the education provider, rather than themselves (Mahida, 2012).

Characteristic 5: Challenging expertise and evidence

So far, the characteristics of new millennial students include: their tremendous capacity to filter information, their accustomed expectation of easy access to others, and their potential transactional approach to life. The fifth characteristic is that of challenging expertise. Referred to earlier by Tulgan, the new millennial student population are "would-be experts on everything" (2016, p. 7) owing to their ability to manage masses of information online. Where this leaves those who are employed specifically to be working towards becoming, and presumably want to be regarded as, 'an expert' in their field is thus problematic, not least because the concept of 'expertise' and evidence itself is open to debate.

At stake here is the very idea of what it means to be an academic; that is, an expert in a field and discipline, based on a long-standing immersion into a topic and area, built upon a comprehensive and critical knowledge base. For the early career academic starting out, as noted in the next chapter, you are likely to be an expert on a specific issue or in relation to a specific problem, item or process, but at the start of your academic career you are unlikely to have the depth and breadth of understanding and experience that justifies a label of expertise within a broader field. When faced with a generation of students who have grown up with easy access to information online, who may regard themselves and be regarded by others as something of mini-experts, you thus have to build up your teaching experience and resilience to be able to continue to pursue your expert goal.

This resilience is vital when one considers the questioning of the relevance and societal worth of academics outlined in chapter 1. Compared to two decades or more ago, as an early career academic you are likely to find yourself – regardless of the size of your respective field – *one of many* would-be experts, both academic and non-academic, and that can include your students.

Pause for thought

Within your field, who else could be considered an expert? Industry? Think tanks? Artists? Politicians? The media? Specific individuals? Your students?

The context in which you teach 39

A devolution of expertise via the online world has been part of, and contributed to, a rise in citizenship journalism, whereby everyone online is now able to share news, their perspectives, their opinions; with every social media post having the capacity to spread at speed and without containment (Ball, 2017). Traditional providers of expert knowledge and comment, namely academics, teachers, politicians, journalists and other professions that require the individual to present their standpoint, are thus now just one of *many* providers of knowledge and comment, and it is left to the consumer of said knowledge and comment to question and establish the legitimacy of their claims alongside others.

At the very heart of this shift towards the consumer's assessment of legitimacy is a questioning of what constitutes evidence and credibility. Most recently, concerns have been raised about this in relation to 'fake news' and 'alternative facts', whereby different interest groups present alternative interpretations of images, policy, statements and so on to promote their own agenda. In the past, as noted in a US study (Wineburg et al., 2016), consumers could rely on publication editors to vet the quality of information being provided but in a time of unregulated information sharing online, the onus is now on the reader to determine credibility. Interestingly, the same study found that teenagers can struggle to recognise and identify the difference between a news story and a piece of advertising, while often not questioning the source of a claim or evaluating news from organisations with political agendas. Not everyone shares this view however. Elsewhere, Kyung-Sim et al. (2014) argue that students who are 'information literate' – as today's new millennials are – have been shown to be competent and capable of questioning information online. Rather, the challenge is whether they actively commit to and practise this questioning, when expediency and ease of access to sources is typically prioritised:

> Being information literate does not hinge on the type of source used, but on whether the source consulted fits the intended purpose of the information seeking and nature of the information needs . . . Researchers have identified key evaluation criteria such as accuracy, authority, comprehensiveness, and so on . . . Studies suggest that college students who have received IL [information literacy] training are aware of key evaluation criteria, as evidenced in findings where students cited accuracy as being more important than accessibility for academic tasks. It should be noted, however, that *the knowledge of important evaluation criteria is not always translated into action*. Students are

still inclined to use convenient and easy-to-use sources, even when they cite accuracy as the most important evaluation criterion.

(Kyung-Sim et al., 2014: 445-446, emphasis added).

The question of the evaluation of evidence is further framed by the broader issue of the social, economic and political value attributed to different *types* of evidence and opinion, namely the worth attached to numerical figures and words. Within the context of social science and humanities teaching the attributed importance of numbers over words (at its most basic) can be seen in social science and humanities students' fixation with word counts and the number of references needed in an assignment rather than quality of the content or the articulation of their argument. At its most vivid, and as a product of the schooling system from which they come, it can be further seen in the importance placed on the mark awarded for a piece of work, rather than the qualitative feedback on why the mark was awarded and how to improve. It can further be seen in the way in which obtaining a degree and the classification of that degree is more important as a vehicle into life beyond HE than the intellectual growth experienced while studying.

This goal orientated, means-to-an-end approach to tasks is not isolated to new millennials or just teaching; it can be seen elsewhere in academic publishing in terms of what is valued and how that is measured (see chapter 5). Moreover, it is not unique to HE, with emphasis on hit rates for online articles (Ball, 2017), viewing figures for television, music downloads and so on. This focus on numbers and volume is thus the product of a society in which political and economic emphasis and determinations of popularity and relevance is placed on output that is archetypally measured by volume; that is, numerically.

Characteristic 6: A language of rights

The final characteristic of undergraduate students is the language of 'rights' that has been readily adopted by the new millennial generation. Colleagues will often talk of this in terms of students' sense of entitlement; indeed, this is perhaps one of the most oft-said phrases within my working week. This discourse of rights extends beyond the rights attached to being a transactional consumer as outlined earlier; framed by the growth in the political discourse and rhetoric of human rights, students in this age group have been born into an era when there is a moral imperative to ensuring that all individuals are equally heard, represented, responded to, and supported.

This expectation of rights has been nurtured by the parents of new millennials. It is highly likely that many of the students you will teach today will have been parented by very hands-on adults, where "every step of the way, they have been guided, directed, supported, coached and protected" (Tulgan, 2016: 58). Sometimes referred to as 'helicopter parenting' as children age and parents remain heavily engaged in their world, this parental involvement has placed emphasis on, their offspring's 'right' to be heard and the importance of their views – which are to be respected and their opinion encouraged. From a very young age, the current student population has thus been encouraged to:

- Assert themselves;
- Voice satisfaction and dissatisfaction when they perceive to experience it;
- Express their feelings;
- Develop their autonomous voice (somewhat ironically, given the level of support and guidance received and required from their parents).

Let's be clear, this right to talk and to be heard is, fundamentally, not a problem. Indeed, it is the product of social and political change where equality between genders, ethnicities, nationalities, class and geography has been sought, promoted and fought for. The challenge lies however in the extent to which individuals who have grown up in this environment have been taught to appropriately moderate, filter and restrain their voice according to the situations in which they find themselves.

Why does this matter for students? Having liberty to pontificate without consequence, because it is a 'right', belies how that opinion can be received and responded to. It also creates a sense of entitlement and privilege. Is that a 'fault' of undergraduate students though? On the one hand, an inability to temper one's voice can be explained by youth and immaturity, a lack of empathy for others that has yet to develop through life experience, and a youthful exuberance and energy that is, as yet, lacking cynicism, scepticism and wariness. On the other hand, however, an expectation that authority accompanies their voice has been exacerbated by this population of students' capacity to express themselves online, on any issue and at any time, without any filter. In that world there exists an ever present audience, waiting and willing to respond, argue, discuss. And in that world they can, as noted earlier, choose to ignore or engage and then move on with speed.

Thus, this is a group of students who have potentially not fully seen, witnessed or understood the impact of expressing their opinion. This, alongside being taught to pass at school, means that they are less likely to have been exposed to checks and balances, criticisms and challenges that can undermine their sense of self-worth and individual ability. It is within this context, and noted earlier, that Sinek (2017) has argued (in a hugely popular viral video) that this generation are at considerable risk from mental health issues owing to their relatively fragile self-esteem. Heavily supported by parents and underpinned by their expectation to be listened to, their sense of self has not been tested, their resilience not built up through adversity, so that they can respond to and address criticism and failure.

As a result, undergraduate students can arrive at university and may, for the first time, be exposed to challenge and critique about their opinion and their ability to communicate effectively. Emotionally unprepared and lacking the resilience to deal with criticism, or the implementation of immovable standards imposed by the institution, they can struggle. Sometimes this can manifest itself in lashing out at the perceived perpetrators, for example in their evaluation of teaching (see chapter 4); at other times, or for other students, it can manifest in stress, pressure and burnout (aka the 'crispie'). One thing is for sure, those employed to teach students need to be attuned to the baggage that those students bring with them to university, and the importance of managing their expectations: of themselves, of the institution, and of academics.

The frontline: managing your students' expectations

While the purpose of this chapter is not to provide 'one-stop' solutions for addressing all the challenges that this generation of students poses for the HE sector, the following suggestions are intended as food for thought: practical measures you can put in place to be able to manage expectations; both of your students, and your own.

Establishing a shared mission: the student's growth and transition

This first challenge requires a conscious effort to encourage students to move away from focusing on their grades and instead emotionally invest in their educational experience. Contrary to their own expectations of themselves as would-be experts, they are *not* expected to know everything, to be able to write to publishable standard at the outset, or to be able to interpret and articulate complex theoretical ideas. Rather, they are expected to come with their pre-existing knowledge and experience, show an interest and engagement in the topics at hand, and participate in an intellectual journey. They are expected to *take responsibility* for their learning – much like gym membership or driving lessons, a university provides the equipment and training, but the outcome is not guaranteed. That takes energy, effort and commitment on the student's part. X input does not automatically equate to Y output.

> **Tip**
>
> The gym membership model is a fantastically easy and relatable way to articulate the relationship between the 'consumer' student and the 'service provider' academic.

For some students this may require some adjustment as to what they perceive to be their own intellectual journey, and what constitutes personal 'success'. For many, a high degree classification and graduate-entry level job is the Holy Grail, yet for many this will not be the reality. For those where it is not, their task – with your help – is to redress their own expectations in light of their ability, focusing on strengths that they may have overlooked in pursuit of a specific grade, emphasising their intellectual and interpersonal skills beyond their marks.

At the outset this requires personal engagement with individual students, in order to establish *their* benchmarks of success and expectations of their educational experience, and to then work with them on (re)framing that according to their ability and interests. Overall, it necessitates a willingness to create a tutor-student team that can identify and share a common mission of the student's growth and transition into life beyond university. Not to be confused with preparation for the labour market, this is about providing students with the space and time to reflect on what intellectual growth looks like for them and, importantly, placing responsibility for that learning onto the student asking, *how can they help themselves*? It is about recognising and developing the 'customisable' goals of the individual student's education. Such an emphasis on managing students' expectations of themselves can be one of the most rewarding and fulfilling components of the job, and can tap into the new millennials' customisable approach to information and subsequent learning.

Your desire to nurture and support may not always be met with enthusiasm however; not every student will wish to engage with you in this way. Furthermore, a willingness to provide and foster such a positive team effort can also be compromised when you are required to assess that same student's work and provide critical feedback. But when you encounter students who take constructive criticism on board and you see them flourish over the period of a few years as they move from being, for example, an over-confident or reserved teenager to a reflective adult, you can gain much inspiration, satisfaction and hope for the future.

> **Tip**
> - Utilise your personal tutor system to engage with your personal tutees. When you meet with your tutee find out about their background and their reason(s) for studying a particular course at your particular institution. Take the time to find out about them and their expectations of themselves and their university experience. Document and reflect on this at periodic points throughout their studies to consider what has changed and why.
> - Use learning journals for students to map out their goals and the resources they need to achieve these. Review at regular intervals. Note however, that this can be challenging without 'student buy-in'. It is likely that you will need institutional support to ensure that learning journals are utilised.

Providing clarity, challenge and boundaries

Connected to your shared mission with the students is a commitment to providing appropriate and – importantly – *continual* clarity and challenge. Such an ongoing commitment to clarity and challenge requires constant energy and teacher input. Moreover, the energy required is multi-faceted. Not just mental and intellectual, it is emotional and physical; it is as much about what you are saying to students as *how* you say it. It is the performance of teaching – the enthusiasm, the passion, the willingness with which you engage others.

Moreover, one of the difficulties of educating with clarity and challenge is that what is learnt requires *time*: time to explain, time to reiterate; time to absorb, time to reflect; and time to implement. To achieve this in the face of a mass of readily available alternative information, where speed and convenience is valued above engagement and evaluation, when students are accustomed to moving on very quickly when it suits them, and when they are used to voicing their dissatisfaction, requires flexibility and fortitude on the part of the early career academic.

One way in which to provide clarity for students is to communicate and continually reinforce expectations and boundaries. As an early career academic you will be required to enforce institutional boundaries most likely as part of your role, but you will also likely have a choice over how to impose your own personal boundaries with regard to, as previously mentioned, email communication and social media contact. When imposing these boundaries it is imperative that you take the time to explain and clarify *why* you are doing so.

> **Tip**
>
> - Make sure to spend as much time as you can to explain why you are challenging students' expectations and setting boundaries. Reiterate this at appropriate points so that they are reminded of this – you cannot assume that telling them once means that it will be remembered.
> - One straightforward action is to manage your own devices to organise how you receive notifications. Many devices offer the ability to silence/nullify any notifications between the hours you set for 'sleep'. How about setting yours so that you either receive no notifications, or are required to actively and purposefully open your emails? Or turning off notifications between, for example, 7pm and 7am?

Providing the authentic 'extra'

When it comes to teaching those with vast amounts of information at their fingertips and where there are many other potential would-be experts and sources readily available, the challenge of authenticity is about recognising your own interpersonal strengths and weaknesses as a teacher. It is about responding to those areas of weakness, addressing them, and capitalising on and utilising those strengths that come more organically, in order for you to provide the 'extra' that comes with face-to-face teaching.

> **Author reflection**
>
> After 15 years of teaching in HE I know that I am not able to humorously 'quip' in the classroom environment. Time and time again efforts to be comical have been interpreted as sarcasm and mockery. This is something that I need to work on and I have made deliberate efforts to only use humour when I am feeling relaxed and positive, so that I do not come across as scornful. On the other hand, I find it much easier to engage with students face-to-face, one-to-one, or in small groups, so I put considerable effort into making myself available to them in that capacity, to work through their issues and questions in person, with my undivided attention. That ability to engage with a student one-to-one is my organic and authentic 'extra' as I know from student comments and feedback that my exclusive attention to their needs is very much valued.

Certainly, taking stock of your respective strengths and weaknesses throughout your career and as your skills evolve through experience is a useful habit to get into. This may be part of a formal appraisal process, but I would recommend that you do this independently so that you can do so without concern that others will see it (in case that could be an issue). A good way to do such an exercise is with a mentor (see chapters 8 and 10) if you feel that you would want and value insight from a more experienced colleague, or a trusted colleague as a mutual exercise, where you can provide constructive feedback on each other's respective skillsets and areas for potential development.

> **Pause for thought**
>
> It is worthwhile reviewing your own qualities as a teaching academic, identifying what comes more easily to you and what you have to work on. For example, can you identify any strengths or weaknesses from this list of adjectives?
>
> Table 2.1
>
> | | | | | | | |
> |---|---|---|---|---|---|---|
> | Kind | Assertive | Informed | Reliable | Maverick | Spontaneous | Organised |
> | Systematic | Enthusiastic | Caring | Talkative | sharp | Creative | Diplomatic |
> | Flexible | Muddled | Sensitive | Feisty | Humorous | Friendly | defensive |
> | Constructive | Methodical | Patient | Clear | Slow | Empathetic | Tolerant |
> | Irritable | Responsive | Placid | Opinionated | Unflappable | Thoughtful | Quick |
> | Logical | Emotional | Calm | Delicate | Warm | Calculating | Passionate |
> | Expressive | Cold | Confident | Unemotional | Robust | Open | Unruffled |

> **Tip**
>
> - Get to know yourself, take up opportunities for training and learning about your interpersonal skills and where your strengths and weaknesses lie. Make the effort and commitment to addressing areas of weakness and capitalise on your organic strengths. Make your interpersonal skills work to your advantage when teaching.
> - Could you ask someone that you trust to look through these adjectives above and ask them to identify three of your strengths and three of your weaknesses? This may help you reflect on how you come across to others.

Practising self-care

Depending on personality type, self-care will mean different things to different people. There is a wealth of information available on suggestions for self-care (for example Reading, 2017; Noakes, 2017), and as noted in chapter 1, it is not solely relevant to teaching – it applies to other facets of the academic role as well. In the context of teaching new millennials however, the would-be experts who value speed, numerical grades and transaction, it is vital that you have the time and opportunity to establish your own core values in relation to teaching, and undertake activities that give your brain and body a break and chance to recover. You need to be able to pace yourself so that you do not burnout in the face of (what can feel like) constant expectations and demands.

Your resilience is thus vital in being able to teach such a potentially vibrant and challenging community of undergraduate students. There are a multitude of ways that you can practice self-care, and I am no expert on the efficacy of techniques. The following have however, worked for me:

Table 2.2

At work	Outside of work
Identify a more senior colleague with whom you can trust to discuss teaching issues and challenges.	Physical exercise
Request and utilise a mentor	Get a pedometer or equivalent – get your sense of achievement from the number of steps you have walked that day
Request and utilise a buddy	Go to the cinema and immerse yourself in a film
Spend time away from your desk, preferably outside	Pets – their unconditional affection and company is priceless, and their needs relatively simple
Have plants in your office, nurture them	Make sure that your home environment is welcoming and relaxing to be in, especially when you walk in the front door
Take the time to walk the corridors and stop to say hello to colleagues	Drink lots of water
Decorate your desk/work space with objects that remind you of non-work interests and activities	Create your own clear boundaries about when you are *not* working

As noted in chapter 1, with such a diversity in departmental cultures, you may find that self-care is something that is actively promoted, practised and endorsed by your colleagues. However, you are just as likely to find that in a competitive environment that values outputs and success that self-care is a misnomer, never spoken about nor acknowledged. Moreover, as your career progresses you may find that your department's compassionate culture changes, or as you move institutions that you are faced with very different expectations regarding collegial support. As such, it is important to get into the practice early on of taking responsibility for your own self-care, to ensure that you have the capacity, resilience and stamina to sustain your job.

> **Tip**
>
> - Work out what self-care means to you and make sure you allocate time to it consciously and deliberately. No one else is going to do this for you.

As you can see from this chapter, the typical undergraduate student now attends university with a particular set of expectations that have come from much wider societal, cultural, political, economic and technological change. The challenge for you is to recognise and respond to these expectations, rather than trying to ignore them and/or expend much-needed energy to fight them. Suggestions in this chapter on how to manage expectations have emphasised the importance of setting boundaries, recognising the emotional, mental and physical energy required to be an excellent teacher, and the need to practice self-care. I cannot stress the importance of this final suggestion. Do it now.

References

Ball, J. (2017) *Post-Truth: How Bullshit Conquered the World* (London: Biteback Publishing).

French, A. (2017) 'Contextualising Excellence in Higher Education Teaching: understanding the policy landscape', in French, A., O'Leary, M. with Robson, S. and Wood, P. (eds) *Teaching Excellence in Higher Education: Challenges, Changes and the Teaching Excellence Framework* (Bingley: Emerald Publishing), pp. 5–38.

Fullan, M. and Langworthy, M. (2014) *A Rich Seam: How New Pedagogies Find Deep Learning* (London: Pearson).

Hargittai, E., Fullerton, L., Menchen-Trevino, E. and Yates Thomas, K. (2010) 'Trust Online: young adults' evaluation of web content', *International Journal of Communication*, 4: 468–494.

Hoffman, T.K., Franks, T. and Edson, B. (2015) 'Cultural Awareness Training: preparing new instructors for the millennial student', *Basic Communication Course Annual*, 27 (7), available online at http://ecommons.udayton.edu/cgi/viewcontent.cgi?article=1479&context=bcca [accessed 01/06/17].

Kyung-Sun, K., Sei-Chung, J.S. and Eun Young Y.L. (2014) 'Undergraduates' use of social media as information sources', *College and Research Libraries*, 75 (4): 442–457.

Mahida, P. (2012) 'Bad Grades: the fault of students or lecturers and tutors?' *Huffpost*, 8 February updated 8 April, available online at www.huffingtonpost.co.uk/priya-mahida/bad-grades-students-lecturers-fault_b_1261045.html [accessed 06/06/17].

Nicholson, R. (2016) 'Poor Little Snowflake' – the defining insult of 2016, The *Guardian*, 28 November, available online at www.theguardian.com/science/2016/nov/28/snowflake-insult-disdain-young-people [accessed 24/05/17].

Noakes, M. (2017) *The Little Book of Self-Care* (London: Ebury Press).

Reading, S. (2017) *The Self-Care Revolution: Smart Habits and Simple Practices to Allow You to Flourish* (Piscataway, NJ: Aster).

Rockquemore, K. (2015) 'Academic Guilt', *Inside Higher Ed*, 1 July, available online at www.insidehighered.com/advice/2015/07/01/essay-academics-who-face-guilt-whenever-they-arent-working [accessed 15/05/17].

Sinek, S. (2017) 'On Millennials in the Workplace', YouTube, available online at www.youtube.com/watch?v=hEROQp6QJNU [accessed 23/11/17].

Tait, A. (2017) 'The Myth of Generation Snowflake: how did "sensitive" become a dirty word?', *New Statesman*, 27 January, available online at www.newstatesman.com/politics/uk/2017/01/myth-generation-snowflake-how-did-sensitive-become-dirty-word [accessed 05/05/17].

Tulgan, B. (2016) *Not Everyone Gets a Trophy: How to Manage the Millennials* (Hoboken, NJ: John Wiley and Sons).

Twenge, J.M. (2009) *Generation Me: Why Today's Young Americans are More Confident, Assertive, Entitled – and More Miserable Than Ever Before* (New York: Artia Books)

Wineburg, S., McGrew, S., Breakstone, J. and Ortega, T. (2016) 'Evaluating Information: the cornerstone of civic online reasoning', *Stanford Digital Repository*, available online at https://purl.stanford.edu/fv751yt5934 [accessed 08/05/17].

Further reading

Aubrey, K. and Riley, A. (2015) *Understanding and Using Educational Theories* (London: Sage).

Bates, B. (2015) *Learning Theories Simplified: And How to Apply Them to Teaching* (London: Sage).

Combi, C. (2015) *Generation Z: Their Voices, Their Lives* (London: Windmill Books).

Seemiller, C. and Grace, M. (2016) *Generation Z goes to College* (San Francisco: Jossey-Bass).

Waring, M. (2014) *Understanding Pedagogy: Developing a Critical Approach to Teaching and Learning* (Abingdon: Routledge).

Useful journals

Higher Education Quarterly

Teaching in Higher Education

3 Finding your feet

The previous chapter explored some of the characteristics of the conventional undergraduate student today, and practical ways in which to manage their, and your own, expectations. It ended on the importance of self-care. This chapter takes this as its starting point, as it sets out some of the contexts in which you may teach and some of the challenges you might encounter early on in your career. It introduces you to all the other types of students you may work with, and the varying teaching methods you might use. Building on the previous chapter it will discuss the topics you teach outside of your area of 'expertise', and how you can learn to teach them with confidence.

Different types of students and different types of teaching

Whereas the previous chapter examined the group you are most likely to teach – the typical undergraduate university population, namely the new millennials – it is important to recognise that university students are not a homogenous group and that there are important and significant variations within the student population at any given time that will affect how you regard and work with each other. Moreover, there are different formats for teaching, and different levels of teaching, which require recognition and attention in the second chapter of this section.[1]

---

[1] For those readers specifically interested in working with doctoral students, PhD supervision will be covered in relation to research capacity in chapter 6.

Mature students and part-time students

Mature students are identified in the UK as anyone over the age of 21 years when they start studying at undergraduate level. At the time of writing 25 per cent of the undergraduate student population was over 21 (Universities UK 2015), with the majority of that population under 25 years old. In 2014/15, part-time students constituted around 25 per cent (a drop from 31 per cent in 2011/12), but these include all registrations on postgraduate courses, undergraduate and foundation courses (Higher Education Statistics Agency, 2017).

In the UK the concept of 'lifelong learning' that was fostered in the early part of the twenty-first century has been diminished with the introduction of the competitive HE sector outlined in chapter 1. Lifelong learning is now confined to specialist institutions, or those that deliberately target older students with provision that can 'flex' around the needs of older or part-time students. Sadly, with a focus on large undergraduate courses many of the top ranked universities (themselves a misnomer, see chapter 1) and/or research-intensive universities are now beyond the reach of older or part-time students.

Why has this happened? With an expectation of exemplar entry grades to enter the top ranked universities and more 18 to 21-year-old student applications than there are places for most of those institutions, mature and/or part-time students are simply not needed for their 'bums-on-seats' student numbers and income. This is because in order to compete many universities have opted to focus almost exclusively on 18 to 21-year-olds as their key demographic target market. With little or limited domestic responsibility, this age group can study full-time and their courses can be structured accordingly. For example, teaching can start at 8am in the morning and go through to 8pm at night; student support services can be focused on the needs of that age group; and childcare does not need to be provided. By focusing on such a limited student population, the well-oiled machinery of the institution does not need to flex or accommodate those who deviate from this full-time delivery model. The flexibility that was once present in many institutions and enabled mature students to return to education after a period of work or parenting, while they still had some domestic responsibility, or to provide part-time options, has thus effectively vanished in some geographical areas, limiting choice of course and places to study.

Conversely, changes to the organisation of HE and the move towards delivering HE level courses within further education colleges means that mature and/or part-time students may be able to study more locally to their home, and undertake degree-level study or training alongside employment. Local further education colleges often provide courses with a vocational emphasis, meaning that a mature or part-time student can undertake (for example) an apprenticeship alongside degree level study. However, it is unlikely that colleagues in those colleges are research-active, meaning that mature or part-time students who want to work with research-active academic leaders in their field are not able to do so.

Teaching mature and part-time students

Having made a conscious and deliberate decision to attend university following a period away from full-time school education, mature students can be a pleasure to teach. They are usually highly aware of the commitment they have made to their studies and are likely to want to engage fully with you and with teaching materials. While they may have additional domestic responsibilities that take their attention away from their studies, they usually also bring with them a perspective that enables them to acknowledge their skillset and areas for development. Mature students have different needs to 18-year-olds, and as a teaching academic it is important to be attuned to these.

> **Tip**
>
> If you teach any mature students make sure that you show a continued interest in their motives to study, what led them to your course, and what they want to get out of it. Likely to have commitments away from their studies, it is important to consistently engage with mature students to ensure that they continue to invest their time and energy in their studies.

It is also important that when teaching mature students that you capitalise on their life experience and perspective(s), to complement the relative immaturity of those who have just left school.

> **Tip**
>
> When teaching mature students, make sure that you give them ample opportunities to contribute to your class, drawing on their life experience, pre-existing knowledge and/or skillset. By simple virtue of living longer and/or partaking in activities beyond their study they will have much to contribute to their own and others' learning experience.
>
> However, make sure they do not dominate group activities owing to, for example, being more confident in public speaking! Remember, your task is to integrate different types of students within your teaching, not to let older students do the teaching for you, nor let them dictate your class.

More often than not, part-time students will be mature students as well, although there may be times when you are teaching part-time 18 to 21-year-olds. Within this group of students retention is a key issue as, as with mature students, other demands on their time when they are not studying (whatever that may be – work, caring, parenting), are likely to be highly consuming. As a result, part-time students have to work doubly hard to remain committed to their studies over a longer period of time. In the UK this equates to a typical part-time undergraduate degree taking around 5–6 years, and a typical postgraduate degree taking around 3–4 years.

If you encounter part-time students as you embark on your teaching career, make sure to pay special attention to their needs and attendance. In a large class this can mean taking the time with the administrative team to identify part-time students by name/face. As part-time students do not have the same day-to-day engagement with the institution, you may be one of the very few contact points they have during a particular term/semester of study. If they are struggling to attend, commit to their studies, or undertake the assessment, it is unfortunately doubtful that anyone else (course mates, personal tutors or other teachers) will pick up on this. Hence, part-time students – although demanding less of the institution at any one point – require *more* attention paid to them on your part as the 'frontline' of teaching, to ensure that they are supported and enabled to continue.

It also pays to ascertain the number of part-time students within your institution at any point and whether there are mechanisms in place to support them. These might include special/additional study sessions, specific forms of personal tutoring, classes outside normal teaching hours and so on. Make it your business to know the make-up of the students in your institution, the likelihood of coming across particular students, and what opportunities exist for meeting their specific needs.

> **Pause for thought**
>
> What is the student make-up of your institution? How are teaching and resources channelled to different student groups?

Students with a disability or long-term condition

Much with the point above, how likely is it that you will teach students with a disability or long-term condition during your career? The answer is: very, very likely. Disabling conditions in HE are not only those limited to issues of access, they also include invisible conditions, syndromes, and learning difficulties that can impact on the educational experience, such as dyslexia and dyspraxia, diabetes, autism and so on. All of these will have an impact on a student's ability to focus, take in information, engage with said information, participate and contribute to class, and prepare/undertake assessment.

Of crucial importance to you is to know how your institution supports disabled students with additional needs. It is highly likely that there will be systems in place to identify additional needs as a result of disability – usually conducted by experts in learning needs. These individuals should be empowered to instruct you and/or your colleagues and department as to how to support a particular student, while maintaining confidentiality.

> **Tip**
>
> Make sure you are clear on the system in place to identify students with additional needs, and the mechanism through which those needs are ascertained and support delivered. Complacency is no excuse.

56   *Finding your feet*

Sometimes there may be occasions where you suspect that a student has additional needs. Alternatively, a colleague may bring it to your attention. Indeed, a course mate may bring it to your attention. This is when you need to be clear about how to act next in terms of managing your responsibilities, confidentiality regarding disclosure, and so on. It is likely that your institution will have written guidance on this, if not – then ask a senior colleague or student services (or equivalent) for confidential advice as to how to handle the situation.

> **Author reflection**
>
> A student from one of my classes once approached me during my office hours to talk to me about their housemate whom, they suspected, had an eating disorder. At that point, my responsibility was to the student in front of me and addressing their concerns – as their housemate's behaviour was creating considerable stress and anxiety in their household. After discussing their concerns, and documenting our discussion in writing (that I subsequently emailed to the student as a record), the student and I agreed that I would contact the programme director for their housemate (who was in a different department) to raise their concerns directly. I did so via phone call and followed up that phone call with an email, to ensure that our conversation was documented.

For students, managing a disability or condition that can impact on their ability to 'perform', academic assessment(s) can be particularly challenging. This is when measures need to be in place to provide flexibility for the student so that they are able to participate to the best of their ability without gaining an unfair advantage. Your institution will have regulations and guidance on how this is managed (see chapter 9).

International students

International students are students from another country who have come to study in your institution. In 2015-16 across the UK, 6 per cent of all students were from the European Union and 14 per cent were from the rest of the world, with 46 per cent of all studying at postgraduate level from outside the EU (UK Council for International Student Affairs, 2017).

From an institutional perspective, international students can be highly lucrative as they typically pay higher tuition fees and contribute to the international outlook (and potential ranking) of the university. For early career academics, international students can be a joy to teach. Bringing with them knowledge and experience beyond the country in which you are teaching, they can question and provide additional/counter evidence and examples that can inform and shape your teaching. They can be a huge asset within your class as they challenge assumptions made by both yourself and the other students. They can also assist you in probing your own innate knowledge of a subject area and normative expectations (that is, things that often go unquestioned because they are so familiar) of issues.

> **Tip**
>
> If you teach any international students it is worth finding out a little about their background and expectations of studying in your institution or country of work. This will hopefully help you to understand any challenges they may face or concerns they may have. You could do this by offering an 'international students' tutorial or office hour, where they could come to meet with you to discuss their prior knowledge and/or expectations of your module.

International students can also bring with them challenges for the early career academic. Their expectations of teaching and learning may be very different to those that you have experienced before. For example, they may assume more or less contact hours with you because that is the norm in their home country. They may feel very uncomfortable calling you by your chosen name (be that your first name as in the UK, or more formal identifiers such as in the US as 'Professor Jones'). They may carry with them an expectation of deference to the academic. They may be reluctant to question issues, or raise concerns about their experience of being taught. In contrast, they may assume that every aspect of HE teaching is open to challenge, dissection, debate and argument, which can be difficult and wearing for the teacher when you have a time-allotted slot in which to complete your class.

If you teach international students or are likely to do so in the future, it is very important to recognise and appreciate the challenges that international students may face when attending an institution in a new country. These may include the most obvious language difference, but could also include more subtle challenges of cultural understanding, social integration and the building of friendship networks. International students can be highly vulnerable to isolation (Bamford, 2008), not only within their institution but also within the country of study – exacerbated by the geographical distance from their familiar surroundings, and family and friends from home. Interestingly, some of the potential issues for international students can be similar for students who are studying while living at home. For these students, their ability to mix with others when not thrust into shared accommodation at the outset of their course, can be difficult and lead to feelings of isolation from the mainstream activities of the university.

Supporting all students

As an academic you are not solely responsible for students' mental health and wellbeing as your focus is on their educational experience and learning. However, you *do* have a responsibility to ensure that all students in your class are included and involved in learning, and to report any concerns you have to those who can appropriately support the student(s). Thus make sure you are attuned to, for example, the student who never sits with other students, does not ask or answer any questions, or who avoids contact with you. Are they ok? It does not take much time to ask.

> **Tip**
>
> Make sure you are clued up on support for different student groups within your institution. Are there societies? Support for academic study? Specialist student support services? You may need to point students to these.

Not all students will tell you if they are struggling. Indeed, many will do the exact opposite, presenting an outwardly confident and outgoing persona. As you become more experienced in teaching you are likely, and hopefully, going to gather up experience of working with students that will help you read the more subtle signs that an individual is having a difficult time. These signs can include facial expressions (or lack of), defeated body language, hostile language, aggressive or confrontational behaviour, nervousness and so on. You are not expected to be a master of these more understated communicative signs, but it pays to be attuned to them.

> **Pause for thought**
>
> What other signs might indicate that a student is struggling?

If you spot something, be prepared that if you ask how a student is getting on that you will need to provide time to chat and further opportunities in the future for the student to engage with you, to voice their concern(s) and to work out how they can make the most of their studies. If you do not have time to talk with a student make sure to ask how they are getting on and be clear that while you do not have a lot of time to go into detail *at that point*, you welcome the chance to speak with them in more depth on a later occasion. You may be the only person who has shown an interest in how they are getting on, so it is important that you offer a follow up opportunity, and honour it.

> **Tip**
>
> If a student indicates to you that they are struggling make sure you get their name and follow up with an email that reflects the content of your conversation. Not only does that document, date and record what was said if needed at a later date, it also provides the student with an opportunity to come back to you for further support once they have had time to reflect.

As with much in teaching there is an element of interpersonal skill required when recognising potential pastoral issues. If you have concerns, make sure to call on more senior colleagues or a colleague who oversees personal issues within your department or faculty. Over time your capacity to recognise potential issues will develop as you become more assured with regard to your own teaching ability and your capacity to identify problems through such subtleties as disengagement in class, body language and so on.

> **Author reflection**
>
> I once had a first-year student who attended my lectures and appeared very down at heart. She was also my personal tutee. I asked to see her, and after some gentle probing it transpired that she was struggling to meet people and make new friends since joining the university. She was very unhappy, and had begun to consider dropping out, which in turn aggravated her unhappiness as she felt she was failing at university.
>
> We devised a plan whereby we would meet for 5-10 minutes every week to update on how she was getting on and to create an action plan for the forthcoming week. During our weekly sessions we discussed her interests, one of which turned out to be volunteering. Over a period of a few months, structured by our weekly catch-ups and her action plans, the student made contact with the university volunteering service, and through them, a local charity. She became involved in the charity's work, doing a volunteer session for them every week. As she did so, her confidence began to grow in meeting new people, and she subsequently joined a university society where she met even more people and made new friends. Her whole body language changed and her energy transformed from an unhappy and lonely student, to one who was engaged, enthused by her work and was supported by friends. She smiled, held her head higher and, quite simply, blossomed.
>
> After that time we no longer needed to meet so frequently, and reverted back to conventional twice-a-term personal tutee meetings. On graduation day, I was delighted to see her celebrating her success with her family and friends.

Different types of teaching

So far, this chapter has covered the different types of students that you may come across during your early career. There are, of course, other different methods and modes of teaching that will impact on your engagement with the students you teach. As there are many specialist resources for these different forms of teaching, they will not be dwelled on here beyond the brief summaries below.

Postgraduate teaching

The extent to which you are engaged in teaching postgraduate students (for example Masters students) will very much depend on the institution in which you work. You may find that you do not teach any postgraduates, or you may find that all your teaching is with postgraduate students. Many of the challenges outlined in this chapter so far are relevant for postgraduate students and sometimes even more so as they typically have less contact time with academic staff (even when studying full-time), are expected to be more self-reliant and self-sufficient, and are likely to be a very diverse student group – consisting of students returning to study after a period of work, those who have come straight from their undergraduate degree, and those who are combining work and study together.

When teaching postgraduate students it is paramount that you have an understanding of the composition of the student group so that you can adapt and tailor your teaching methods to suit their respective needs. This can mean finding out details about the students in advance from those who provide administrative support for the cohort or from colleagues. If that is not possible, it means going into your first session with them with a top priority aim to discover their respective backgrounds, so that you can adjust your subsequent teaching if needed. Importantly, you need to be mindful of being flexible with postgraduates, as you cannot make assumptions about their age, demographic background, previous education, ethnicity, belief systems, motivations for studying and so on.

Distance learning

In the UK, distance learning has often been linked to the activities of the Open University which was established in the 1960s to provide education for all adults. Nowadays, many universities offer distance learning, not least because of the availability and accessibility of learning materials online, and the potential for collaboration through shared working, seminars and interaction that can be facilitated via online communication tools.

The structure and content of distance learning courses will vary considerably between institutions depending on the topic and size of the course. If you are tasked with delivering or creating distance learning materials it pays to be skilled in the challenges and possibilities associated with this mode of teaching and learning.

Open access learning

In recent years there has been a growth in the number of learning resources placed online for free. Many universities, such as the Open University, have been committed to making available parts of their teaching for a very long time; for others, it is a newer endeavour. Often referred to as MOOCs (massive open online courses), they are in part driven by the need to educate and widen participation (that is, get more people interested in a topic area and open up study options to non-traditional audiences), and also as a marketing tool to promote the education provided by the institution. As with distance learning, if you are tasked with taking on the creation or management of open access learning, you will need to be schooled in teaching online; delivering ideas in this forum; formative assessment and appropriate online exercises; and methods of assessment.

Teaching beyond your specialist topic/area

Unless you are employed on a research-only contract, it is likely that when you are hired you will be required to teach specific modules or courses, which may or may not be within your existing knowledge set and area of expertise. Teaching in areas tangential to your field may require a significant amount of work and, as Grant with Sherrington (2006) note, you need to be mindful and realistic (of which more later) of how much effort and energy that work may demand.

There are challenges, risks, or at least potential disadvantages, of teaching outside of your specialist area. As identified by Huston (2012) these can include:

- Being outsmarted by students;
- Being asked a question you cannot answer;
- Time taken to prepare for every class;
- Difficulty in explaining key concepts;
- Worry and associated impact on mental health.

I would add to this the challenges and risks of:

- Over-preparation;
- Self-sabotage such as undermining yourself to colleagues (for example indicating to colleagues that you are struggling to understand material);
- The potential impact on your own self-esteem and self-worth;
- Loss of up-to-date knowledge and expertise in specialist area as time directed learning new material;
- Overload;
- Burnout.

Some of these challenges are practical and ways to address these challenges are identified shortly. Self-care was covered in the previous chapter; this, along with self-preservation, is important in relation to teaching and is covered later in this chapter and in chapter 4 in how to develop a thick(er) skin.

What is important to acknowledge here is that there *are* challenges and risks associated with teaching beyond your subject comfort-zone; it is important to recognise these rather than pretend they do not exist or that you are an expert in everything. To ignore challenges and risks creates both internal pressure as you set yourself higher and higher expectations as to what and how much you know, and this also feeds into pressure from others as it makes it very difficult to disclose the difficulties you are experiencing to colleagues. In turn, without recognition, over time colleagues can come to hold very high (maybe even impossibly high) expectations of you and your teaching – assuming, for example, that you can teach any subject at 'the drop of a hat'. These pressures contribute to overload, as you put more and more energy and time into your teaching activities, creating ever higher demands of yourself, and which may ultimately lead to burnout.

Having said that, while there are numerous challenges to teaching unfamiliar areas there are *significant* advantages. Huston (2012) identifies the opportunities and advantages to 'teaching what you don't know' as:

1. Learning something new and interesting.
2. Connecting with colleagues outside your specialist area.
3. Broadening your CV (which is covered later in this chapter and in chapter 4).
4. Developing a new area of research.

64 Finding your feet

Teaching beyond your specialist area means that you are required to engage with new ideas, new theories, new scholars and new paradigms. It can open up opportunities for new collaborations with colleagues both internal and external to your institution, enabling you to expand your research interests. It can enhance your CV in that you can demonstrate the *breadth and volume* of your teaching experience and subject areas.

The importance of breadth: knowing a little about a lot

According to Huston (2012) an important advantage to teaching what you do not know is that you move away from the highly specialist model of expertise (depth) perpetuated in and by higher level postgraduate study (and, I would add, research). This expert model may be critical to your research career in that you are/want to become a world-leading expert on a highly specific issue, subject or problem; but for teaching it is typically more important to your students, your institution and your discipline that you are able to make connections *between* issues, subjects and problems. Thus, having a breadth and diversity of knowledge, rather than specialism and depth, may be of more use and value to you and your students. Teaching subjects that are unfamiliar to you can become a way of developing and extending the breadth of your knowledge, enabling you to more readily and easily make connections between issues, questions and problems.

> **Pause for thought**
>
> What connections are you making or could you make between the different topics that you teach?

According to Huston, those people who feel most comfortable teaching outside of their comfort zone do so because they do not feel the need to master their material. This can be because they may not value mastery of material when they walk into their classroom, or because they do not subscribe to a "teaching as telling" model (p. 41). Rather, these individuals value student engagement and what is often referred to in the UK as 'student-centred' learning and teaching. This approach means that you ascertain your students' knowledge and expectations, helping them to learn through your teaching as facilitation rather than simply disseminating information. Taking this approach moves you towards a more cyclical model of teaching and learning, where you engage then give students time to reflect, and then let them re-engage with you. It moves teaching away from a mono-directional dissemination-of-knowledge teaching model, to a reciprocal model that encourages 'deep' rather than 'surface' learning (see chapter 2). You are seeking student understanding rather than knowledge mastery – and are in effect modelling that to the students through your approach to teaching.

Expectation management

An emphasis on your own breadth, deep learning and student-centred approaches to teaching means that both you and your students can have more realistic expectations about what they are going to learn and how they are going to do so during your time with them. It requires effort on your side to ensure that you have the breadth of knowledge, but also shifts the emphasis onto students as active agents responsible for their own learning. This, in turn, can lead to more motivated students. For Huston (2012), this motivation stems from:

1. You having clearer expectations about how long their learning tasks will take – not least because you have had to do it yourself.
2. You being better able to articulate connections between topics and issues – again, not least because you have had to learn them yourself.
3. You being able to judge their efforts as you have had to go through a similar experience of learning.

Thus, counter to a perhaps more instinctive expectation that specialist knowledge equates to high quality teaching, your ability to convey ideas clearly and without jargon in unfamiliar areas is likely to be *enhanced* because you lack specialist knowledge.

Bearing this in mind, it is important to reflect on how much time you expect, how much time you take, and how much time you need to prepare your teaching (Grant with Sherrington, 2006). As Huston notes, 'content novices' who feel anxious about their teaching (see below) are likely to spend significant amounts of time preparing, to make sure that they are not caught out by students. What this can do however is lead to information overload, surplus detail for the tasks at hand, and over-preparation of teaching materials so that when you come to actually teach you end up reading your notes, fearful of missing something out or explaining something incorrectly, rather than engaging with the students in front of you. Your expectations of yourself become so high that they can become a hindrance.

> **Tip**
>
> A good way to manage preparation is to focus on what needs to be taught in class and what you can provide/require of students away from their contact time with you. Does *everything* on a topic have to be covered in that precious contact time you have with students? What can students do to prepare in advance, or follow up problem-solving activities that consolidate their learning?
>
> If you take the pressure off to teach *everything* on a topic matter, what are the 2-3 key things they need to take away from their time with you in each class or lecture? Remember, many students enjoying discussing ideas and will willingly respond to your questions and challenges. You do not need to tell them *everything*. Huston calls this 'backward planning', with an emphasis on what you want the students to be able to *do* (rather than know) after their time with you.

When teaching not only do you have to carefully manage the expectations of your students, you also need to manage your own expectations of *yourself*. Sometimes your teaching has to be and can be exemplary, sometimes it just needs to be good enough; sometimes you need to lead the way, other times you can sit back and let the students take the lead. The skill to learn in the early part of your academic career is about how to differentiate and organising your time, preparation and actual teaching method/materials accordingly.

Imposter syndrome

Where does being and accepting being 'good enough' at times in your teaching leave you? It may appear that so far in this chapter I am advocating slovenly or lazy teaching. Far from it, this is about managing your time day-to-day to ensure that you are consistently and dependably good (enough) at what you do, have a vision of where you are going with your career, and to make sure you do not burnout in the early years of being a teaching academic.

Without doubt, being good enough can be an uncomfortable position to occupy, particularly if you are used to being highly competent and skilled in your research or other areas of your life. Certainly, when teaching an unfamiliar topic you may sometimes only feel one step ahead of your students. However, it is important to realise that there are times when *that is only as far as you need to be*. While you may be aware of your own limitations and gaps in knowledge, your students are not. Thus, the way in which you convey confidence and self-assurance in your teaching can be as important as the information you are disseminating. This performative element of teaching and what you can do to help you feel (more) confident in front of a class is covered in greater detail in chapter 4.

This is not to say that HE teaching is all about performance and nothing about the content; rather that you can be your own worst enemy in convincing yourself that students and colleagues are aware of the gaps in your knowledge and perceived inadequacies/deficiencies. Feelings such as these are often referred to as 'imposter syndrome'. In relation to managing feelings of being an imposter when teaching, in 28 interviews with academics Huston identified three types of people when it came to teaching outside of their subject area. They were the:

1. Poised and Confident group, who were un-phased by teaching topics and actively sought them out.
2. Undecided but Untroubled group, who felt comfortable teaching outside of their specialist area sometimes but not always, and
3. Strained and Anxious group, who were unhappy teaching unfamiliar topics and were tired and overstretched as a result.

Huston argues that there are ways to avoid being in group 3, contingent on factors that are both inside and outside of your control. Those outside of your control include being assigned to teach a topic/module/course as opposed to it being a choice. Being assigned a topic can lead to feelings of frustration, insecurity, and being exploited by colleagues because no one else wants to teach that course. In contrast, she found that *choosing* to teach outside of an area can lead to academics feeling energised, enthused and willing to engage and continually update and revise their teaching.

68 *Finding your feet*

As an early career academic it is highly likely that you will not yet have the esteem, reputational currency or capacity to negotiate your teaching topics, and you may even have been specifically hired to teach specific modules. Having choice over what you teach may therefore feel unrealistic or a long way off. When that is the case, it is important to focus on the things that you *do* have choice over: your attitude and approach to teaching, how you manage any feelings of imposter syndrome and the practical ways in which you can handle teaching unfamiliar topics.

> **Pause for thought**
>
> What is your approach/attitude towards teaching right now? Is it something you enjoy or look forward to? Is it something you feel is a burden or responsibility? What changes could you make to help shift your attitude towards your teaching?

Huston (2012) identified that, for those in the poised and confident group, dealing with rather than ignoring their feelings of imposter syndrome was key. In addressing your sense of imposter syndrome, she advocates that your emphasis be on honesty and humility, without shame or embarrassment, all the time avoiding any self-sabotage of your credibility.

> Instructors who found a way to be honest with their students about their limited knowledge were much more comfortable teaching outside of their expertise. In contrast, content novices who pretended to be content experts were more likely to be Strained and Anxious. They felt it was important to appear more knowledgeable than they actually were, and this created tremendous pressure and more work, as you might imagine.
>
> (Huston, 2012, p. 38)

Being upfront with students in this context does not mean declaring to that you are out of your depth, or that you are struggling to teach them. This can potentially lead to a loss of credibility in their eyes and damage to your own sense of worth as a teacher. It could, however, mean that you acknowledge your existing specialist background and recognise that you are branching into new and exciting areas with them – and that you are looking forward to learning *alongside* them and hearing their ideas. Identifying the limitations of your knowledge therefore not need be an additional source of pressure; rather it can be a liberating opportunity to articulate your shared passion for learning with your students.

Managing your own expectations and the extent to which you feel it is a necessity to appear to students to possess greater knowledge than you have is thus critical. Ways in which you can do this authentically in front of students with a little help from 'stock phrases' are covered later in this chapter.

Pause for thought

What are your own expectations of yourself when it comes to teaching? How realistic are your expectations about your knowledge base? Can you identify gaps? What do you absolutely need to make sure you know, and what can you admit to *not* knowing?

Practical ways to address the challenges of teaching

Time management: managing your teaching workload

One of the biggest challenges you can face when you commence your academic career is the sheer amount of time it takes to teach. While your timetable may suggest that you teach a specified number of hours a week, this does not account for the time it takes to prepare for teaching, deal with students during tutorials or office hours, answer emails, set assignments, mark papers, and perform the administrative tasks that accompany organisation and delivery of teaching. As noted earlier, within this,

> . . . there is an inherent danger in over-preparing. If you have a brand new lecture to write, this could consume your entire day . . . The trick is to set yourself a time limit, say three to four hours, for writing a lecture, and stick to it. By doing so, not only do you 'temper ambition' but you do not allow teaching preparation to encroach on your other activities and commitments.
>
> (Grant with Sherrington, 2006: 81)

The immediacy of teaching and its associated demands mean that it is very easy to slip into 'responsive mode' and prioritise teaching above all other demands on your time. This can be a slippery slope as other activities, and for those on research and teaching contracts your more long-term goals such as research paper writing, can be sidelined and ultimately shelved altogether in favour of teaching. The importance of being realistic in what your teaching can cover, and tempering your ambition in what you teach, cannot therefore be overestimated.

There are a multitude of texts on how to teach, how to prepare teaching materials and so on. This chapter does not seek to replicate these (see the suggested further reading at the end of this chapter), but there are ways to make your life easier when it comes to managing your teaching load and building up your teaching repository.

> **Tip**
>
> In terms of building up your teaching repository, there are a number of possible ways to achieve this:
>
> - Find core teaching materials that do not date too quickly so that you can update them (for example) every other year rather than every time you teach a course.
> - Make sure that you have a number of activities within your modules that explicitly address the learning outcomes for the module. This ensures that you can evidence to your students and to colleagues that the learning outcomes are being met if requested.
> - Periodically check your library and/or publisher websites to ensure that you are using the most up-to-date core teaching materials/textbooks. Most publishers provide (free) inspection copies of their bestselling textbooks as a way of promoting the book to academics and potential library purchases. Request inspection copies and use them in your teaching if appropriate. Make sure your library has copies of the most up-to-date texts available.

- Many publishers also provide complementary websites/activities for key textbooks – seek them out make use of them if appropriate. You do not need to (re)invent the wheel every time you create/revise your teaching materials.
- Make sure you keep an index of key sources such as journals, publishers, news websites, and so on. This means that when pressed for time you can refer to reliable and trustworthy sources rather than having to (re)identify sources.
- Periodically check your disciplinary association/teaching accreditor for newly released materials that can be used in or to inform your teaching.

So far this chapter has examined some of the issues involved with teaching different groups, at different levels, and in different subject areas, with a view to building up your experience and expertise in teaching first-hand. For some readers, this will be more straightforward, depending on their extrovert personality, their ability to organise, their institution, their job role and so on. If you struggle to teach or feel yourself floundering however, know that you are not alone – although it can be easy to assume you are the first to feel this way when others appear so self-assured in their knowledge base and teaching experience.

> It's easy to assume that your senior colleagues have somehow always been content experts in their courses. This assumption leaves a new instructor thinking that she is somehow the first person in her department to machete her way through a new topic after being hired.
>
> (Huston, 2012: 39)

It can also be easy to assume that teaching will always feel overwhelming, stretching, and energy-sapping. It will not. The more materials you amass over your career, the more you will have to draw on and update in future teaching.

> **Author reflection**
>
> As a very early career academic one very senior colleague told me that in their experience the first few years of an academic career are some of the most challenging – not least because you are developing your ability to teach in HE and building up your teaching repository. Once you have several years of teaching 'under your belt' and a range of teaching materials saved, alongside experience of efficiently sourcing and (re)interpreting materials for class dissemination and discussion, you will (hopefully, likely) feel much more confident in your ability to teach. This is turn will influence how long it takes you to prepare teaching materials, and the extent to which you feel the need to prepare – because you feel more assured in being able to handle unfamiliar information, address challenges with students and manage setbacks.

Boosting your confidence

In the meantime, before you arrive at such an experienced place, there are ways to boost your confidence, and in turn your credibility with colleagues and students as a good, competent and reliable teacher.

Stock answers

There will be times when you are asked a question by students to which you do not know the answer. Not knowing everything is perfectly reasonable and being caught off-guard is something that you can anticipate happening in all teaching (regardless of your experience and knowledge) in advance. A good way to handle such situations is to make sure you have some 'stock answers' or responses ready for when you are put on the spot. Huston (2012) provides some really good examples of stock answers, and how to set the tone with an opening positive response. To paraphrase some of her suggestions, for example you could respond as follows:

- "That's a really interesting question, what does everyone else think?"
- "That's a really good point Sarah, we will address that next week"

- "What a great question. I wish I had a great answer!"
- "I'm not quite sure about how to respond to that. Let me have a think and get back to you on it"
- "That's a good point, here's a tentative answer as it's something I'll need to look into more and come back to you on".

Of course, critically, if you say you will get back to the class on a question – make sure you do! This can either be a follow-up message or email to the whole class, or address it again in a following lecture/session. Importantly, make sure you respond publicly and not just to the student who asked the question – so that all the other students benefit from your response, and are witness to your efforts in getting back to the original questioner.

Avoiding mistakes

There are some pretty basic ways to undermine yourself and your students' confidence in you, such as:

- Turning up late to your class or going to the wrong room;
- Not knowing how to use the technology in the classroom provided;
- Running out of time to give the complete lecture;
- Not having read your own suggested materials in advance;
- Not adhering to standard practices within your department/institution;
- Not knowing how assessment is managed;
- Not being aware of assessment deadlines.

All of these can be addressed in advance of your teaching: check the room you are teaching in; make sure you are familiar with the technology; double-check assessment deadlines and how assessments are submitted, marked and returned; run through your lecture in advance and/or make sure you have a clock to hand when teaching; read through materials in advance, and so on. Huston (2012) further advises against the four common mistakes that more inexperienced teachers in HE can make:

- Underestimating the time it takes to prepare your teaching;
- Assigning too much work to the students;
- Not managing others' expectations;
- Forgetting what you've learnt from other experiences.

> **Tip**
>
> If any of the above are a potential risk for you then you need to get into the practice of documenting how long it takes you to complete tasks, seeking feedback from students on how long it takes them to do tasks, and recording 'lessons learned' (for example, whether or not to provide hand-outs).

Publishing on teaching related topics

Another way to boost your confidence (and credentials) is to publish on teaching related matters. This is an excellent way to stay on top of your field as reading-for-writing-for-publishing can help you stay up-to-date on a particular theory or method, or some element of the practice of teaching. Not only that, it establishes you as a reflective teacher engaged with your field of enquiry/teaching practice and is a useful addition to your CV in terms of your experience, skillset and ability to connect your teaching to wider theory, methods, policy and practice debates.

> **Pause for thought**
>
> If you were to publish on aspects of teaching, what kind of topics would they be? For example, how to teach specific techniques or research methods? Or even book chapters like this one, on how to manage teaching in HE?

Get involved in team teaching

The extent to which the opportunity to teach as part of a team is available to you will depend on your topic and how teaching is organised within your department/institution. Working with colleagues can be a really useful way to manage your teaching load, sharing marking, and learning from each other. It can also make for really great courses as you put your collective knowledge, experience and energy into creating curriculum and assessment plans, and can help boost your confidence in both giving and receiving constructive feedback from colleagues.

> **Tip**
>
> Ask your line manager or whoever allocates teaching about the possibility of team teaching – is this something that is commonplace in your department, or something they would consider introducing?

Team teaching can also be difficult however, in terms of coordination, overload, managing expectations and working with colleagues who may have very different ideas as to the priorities of a course or methods of teaching. So if your department or institution actively practices team teaching, or is bringing it in, then make sure you have very clear agreements in place regarding ownership, responsibilities, deadlines, communication and so on.

Teaching observations

It is likely that at some point you will be observed by a peer when teaching as part of a formal documentation process to demonstrate that you are up to the job and to provide feedback on where you could improve. It is also likely that your institution will have quite a prescriptive teaching observation form and protocol for including observations in any recording of your teaching performance (see chapter 1).

> **Tip**
>
> Make sure you are familiar with your institution's expectations regarding teaching observation(s), probation and promotion. Are you required to have a specific number in any given period? Who decides who the observer is? How are observations fed into processes that assess your overall performance?

Beyond acting as a tool of surveillance however, teaching observations can be a really helpful way of seeking and receiving feedback from more experienced HE teachers, and should be regarded as such. They can help boost your confidence in terms of identifying your skills, your abilities and your engagement with students, as well as how to tweak your teaching here and there. Having had my teaching observed many times, I can also say that it can be quite nerve-wracking. It is therefore paramount that you have confidence and trust in your observer, so that you feel comfortable teaching in front of them. Let them know if there are any issues with the class beforehand (are they are very vocal class that you struggle to manage? Or a very quiet group of students that require a lot of prompting?), and any topics you would like specific feedback on, for example:

- Time management;
- Pace and clarity of communication;
- Presentation skills;
- Use of prompts;
- Student engagement;
- Handling questions;
- Opening and ending the session.

Teaching observations should be a win-win scenario, as a tool for your institution in terms of your teaching being validated, and for you to gain insight and supportive feedback that helps you feel more confident when teaching.

> **Tip**
>
> Why not get involved with observing others? This is a really great way of observing and exploring teaching techniques, interpersonal skills, and reflecting on your own practice.

Undertaking continuing professional development (CPD) on teaching

Alongside teaching observations it is probable that your institution will provide opportunities to develop your teaching through educational courses, one-off sessions and so on. Depending on your background it may be mandatory for you to attend some of these in the early phase of your career. Indeed, with the introduction of the Teaching Excellence Framework in the UK (see chapter 4), the importance of education for HE educators and ongoing professional development is likely to become increasingly important across the HE sector, as institutions are tasked with demonstrating the professional credentials, capacity and skillset(s) of their teaching workforce.

> **Tip**
>
> It is worthwhile acquainting yourself of your institution's expectations regarding Continuing Professional Development (CPD) in teaching. Are you expected to have or be working towards a teaching qualification? Are you expected to undertake specific CPD activities otherwise?

Whether or not you are expected to take part in CPD, it is necessary to consider how important you regard teaching within your career, and what experience, knowledge and credentials will make you an attractive asset to your employer or future employers.

> **Pause for thought**
>
> If you foresee teaching as part of your future academic career, what could you do to go above and beyond what is expected in your institution or across the HE sector? Are there courses you could go on, activities to undertake or qualifications to pursue?

Chapter 4 will provide further examples of how you can expand your CV through taking on teaching related activities.

Become a member of a teaching body

In terms of establishing your credibility as a teacher there exist national bodies on teaching practice of which you can become a member, associate or fellow depending on your experience and skills. In the UK, the body that provides official recognition of teaching competency is the Higher Education Academy. Your own disciplinary organisations may have teaching qualifications or membership options that highlight your teaching role. Becoming a member of such bodies is a highly visible way to establish, identify and promote your teaching ability, thereby boosting your confidence in your own ability along the way.

> **Pause for thought**
>
> What teaching organisations are available to you, what is their currency in terms of their credentials, and what do you need to do to become a part of them?

Getting involved

Involvement in curriculum development such as setting learning objectives and methods of assessment, and revising degree courses or codes of practice, are a great way to understand how teaching is managed and organised within an institution. It is likely that your institution will have a clear committee pathway where decisions about teaching are made (see chapter 8). Access to the committees may depend on being allocated an administrative role, or they may be open to any interested member of staff.

Getting involved in such activities can be a way to feel valued in terms of your input into teaching, receiving feedback on your ideas, and boosting your experience and confidence all at the same time. However, such involvement can also come at a cost in terms of energy and time to do other tasks, so it requires an informed and considered decision and commitment (see chapter 4).

> **Tip**
>
> Find out what opportunities are available to you to get involved in curriculum development, and if you have the capacity to do so volunteer if you have an interest in this area. Not only will you contribute to the organisation of teaching where you work, and (hopefully) have

> some influence over what is taught and how, getting involved in this is an excellent way of developing your transferable skills and evidencing your CV as a competent and capable HE teacher, as you head beyond probation or towards promotion.

While this chapter has taken you through some of the realities of teaching in HE, remember that all HE teachers have to start somewhere, and it is highly unlikely that your more experienced colleagues will not have encountered many of the hurdles that can and will come your way. No one is born a teacher, it is a skill that is learned and refined over time. Becoming a better educator is always a process. Do not expect yourself to be utterly infallible at the outset of your career. Make sure you enter the classroom prepared in terms of knowing who your student group is, understanding their expectations, understanding your own expectations (including those of yourself), and what needs to be taught. Moreover, as you embark on your early academic career, actively seek out and give yourself as many opportunities to feel confident in your own teaching ability – this will be critical when you encounter challenging periods, as the next chapter will show.

References

Bamford, J.K. (2008) 'Improving International Students' Experience of Studying in the UK', *The Economics Network*, available online at www.economicsnetwork.ac.uk/showcase/bamford_international [accessed 01/07/17].

Grant, W. with Sherrington, P. (2006) *Managing your Academic Career* (Basingstoke: Palgrave Macmillan).

Higher Education Statistics Agency (2017) 'Higher Education Student Enrolments and Qualifications obtained at Higher Education Providers in the United Kingdom 2015/16', available online at www.hesa.ac.uk/news/12-01-2017/sfr242-student-enrolments-and-qualifications [accessed 08/07/17].

Huston, T. (2012) *Teaching What You Don't Know* (Cambridge, MA: Harvard University Press).

UK Council for International Student Affairs (2017) *International Student Statistics: UK Higher Education*, available online at https://institutions.ukcisa.org.uk/Info-for-universities-colleges–schools/Policy-research–statistics/Research–statistics/International-students-in-UK-HE/#International-(non-UK)-students-in-UK-HE-in-2015-16 [accessed 08/07/17].

Universities UK (2015) *Patterns and Trends in UK Higher Education* (London: Universities UK)

Further reading

(Please note some of these texts are intended for students, but will provide you with useful insight from their perspective)

Becker, L. (2004) *How to Manage your Distance and Open Learning Course* (Basingstoke: Palgrave Macmillan).

Becker, L. (2004) *How to Manage your Postgraduate Course* (Basingstoke: Palgrave Macmillan).

Becker, L. (2009) *The Mature Student's Handbook* (Basingstoke: Palgrave Macmillan).

Biggs, J. and Tang. C. (2011) *Teaching for Quality Learning at University*, 4th edn (Maidenhead: Open University Press).

Binns, C. (2017) *Module Design in a Changing Era of Higher Education: Academic Identity, Cognitive Dissonance and Institutional Barriers* (Basingstoke: Palgrave Macmillan).

Gatrell, C. (2006) *Managing Part-Time Study: A Guide for Undergraduates and Postgraduates* (Maidenhead: Open University Press).

Goyder, C. (2014) *Gravitas: Communicate with Confidence, Influence and Authority* (London: Vermilion).

Hunt, L. (ed.) *University Teaching in Focus* (Abingdon: Routledge).

Falk, E. (2012) *Becoming a New Instructor: A Guide for College Adjuncts and Graduate Students* (Abingdon: Routledge).

Fry, H., Ketteridge, S. and Marshall, S. (eds) (2014) *A Handbook for Teaching and Learning in Higher Education: Enhancing Academic Practice* (Abingdon: Routledge).

Kettle, M. (2017) *International Student Engagement in Higher Education: Transforming Practices, Pedagogies and Participation* (Bristol: Multilingual Matters).

Lea, J. (ed.) (2015) *Enhancing Learning and Teaching in Higher Education: Engaging with the Dimensions of Practice* (Maidenhead: Open University Press).

Light, G., Cox, R. and Calkins, S. (2009) *Learning and Teaching in Higher Education*, 2nd edn (London: Sage).

Pokorny, H. and Warren, D. (2016) *Enhancing Teaching Practice in Higher Education* (London: Sage).

Pritchard, L. 2006) *The Mature Student's Guide to Higher Education* (Maidenhead: Open University Press).

Race, P. (2014) *The Lecturer's Toolkit*, 4th edn (Abingdon: Routledge).

Ramsden, P. (2003) *Learning to Teach in Higher Education* (Abingdon: Routledge).

Reinders, H., Moore, N., and Lewis, M. (2012) *The International Student Handbook* (Basingstoke: Palgrave Macmillan).

Riddell, S. (2005) *Disabled Students in Higher Education* (Abingdon: Routledge).

Young, V. (2011) *The Secret Thoughts of Successful Women: Why Capable People Suffer from Imposter Syndrome and How to Thrive in Spite of It* (London: Crown Publishing Group).

Useful journals

International Journal of Teaching and Learning in Higher Education
Journal of Diversity in Higher Education
Journal of Further and Higher Education

4 Behind the scenes of teaching

As noted in previous chapters there is a wealth of instructive guidance available on 'how to teach in HE'. Indeed, as an early career academic you may already be familiar with this literature having been required by your institution to take part in formal training on how to teach. Drawing on these and the previous chapters in this section, the chapter first examines the impact of measurement and teaching evaluations of your work. It then explores some of the diverse teaching responsibilities and activities that you can take on as an early career academic, and the challenge of establishing when to agree to undertake teaching that will be beneficial for you/the students/the department/the university, and when to negotiate (and how!). It will, in essence, share with you some of the less visible parts of teaching, the parts of which you may not yet be aware of, and the bits you may have some autonomy over (and the bits you don't).

The surveillance and evaluation of teaching

As alluded to in chapter 1, there is an increased evaluation of all aspects of HE, corresponding with moves towards rankings and commercial imperatives showing 'value for money' for the student 'consumer'. Teaching, in particular, is coming under greater scrutiny than ever before as, in the UK at least, the burden of financing HE has shifted from the state to students. As a result, scrutiny – with the intention of ensuring quality and standards – has permeated almost every level of teaching and institutional bureaucracy, so at any one point your teaching will likely be being monitored, assessed and evaluated via a number of channels. These include but are not limited to:

- Course evaluation by students;
- Peer observation/evaluation by colleagues (to conform to either institutional or external requirements regarding teaching proficiency and continuing professional development, see chapter 3);
- Moderation of assessment marking by colleagues;
- Evaluation of teaching materials and assessment by external examiners;
- Course/degree evaluation by Programme Leaders (see chapter 8), or others in the department;
- Course/degree evaluation by an institution committees that sit above the department;
- National student evaluation such as the National Student Survey;
- National institutional evaluation such as the Teaching Excellence Framework.

The extent to which these practices shape your own teaching will be dependent on your institution and where you are in your academic career. As noted in chapter 1 however, it is worthwhile recalling at the outset of this chapter some of the difficulties of measuring education and 'quality' in HE, with a view to you not losing sight of the social, economic and political contexts in which these evaluations take place.

> **Pause for thought**
>
> What would truly excellent teaching look like to you? Could this be measured? How?

At the level of the individual, surveillance activities undertaken by colleagues such as peer observations, assessment moderation and external examiners (of which more later) are akin to a 'peer-reviewing' of teaching. Such peer-reviewing is reliant on a supportive community of academics who are actively engaging in 'collegial governance' (Rowlands, 2015). Within this collegial governance model academics can provide agreement (or not) regarding standards with recommendations for improvement, along with guidance, support and insight into teaching practice and standards.

Rather than measuring value per se, this exercise is about validating and confirming each other's work, in turn legitimising the academic's role as a source of expert teaching experience and knowledge. It is arguably central to the development of academic practice in that is provides mechanisms to share experience and expertise across the sector, further acting as a professional developmental exercise for individuals who are both scrutinised and scrutinising. Such endeavours are thus less about measurement of practice, and more about collaborative improvement.

> **Tip**
>
> If you are asked to take on peer observation of teaching, do it. As with above, it can be a very constructive experience in terms of observing how others teach (see chapter 3).
>
> Even if you are not tasked with undertaking peer observation of a colleague's teaching for the purpose of your institution, it can be very helpful to occasionally sit in on colleagues' classes to observe how they teach. As a matter of courtesy do not forget to ask if it is ok to do so first!

Beyond such collegial activities, which also includes assessment moderation and external examining, an increased emphasis on national student surveys and institutional surveillance (see chapter 1) means that the appraisal of teaching quality is slowly shifting upwards to students, vice chancellors and senior management teams (Rowlands, 2015), and towards external agencies. In terms of student evaluations, this can include evaluations of the course(s) you teach, your teaching, the department, their degree and the institution overall. Student comments can be very helpful in seeing how they engage with their educational experience, and can often provide some useful suggestions for tweaking teaching to accommodate perceptions, challenges and difficulties they may share with you. They can, however, also be damning and highly critical, and this is something that you need to be prepared for when you 'put yourself out there' as a HE teacher. Mechanisms for how to utilise student evaluations are discussed shortly.

In the UK, an external assessment of quality has been formalised via the Teaching Excellence Framework. Introduced in 2016, the TEF intends to define, measure, document and rate teaching within institutions and departments across the country. It is envisaged that the rankings will be used to inform league tables on teaching (see chapter 1), and provide potential applicants with additional guidance regarding the quality of teaching within their prospective university (French and O'Leary, 2017).

For you as an early career academic, one potential outcome of all this surveillance and evaluation is that it can create ever-growing expectations and pressures to perform excellently in your teaching, at all times. Although striving for brilliance is not to be admonished per se, a stress on *continued* excellence can make it very difficult to acknowledge times when teaching is anything *less* than excellent; when mistakes happen; or times when you perhaps have not performed at your teaching 'best' because (quite reasonably) you were putting your energies into research or an administrative task.

As noted in chapter 1, such an emphasis on excellence can further contribute to an increasingly competitive working environment as academics, departments and universities are measured and ranked *against* each other. Such competition can dampen collaboration and innovation because change may involve risk, risk may result in less than excellent teaching and a less-than-excellent learning experience for students, and a less-than-excellent learning experience for students may result in a poor evaluation. It is therefore something of a paradox that striving for excellence may actually *hinder* the development of new, exciting and inventive teaching.

> **Pause for thought**
>
> If you had the chance to be completely innovative with your teaching without risk of poor evaluation from others, what would you do differently? What risks would you take with content, delivery, and assessment? Could you mitigate any of those risks in advance? How?

Moreover, such pressures of sustained excellence are arguably contributing to a growing fissure between those delivering teaching and those individuals and agencies, both internal and external, who are defining and measuring excellence and 'quality'. Certainly,

> ... it should come as no surprise to anyone involved in HE that agreeing on a standardised definition of teaching excellence should be so problematic. It is precisely because teaching is a complex, multi-faceted and contextually dependent process that reaching a consensus on a common definition in a specified context is an incredibly difficult task, let alone extending this to a country's education system.
>
> (O'Leary, 2017: 78).

As an early career academic a culture of evaluation can perpetuate a sense of 'us' and 'them' with your students, whose ratings of your teaching become ever more important for your career and your institution. What is more, scrutiny and ongoing measurement can lead to increased adjustments to an academic's teaching activities to mitigate potential risk, such as changing topics, content, assessment and so on. Writing from the US vantage point (hence the terms used below), Huston (2012: 18) notes how:

> Administrators carefully watch a variety of indicators to see how their institution compares with competing institutions, numbers such as their student enrolments, graduation rates, and national student surveys. Quite reasonably, colleges want to enrol the most desirable students, graduate more of them, and ensure that they are satisfied with their education. So these numbers are brought to the attention of the president, provost, and vice presidents as they do their strategic planning for the year. One result of this number-crunching is an increasing number of top-down initiatives to improve said numbers. Some initiatives lead to adjustments in curricula and changes in the kinds of courses that faculty are required to teach, the way these classes are structured, and the types of learning activities that the instructors are expected to incorporate.

One significant outcome of this increased input into the development and delivery of teaching in HE has been a gradual erosion of academic autonomy in teaching (Rowlands, 2015). Indeed, with the introduction of higher tuition fees in England and Wales we may be witnessing a move towards more standardised curricula to afford congruence and comparison between teaching institutions. Time will tell whether this will extend into more specific requirements regarding degree content.[1]

> **Pause for thought**
>
> In what areas of your teaching do you have autonomy? What can you control within the course(s) that you teach? In an ideal world, what topics would you teach?

In the face of at times (what can feel like) relentless evaluation, it is of course important to recognise that while there are institutional requirements for evaluation you can also use the experience of evaluation constructively. For example, if you can see opportunities for development in your teaching or the courses you are involved in, a case for making change can be validated by seeking input from colleagues, external examiners and students. They may also give you useful insight and guidance on topic areas to develop and so on.

Working with evaluations

Thus, evaluations of your teaching can be constructive, but also demanding. In terms of utilising evaluations effectively rather than feeling at the whim of all those who are evaluating your teaching, it can help to get into the habit of *evaluating the evaluations* of your teaching periodically so that you do not lose sight of (1) your priorities and (2) areas you need to develop. This suggestion for personal reflection does not need to be shared with anyone else and is going above and beyond what the institution might instruct that you do to respond to student, external examiner and external evaluations. Moreover, while this extra task can *feel* onerous, it need not take more than 20 minutes over a cup of coffee and with a 'light touch approach'.

---

[1] It is important to note that the conceptualisation of academic autonomy in teaching will depend on your discipline and the vocational features (if any) of the degrees on which you teach. For example, there are some degrees that lead to professional or practitioner qualifications and therefore the content of the teaching is determined by the accrediting authority/organisation/body.

> **Tip**
>
> Questions you may want to ask yourself when reflecting on evaluations of your teaching could include:
>
> - What has been identified as something I excelled at with this particular task?
> - What I am most proud of within this evaluation?
> - What areas were identified for potential improvement?
> - Beyond the evaluation, what further evidence is there for the need to change/improve?
> - How could I make these improvements in the future? Do I need to have a short and long-term strategy and vision?
> - What do I need to do right now? What do I need to plan in for the medium term?
>
> It is worthwhile either creating a diary or a folder of some kind to keep a note of your reflections, so that you can go back to them several years down the line and see how far you have come. You can then assess your own development and generate your own sense of fulfilment, achievement and satisfaction, rather than being reliant solely on external evaluators.

When working in an environment of evaluation it is imperative to grow what has been referred to me by a more senior colleague as a 'rhino hide'. This metaphorical thick skin is worth spending time cultivating, especially if you personally rely heavily on external validation and know that you are easily bruised by critical comments from others. It is important that you have techniques in place that you can refer to/undertake periodically throughout the academic year so that you can either prepare for, or respond to, evaluations of your teaching.

There are many ways of developing these techniques. Some lucky people, some of whom will be your colleagues, appear to have a more innate resilience when it comes to dealing with evaluation from others, and it is worth seeking their perspective on how they nurture and sustain that their rhino hide.

> **Tip**
>
> Ways in which I have heard colleagues nurturing their rhino hide include:
>
> - Seeking input and feedback from senior academics or academics tasked with teaching administration.
> - Seeking development opportunities, internal and external, that relate to teaching and enable you to contextualise your own teaching practice and feedback received.
> - Undertake recognised and accredited courses on teaching that provide validation for your own skills, knowledge and expertise.
> - Seeking feedback on your teaching from a trusted and knowledgeable colleague who will be able to give you fair and supportive comments on strengths and areas for improvement.
> - Seeking a mentor or coach (see chapters 8 and 10) where you will have the opportunity to reflect on teaching.
> - Undertaking self-care activities (see chapter 2) that will enable you to reflect and build your self-esteem.

All of these types of activities should enable you to contextualise your own teaching and the evaluations of your teaching, with a view to regarding evaluations as a positive developmental experience. The idea is to move beyond the temptation to be simply responsive and instrumental with teaching evaluations, from:

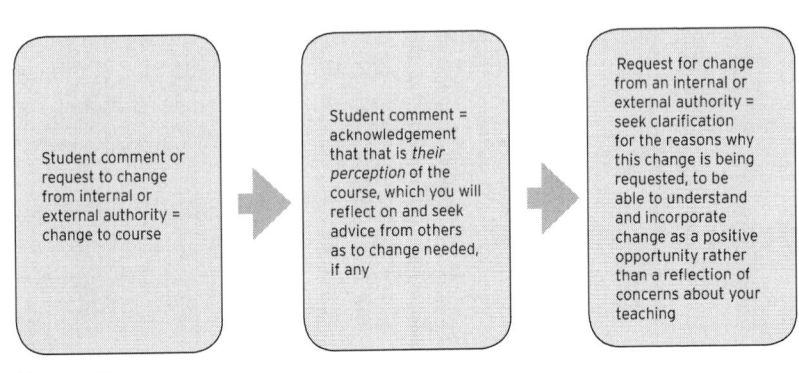

| Student comment or request to change from internal or external authority = change to course | ➔ | Student comment = acknowledgement that that is *their perception* of the course, which you will reflect on and seek advice from others as to change needed, if any | ➔ | Request for change from an internal or external authority = seek clarification for the reasons why this change is being requested, to be able to understand and incorporate change as a positive opportunity rather than a reflection of concerns about your teaching |

Figure 4.1

When it comes to potentially bruising student comments in evaluations it is really important that you feel able to deal with them appropriately, both for your own wellbeing and to ensure that you can differentiate between comments that require a response and those that do not. Your aim here is to move from:

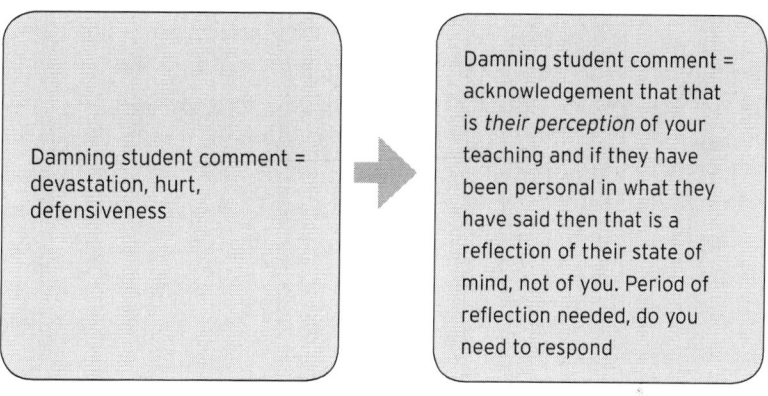

> Damning student comment = devastation, hurt, defensiveness

→

> Damning student comment = acknowledgement that that is *their perception* of your teaching and if they have been personal in what they have said then that is a reflection of their state of mind, not of you. Period of reflection needed, do you need to respond

Figure 4.2

If you receive personal comments in your teaching evaluations, make sure that (1) you discuss these with your line manager and document your concerns and (2) check to see if the comments adhere to your institution's guidance on good IT citizenship (if it has one – if not, then find out why and suggest one is created!). Such guidance on IT citizenship is one mechanism through which you and your institution can set clear boundaries regarding appropriate conduct for students and their feedback.

Author experience

One key practice I have put in place to help me reflect on evaluations of my teaching is regular coaching sessions with an individual external to the institution where I work. In these sessions I am not accountable to anyone but myself. Having received some challenging student feedback, I was able to reflect on the discouraging comments with the coach's help, disentangling my own emotional response(s) and putting their comments in context. Together with my coach we covered similar ground to those questions above. I make notes during and following these coaching sessions and I see this as an investment in my career, to help me develop the resilience and aptitude to know how and when to respond to evaluations, and how to do so appropriately.

90 Behind the scenes of teaching

Within this evaluative context, it is important to remember that there is a substantial performative element to HE teaching, and whether fairly or unfairly this is often what students will be evaluating you on. Indeed, sometimes your colleagues will be doing so too if your institution requires peer observations of teaching (see chapter 3). When it comes to your teaching performance you are establishing, (re)producing and (re)conveying your credibility as an academic with expert knowledge to your student audience. They are an audience who is likely to engage with, question and evaluate you – so how you are received by them and their perceptions of your authority and expertise matter (see chapter 2). It is most likely that in considering your authority on a topic, students will be observing your ability to:

- Communicate clearly;
- Present ideas with clarity;
- 'Work the room', engaging with everyone in it;
- Use the space appropriately;
- Draw on technology to support your teaching.

You may find that peer observations from colleagues can even include questions regarding eye contact with students, hand gestures and body language. All of these point to the performance that you are giving when you teach, the way in which you present yourself, the confidence that you can instil in others and their resulting confidence in you as an authority on a subject.[2]

What can you do to enhance your teaching performance as an early career academic? Beyond knowing your topic, preparing your teaching in advance, and using some of the techniques in chapter 3 for dealing with questions, there are a number of more subtle and interpersonal ways in which you can instil others' confidence in you as a source of knowledge and authority. This can include paying attention to details such as:

---

2 It is important to briefly recognise at this juncture that research has shown that time and again student evaluations and perception of teachings are influenced by gender (Mengel et al., 2017), and 'race' and ethnicity (Deo, 2015). I am not proposing here how to combat the significant and concerning discriminatory biases that some students can hold as this has been done elsewhere (see references at the end of this chapter). However, it is important to acknowledge that they exist and they will shape the lens through which some individuals will judge your teaching performance.

- Academic dress – is there a norm within your department or institution for how to dress? Some Management Schools are known for encouraging academics to wear suits. Other departments are more casual. Do you want to conform or do you want to be a nonconformist? This is up to you – but it is worthwhile reflecting on the message you want to give to students (and colleagues) via your dress choices and why.
- Personal grooming – this is completely a personal preference as to how you wish to look, but again your performance and how it is received may be influenced by how you look (sad but very true).
- Pace of speech – this can be hard to do when you are passionate or enthusiastic about a subject. Moreover, often that enthusiasm is infectious and can enthuse students. However, it is important to remember that enthusiasm (or nerves) can result in fast speech, which can be difficult for others to follow, or at worst be received as incoherent babbling. Measured and slower speech is usually better received as it conveys an informed, considered and knowledgeable speaker.

With time the performance of teaching usually gets easier as you develop some of the techniques of teaching outlined in chapter 3, and practice, repeat and improve your 'routine'.

> **Tip**
>
> Get one of your lectures recorded visually. It may already be recorded as a matter of course within your institution. Watch it back and focus specifically on your 'teaching performance' rather than the topic content. How much do you move around? How fast do you speak?

Establishing credibility

Of course, credibility when teaching is much, much more than simply your performance, interpersonal skills and personal confidence. It is about your background, your experience(s), the ideas you are able to convey and so on. It is also about how well you are able to practically teach. For example, can you:

- Use teaching methods that engage with all types of learners within your class?

- Utilise teaching materials that are appropriate to their learning needs?
- Design and deliver teaching that meets the learning outcomes of a course?
- Set assessments that assess students' understanding of the learning outcomes?
- Be inclusive in all aspects of your teaching?

There are many excellent HE handbooks available to explore some of these questions and how to address them. There are also excellent courses on teaching in HE. What is more, as noted at the outset of this chapter and in chapter 3, your institution may require you to possess a teaching qualification or undertake some form of continuing professional development (CPD), to demonstrate that you have the knowledge and skills to be able to teach effectively. With the introduction of the Teaching Excellence Framework in the UK, this is being formalised through the expectation that teaching individuals are members of a respected educational organisation (see below) and/or hold a teaching qualification (which can also come with accreditation from one of the educational authorities).

> **Author experience**
>
> Having two postgraduate level teaching qualifications myself, I would strongly recommend studying a course on teaching in HE and using the opportunity to focus on your strengths and areas for development as a teacher (see chapter 3). Not only did studying and attending these courses contribute to my knowledge of some of the resources I have drawn on in this book and, indeed, my writing of this book, I met peers from across the two institutions where I took these courses, including people from departments with whom I would not normally come into contact. One of my closest academic friends of 15 years standing came from one of these courses, and they have been a valuable sounding board over the years as my career has evolved.

Beyond completing a teaching course, there are a number of ways that you can establish credibility as a teaching-active academic.

Membership of professional associations and bodies

With moves towards professionalising teaching in HE, a helpful way to establish and cement your professional credentials is to join a relevant professional body and association. As noted in chapter 3, in the UK the most commonly recognised authority is the Higher Education Academy. Another organisation to consider joining is the Staff and Educational Development Association (SEDA). There may be discipline/subject specific equivalents in your own field (see chapter 9).

Different organisations will provide different validation(s) of your credibility – for example some will *only* allow you membership if you have a qualification in an identified area. Others are subscription-based and do not require a specific qualification to join. One thing is for sure, membership of associations will enable you to keep abreast of developments within your field and apply them to your teaching.

Opportunities external to your institution

There are a number of opportunities for expanding your experience and knowledge of teaching that are external to your institution. These are all ways of building up your expertise, involvement and understanding of teaching standards, practice and quality, and how these can and do evolve over time. Please note though that before you take on any additional task it is worthwhile ascertaining the commitment required – see later in this chapter for the kinds of questions that are worth asking yourself before you take these types of tasks on.

External examining

As noted earlier external examining is effectively a peer-review exercise that involves academics from other institutions reviewing teaching practice and standards. The practice itself has been open to debate regarding its effectiveness (see Bloxham and Price, 2013; Bloxham et al., 2015) with efforts being made across the England to formalise the process (see Higher Education Funding Council for England, 2017). At the time of writing, external examining remains one of the most well-established methods through which the 'frontline' of teaching is evaluated and supported.

Typically, external examining involves a consultation in the setting of learning outcomes, the establishment of course content and the creation of assessment(s). It will most likely also involve reviewing marking and moderation of assessments to ensure that academics are consistent in their marking within and between assessments and courses. It can mean being consulted when changes are made to courses, and attending exam boards to ensure that standards are upheld.

External examiners usually have a term of post, or office, between 3-5 years. Sometimes vacancies are advertised via general or subject specific mailing lists, and/or expressions of interest encouraged. On other occasions individuals are contacted directly. They may be approached owing to:

- An existing working relationship with academics in the institution (although the type of relationship and history is usually specified in institutional regulations and/or codes of practice);
- Their academic standing;
- Their external reputation in their field;
- Their specific expertise;
- Gaps in the external examiner team within a department (for example, some degree courses require two or more external examiners and their skills/expertise are split so that they are complementary).

> **Pause for thought**
>
> How are external examiners in your institution and/or department (current or previous) recruited? Is there anything you can take away from how external examiners have been recruited in terms of their skill set, the criteria used for selection and so on, and how you can relate this to your own career?

Taking on external examining is a commitment, so it is important that before you volunteer or respond positively to a request that you find out as much as possible about what will be asked of you, and take time to consider how you will fit this in around your existing obligations.

Reviewing textbook proposals

A very useful and (usually) relatively straightforward task – and one that is flexible in that you can accept or turn down depending on your other commitments – is reviewing teaching textbook proposals for academic publishers. When publishers receive a new proposal or seek to update an existing version of a textbook used in teaching, they will often seek external opinion on the quality of the proposal/proposed additions and how these could be utilised in teaching. This is a really useful way of both inputting into the development of teaching materials beyond your institution, and at the same time learning about where developments in your area of teaching are heading, and how you could incorporate that into your own teaching.

> **Tip**
>
> Identify a handful of key textbooks in your field or area of teaching, and the publishers and editors. Make contact with an editor to volunteer as a reviewer for them in the future should they publish subsequent, expanded editions of that textbook or others similar, and classify your specific areas of expertise/interest. The editor is likely to add you to their database of reviewers and could call on you should the need arise. The editor may also call on you if new authors or contributors are needed for a teaching textbook, so it is worthwhile making your name and interests known to them.

Academic news sources

Academic-focused news publications such as the UK-based *Times Higher Education* and the US-based *Chronicle of Higher Education* have a wealth of first-hand articles on teaching in HE. They are also always in need of 'copy'. That is, they need academic contributors and reviewers, as are online sites such as *The Conversation*, *Inside Higher Ed* and the *Huffington Post*. You can therefore not only read but also write articles, commentaries or review works, papers, and books for some of these outlets, acting as a good opportunity to engage with others outside of your specialist area/discipline, while also refining your written communication skills and style for different audiences, and expanding your network.

Why should I take on more teaching-related activities?

Alternatively, the question could be 'why *not* take on more work?' The relative autonomy for most academics (which can fluctuate at different points in your career) means that you can find yourself in a position where you have the option of agreeing to, or declining, opportunities and approaches from others. Sometimes you may even be actively seeking them out. The difficulty when you are early in your career however, is that you do not yet have the first-hand experience to know when to pursue something and when to hang back. Ascertaining when to say 'count me in!' or 'on this occasion I will have to decline' is critical to ensuring that your teaching commitments and overall workload are manageable.

Spotting opportunities and when to say no

So far this chapter has explored some of the ways in which your teaching is assessed, how you can potentially expand, develop and improve your teaching, and why you may wish to do so. Sometimes you will seek out opportunities yourself, other times you will be asked to take them on. It is important to recognise that there are often risks associated with taking on new commitments – commitments that can overload you, distract you from what your institution (and employer) is requesting from you, and can possibly even be detrimental to your career. On the other hand, they may be energising, exciting, fulfilling and a real source of personal growth and achievement. The key is working out when to take something on and why, and when to resist or negotiate.

If you are good at engaging with students, or show an aptitude for teaching, you can expect that you will be in demand within your department. This can be a valuable and much needed recognition of your (potential) contribution to the department, institution, student population, discipline and sector as a whole. It can contribute to your sense of self-worth and external credibility, after all you are in demand! However, it also can be overwhelming and detract from other commitments, which may be more important to you personally and be more important to the longevity of your academic career. So how do you know what to take on and what to resist?

How to spot an opportunity in teaching

Unfortunately, there is no perfect formula for recognising an unmissable teaching opportunity, nor for automatically recognising a request from which to steer clear. One thing is for sure, teaching opportunities will continually present themselves and depending on where you are in your career you may feel very differently about them and approach them accordingly. It is therefore important when you spot an opportunity to take stock and reflect on why you are wanting to do it, or why you are being asked to do it, before committing.

Author reflections

When I started at one institution I was tasked with convening a compulsory module on a specific topic. I jumped at the opportunity as I saw it as a chance to (1) develop my experience of teaching large classes in large lecture theatres, (2) write lectures within this context, and (3) grow my knowledge and expertise in the topic. The scope of the module was quite limited in that it had to complement and correspond with subsequent compulsory modules within the degrees offered. I taught that module for several years, and with significant time, energy and investment I was able to develop and refine the content and techniques used so that I could help the students relate quite 'dense' topic material to their everyday world. For those years I enjoyed teaching the module and developing it, and felt a lot of satisfaction when I received positive student feedback.

Nearly a decade later, and at a point in my career when I want to prioritise research, I no longer feel the same eagerness nor the need to learn about teaching large compulsory classes (although I do), and if I were tasked again with teaching this module or similar I would likely approach the task very differently. I would draw on my teaching experience over the last 10 years, and the shifting expectations of undergraduate students outlined in chapter 2, to build and teach quite a different module to that of 10 years ago. Why? Because I would want to ensure that while I was meeting the learning outcomes and supporting students, I was also ensuring that I was protecting time and energy to put into research activities, which have now become more of a priority.

When you spot, or are approached to take on, a new teaching task you thus need to ask yourself, why *now*? Opportunities continually arise in teaching owing to the cyclical nature of the academic year and turnover of degree courses. External examiners are always needed for courses; there will always be more textbook proposals. If you are attracted to an opportunity think carefully about how you can add it into your existing commitments and whether there would be any short or long-term cost, be that personal or professional. The academic year has a structure to it that means that certain aspects of the teaching role can be predictable and timetabled/scheduled in well in advance – sometimes to the day or week (for example, annual exam boards, assessment setting, reading weeks, and so on). If you want to do something beyond your existing commitments, or are being asked to, how can this be accommodated within this structure?

> **Tip**
>
> Pay attention to the demands of the academic year and its structure, and make note of teaching-heavy periods and times when teaching demands drop off. This is highly likely to repeat itself every year and you can therefore plan in advance as to how to manage your time and other research and administrative tasks. I know of one colleague who was so confident in their advance planning and knowledge of teaching demands that they were able to schedule in a few days of annual leave for a much-needed break, just around an assessment period. For my part, I am continually amazed at how email requests from students cease, almost overnight, at specific points in the academic year, year on year.

An opportunity arising that may not be at the right time for you professionally (for example, you have committed to writing a book, or have a looming research bid deadline) thus might come up again at some point in the academic year, or the next academic year. You can always check to see if it is possible to delay taking something on owing to other priorities; there is no harm in asking if you have a clear and rational explanation for why you are doing so.

If you are asked to take something on, tasked with a teaching duty, or approached to take part or contribute, you need to consider:

1. Timing, both short and long(er) term. How long is the commitment for? Is it one that will come up again? How will it contribute to the development of your academic career?
2. How you could include the activity within your existing workload.
3. What, if anything, would have to 'give' to accommodate the new task.
4. Any personal cost that you may need to recognise in taking on a new commitment.

Depending on where you are in your career, opportunities that might be too good to turn down could include:

- Leading and developing a particular module;
- Contributing a specialist lecture to a module;
- Teaching a particular size of class;
- Teaching a particular type of class;
- Dissertation/thesis supervision;
- Contribution to a teaching textbook;
- Assessment marking;
- Assessment moderation.

Such a strategic approach to teaching and the development of your academic career is to ensure that you avoid over-committing, under-delivering, or end up prioritising short-term gains over long-term goals. You do not always need to be so strategic however, and there might also be times when you want to volunteer or feel compelled to support a colleague, for example in taking on some of their lectures or sharing assessment marking. These actions are principally driven by collegiality and being a 'good citizen' of the department, and when you take them on reflect your personal and professional commitment to colleagues and the department. However, you need to be mindful that when you do this you are not automatically setting a precedent as the 'go to' person that will pick up extra tasks or step in when there are issues, nor that you are committing to anything beyond your helpful act. For example, make sure that sharing assessment marking to help a colleague out in a difficult situation one year does not routinely become shared marking *every* year – or at least if it is, make sure that is recognised (ideally in writing) by your line manager and accounted for within workload planning and models.

> **Tip**
> - If you are invigorated by the thought of a teaching opportunity but have concerns about the level of commitment required and your capacity to do so, *say it and make sure it is documented*. Do not take on tasks and duties without acknowledging the impact on your other responsibilities and priorities.
> - If it is not the right time for you owing to your other research and administrative commitments, can you negotiate taking on the opportunity at another point in the future? Can the task be handled by others (with or without your input) in the short term, with a view to you prioritising other activities and getting on board fully at a later date?
> - Remember not to over-commit yourself! It is very easy to accept exciting opportunities and end up with little time and 'brain space' to engage with them.

How to spot a risk and how to learn from experience

What might a risk look like when it comes to teaching? Here are a few examples:

- Being asked to 'co-convene' a module without clarity about your input or responsibility;
- Taking on a teaching duty from someone who has not been very 'present' within a department for the preceding six months;
- Agreeing to supervise students who have personal issues, or have past histories of difficulties with other colleagues;
- Being asked to moderate a course where there has been a problem with the marking of assessment in the past.

As with opportunities, there is no fool-proof formula for what constitutes a risky task. Overall, a risk is an endeavour that may:

- Distract you from other activities;
- Consume more time than the output/goal warrants;
- Lead to your personal sense of integrity being challenged;
- Lead to your public standing and reputation being compromised.

In common for all risks is that they are energy sapping, and in a role that requires considerable energy for your teaching 'performance', attention to detail and time management skills, taking on tasks that require a re-prioritisation or divert you from your own professional goals always require thought and reflection before commitment.

A key way to recognise previous teaching risks you have committed to, and to learn from experiences that have sapped your energy, is to make sure you adequately review what happened and why. Most institutions are likely to have a formal appraisal process, and if you are lucky and are matched with a more senior colleague who can help you make sense of your experience and what you can learn from it, then make sure you use that opportunity. It is important to make sure you document your reflections, lessons learned and concerns not only for yourself and your own learning, but so that your colleagues, line manager, and the institution over all can be made aware, and learn too.

> **Tip**
>
> - Use your institution's appraisal process to review your teaching commitments regularly, and what you can learn from your experiences.
> - Make sure your reflections and any concerns you may have about your teaching commitments are fully documented in your appraisal. If your appraisal is too far in the future and you have concerns, make sure that you document your concerns via email to your line manager or an appropriate colleague so that you can refer to these at a later date. If a response is required from them, make sure that you are absolutely clear about your expectation that they act.

There is much to be learnt from experiences when perhaps you should have said 'no'. First and foremost is the importance of time – both in terms of allowing time to elapse before you commit to something, and for time to elapse before you fully reflect on lessons learned. Often emotional responses to concerns or problems can be overwhelming, excessively negative, unconstructive and ineffectual, blinding you to the lessons you can take forward in your career. While Berg and Seebers (2016) suggest that admitting to struggling as an academic "undermines our professional identity" (p. 2), I disagree in that it is *not* a failing to have committed to a teaching task and struggled with it, nor is it a failing to admit this to yourself or a trusted colleague or line manager. Indeed, from my experience most colleagues and line managers would rather know how you were doing and help you to address any challenges you were facing, rather than you internalise your struggles, suffer, and potentially burn out. Losing a colleague to sick leave, or the university altogether if they move elsewhere, is something to be avoided via support, good line management and collegiality.

> **Tip**
> - If someone asks you to do something, thank them for the invitation and ask to think about it. Give yourself at least 24 hours to work out the advantages and disadvantages of taking on an additional task, including short-term priorities and impact upon those and on your long-term goal(s) and how it might help you develop your teaching experience.
> - Set up a working relationship with a trusted colleague that you can bounce ideas off, so in the instance above you can consult another person to see if they agree with your decision and why.
> - Listen to your gut feeling when you think about a new task or project. If it fills you with dread then pay attention. Sometimes you may be asked to take something on that feels like this and you have little or no room for negotiation. In those cases make sure the task is time-limited and you have clear boundaries and expectations agreed with your colleague as to your role and level of commitment and responsibility.

Sometimes, and for some people, saying no when they are asked to do something or approached with an opportunity can be extremely difficult. They may have a very strong sense of duty and responsibility. They may find it very difficult to question a request from a more senior colleague. They may simply find being assertive and saying 'no' challenging. There are ways to do so however that are more than simply shutting the door in someone's face. When dealing with students, it is useful to have stock phrases to hand to call on if you are put on the spot, or when you need to challenge a request (see also chapter 2). For example, rather than saying 'I don't want to', you could say:

- I have to decline the invitation/opportunity to work on . . . (for evermore? Or on this occasion?).
- Owing to workload/other commitments I am unable to take on . . . (ever? Or at this time?).

Depending on how much negotiation you want to enter into, it is advisable to avoid non-committal phrases such as 'I would prefer not to' as this indicates that while you may not want to do something, you will do so if pressed.

The important thing to remember is that you need to be able to work with your colleagues and networks in the future so if you are declining, you should do so politely, with good grace, and for an informed and sensible reason. Sensible reasons could be time management, prior commitments, workload, priorities, areas of specialism, and so on. Of course, on a personal level you may have other reasons for turning something down, such as concerns about working with particular students or colleagues, but you need to be diplomatic and considered if you decide to voice this or use this as a reason.

> **Tip**
>
> Remember, never put anything in an email that you would not be willing to say to someone in person.

When it comes to negotiating teaching tasks, your ability to work collegially will be crucial. Throughout your career it is highly likely that you will encounter colleagues that you instantly 'click' with and others with whom you find it more challenging to work. Sometimes teaching may be the only time you encounter the people you find challenging, for example if you are required to co-teach a course, or support each other with marking an assessment. Difficulties with teaching colleagues (as noted in chapter 3) can include:

- Varying approaches to teaching preparation, including how much and how far in advance;

- Different expectations about communication with students, including how often and by which means;
- Differing views on the purpose and quality of feedback to students in assessment marking (even if there are standards set by the institution).

It is important therefore that when you negotiate teaching responsibilities and you teach with others that you are clear about how you like to work, and to find common ground on which you can agree so as not to make yourself/yourselves vulnerable to accusations of bias or preferential treatment.

Finally, to note, it is important to recognise at this point that decisions about teaching, beyond the specific lecture content, are very rarely now made in isolation or by an individual alone. Decisions regarding learning outcomes, overall module content, assessment format, and examiners are typically subject to scrutiny via others and institutional committees. There are likely to be processes and procedures in place to ensure that students, colleagues, examiners and other stakeholders are consulted regarding change and development, to ensure consistency, clarity, coherence and reason. Covered in more detail in chapter 8, it is worthwhile understanding how these chains of command work, so that (1) you can shape change and (2) if you wish to get involved in teaching administration, you have a reasonable knowledge of how you might do so.

> **Pause for thought**
>
> You want to make a considerable change to a course you teach, including learning outcomes, organisation and content of lectures, and assessment. How are you expected to go about this within your institution? What are the quality assurance processes? Who else needs to be involved in the decisions made, and how do you need to present your proposals?

In an environment and climate where your teaching will come under increasing scrutiny, it pays to extend your know-how and negotiation when it comes to teaching. There is no doubt that teaching in HE is one of the most time-intensive parts of the job, and you can find yourself making considerable personal and professional sacrifices to accommodate the demands of lecture writing, student support, module development and so on. Structured by the shape and rhythm on the academic year, teaching demands are nearly always more time-specific and pressing than other parts of the academic role. Different individuals will have different approaches to teaching, and the extent to which they enjoy it and wish to prioritise it as a part of their job. In the early phase of your career, the key balance for you is to take on teaching and associated activities that enable you to develop and learn as a teacher in HE, while also ensuring that you do not over-commit or take on activities that detract from your other (sometimes competing) responsibilities and priorities.

References

Berg, M. and Seeber, B.K. (2016) *The Slow Professor: Challenging the Culture of Speed in the Academy* (Toronto: University of Toronto Press).

Bloxham, S., Hudson, J., den Outer, B., and Price, M. (2015) 'External Peer Review of Assessment: An Effective Approach to Verifying Standards?', *Higher Education Research and Development*, 34 (6): 1069-1082.

Bloxham, S. and Price, M. (2013) 'External Examining: Fit for Purpose?', *Studies in Higher Education*, 40 (2): 195-211.

Deo, M.E. (2015) 'A Better Tenure Battle: Fighting Bias in Teaching Evaluations', *Columbia Journal of Gender and Law*, 31 (1): 7-43.

French, A. and O'Leary, M. (2017) 'Introduction', in French, A., O'Leary, M. with Robson, S. and Wood, P. (eds) *Teaching Excellence in Higher Education: Challenges, Changes and the Teaching Excellence Framework* (Bingley: Emerald Publishing), pp. 1-4.

Higher Education Funding Council for England (2017) *Quality Assessment*, available online at http://www.hefce.ac.uk/reg/QualityAssessment/ [accessed 10/12/17].

Huston, T. (2012) *Teaching What You Don't Know* (Cambridge, MA: Harvard University Press).

Mengel, F., Sauermann, J. and Zölitz, U. (2017) 'Gender Bias in Teaching Evaluations', IZA Institute of Labor Economics, Discussion Paper No. 11000, available online at SSRN: https://ssrn.com/abstract=3037907 [accessed 23/11/17].

O'Leary, M. (2017) 'Monitoring and measuring teaching excellence in Higher Education: from contrived competition to collective collaboration', in French, A., O'Leary, M. with Robson, S. and Wood, P. (eds) *Teaching Excellence in Higher Education: Challenges, Changes and the Teaching Excellence Framework* (Bingley: Emerald Publishing), pp. 75-108.

Rowlands, J. (2015) 'Turning collegial governance on its head: symbolic violence, hegemony and the academic board', *British Journal of Sociology of Education*, 36 (7): 1017-1935.

Further reading

Ashwin, P. (2015) *Reflective Teaching in Higher Education* (London: Bloomsbury Publishing).
Brookfield, S.D. (2017) *Becoming a Critically Reflective Teacher, 2nd edn* (San Francisco: Jossey Bass).
Philipsen, M.I. (2008) *Challenges of the Faculty Career for Women: Success and Sacrifice* (San Francisco: Jossey-Bass).
Riniolo, T.C., Johnson, K.C., Sherman, T.R. and Misso, J.A. (2010) 'Hot or Not: Do Professors Perceived as Physically Attractive Receive Higher Student Evaluations?', *The Journal of General Psychology*, 122 (1): 19-35.
Rosen, A.S. (2018) 'Correlations, trends and potential biases among publicly accessible web-based student evaluations of teaching: a large-scale study of RateMyProfessors.com data', *Journal of Assessment and Evaluation in Higher Education*, 43 (1): 31-44.
Wilson, J.H., Beyer, D., and Monteiro, H. (2014) 'Professor Age Affects Student Ratings: Halo Effect for Younger Teachers', *Journal of College Teaching*, 62 (1): 20-24.

Useful journals

International Journal of Teaching and Learning in Higher Education
Journal of Assessment and Evaluation in Higher Education
Student Engagement in Higher Education Journal

Section 2
Research

The second section of this book turns to the research elements of the early academic's career. Depending on your contract, the demands to undertake research will vary considerably, with some early academics (such as post-docs) tasked solely with undertaking research and others (such as lecturers in teaching-intensive universities) having minimal expectation to conduct research with outputs and research funding being largely regarded as a 'bonus'. One thing is for sure, unless you want to focus explicitly on teaching or are content being an academic who only teaches, it is highly likely that at the start of your academic career you will have an ambition (however large or small) to undertake some form of research and contribute to society in this way. Wanting to make a difference to the world via developing existing ideas or establishing new knowledge, fresh partnerships, and innovative practices is an admirable and laudable goal.

The next three chapters explore some of the realities of this pursuit, including how to find your research niche, publishing culture(s), and building up your networks both within your institution and externally. A core theme running throughout all three is the need and importance of establishing research credibility early on in your career.

5 Establishing your niche

The first of three chapters on research, this chapter will examine the process of establishing yourself as a bona fide and fully-fledged research-active academic with a sustainable career trajectory ahead of you (see Gilbert, 2006 for a good example of how this has been done elsewhere). Exploring current publishing cultures and the pursuit of research funding, and contextualised by the ongoing issues of the Research Excellence Framework in the UK, open access publishing and journal citation rankings, it will consider the tensions of credibility and popularity, alongside targeting journals and handling rejection.

The chapter has a distinctive water theme running throughout it, as you will see. This is intentional, aiming to encourage you to recognise and appreciate the ways in which research ebbs and flows in terms of ideas, outputs, environments, and cultures. As this chapter will show, there is a 'political economy' associated with academic research, in that the political and economic systems and structures influence one another and the shaping of the academic research environment and agenda(s). This chapter aims to shed some ray of light on this political economy, and your place within it.

Establishing yourself and your research

There is a significant difference between being a PhD student, a research assistant, an employee of a research agency or a consultant, and an employed, 'jobbing' academic. As an early career academic, it is likely that you will be balancing a multitude of demands that require different skills, such as teaching and administration. If research is part of your remit, or if you want it to be future employment, it is vital that you create and maintain a momentum within your research, be it bidding for research income, publishing, collaborating with others, networking or providing conference papers.

The intensity with which you approach research as part of your everyday work will ebb and flow throughout the academic year and over the early part of your career. Whether you are in a particularly fertile period of research or are experiencing a slump, if you wish to sustain a career that includes research you need to be mindful of it, and where you are going with it, at all times.

> **Tip**
>
> At the outset of your employment make sure you have (and keep) a copy of your job description, contract, and probation/promotion requirements. Make sure you are fully informed as to what your employer expects with regards to the various parts of your role. If research is part of your role this includes expectations and obligations regarding grant income, publications and their ranking, public engagement, impact and so on.

However you start your academic career, and whatever experience you have already amassed, if you want to build a career to include research there is nothing quite like the first few years both in terms of the excitement and intellectual stimulation you can feel as you move into new topics and areas, and establish yourself as a bona fide research-active academic with something to say. At the same time, this enthusiasm and drive can be challenged, stifled, and suppressed in the face of the sometimes overwhelming pressures to raise research funds, to publish in peer-review journals and to establish your track record. You may find yourself being pulled into bids and papers that you have little intellectual interest in, but will support the direction of your team, department or institution more broadly. You may find yourself struggling to write exhaustive research bids that you know have a very low chance of receiving funding; or find yourself moving from post to post in search of that all-elusive permanent position.[1] If you are

---

1 A good account of the first couple of years of a research-active early career academic's life can be found in McLachlan (2017).

employed as a lecturer or assistant professor, with the immediacy of teaching demands outlined in section 1, it can also be the case that your research priorities take a backseat, let alone allowing you the time to reflect on the type of researcher you want to be, and how important research is to you as part of your academic identity. You may struggle to carve out the time to think, write and progress intellectually.

Given these joys and pressures, if you wish to be research-active it is important to establish your research career and develop your academic identity via your research activities. Moving beyond research being something you do as a gateway into a role (much like the PhD is today), this is about embodying the identity and culture of being a fully paid-up researching academic, and giving you the opportunity to consider where you want to go, why, and how you could get there on a 'research ticket'.

> **Pause for thought**
>
> Picture yourself in five years' time. What do you want to be researching? What does your working environment look like? Are you a lone researcher or working in a cluster of people? Are you a team member or a leader? A risk taker, maverick innovator and pioneer, or a steady, reliable pair of hands?
>
> Your ambition and goals do not need to necessarily correspond with your current employment, but having something that *you* want to work towards will help when you are faced with competing pressures on your time and when tasked by your institution.

Although I have noted the tendency towards ranking within academia in chapter 1, and the insecurity and competition it breeds, in the early phase of your career it can be helpful to do a little investigative work to understand your colleagues' career trajectories, or to understand how an academic you admire has established their research credibility. This has to be done within the context of recognising when they entered academia and the evolution of academic research culture over the years they have been working (more of which next), as this will inevitably have shaped their productivity and the types of projects conducted and outputs produced. With this in mind, it can be helpful and inspiring to establish what constitutes and has contributed towards a 'successful' career for others, and what you want to aspire to personally.

> **Tip**
>
> Ways to explore colleagues' career trajectories include:
>
> - Looking up academics' institutional staff profiles and personal webpages.
> - Looking up academics and their narratives (that is, the way they present themselves) on professional networking sites such as LinkedIn.
> - Understanding academics' networks and who they have cited for support and inspiration – for example in book and paper acknowledgements, then exploring those inspirational individuals.

Nurturing an interest in peers and colleagues, both within and beyond your specific discipline and expertise, is an important activity in terms of your own growth as an academic and learning from others, and is a habit worth getting in to.

Academic research culture: scholarship to productivity

There are many available texts that explore how academic research has changed over the last 30 years, in which a common theme is that in almost all HE sectors around the world there has been a shift from an environment of scholarship towards a managerial culture that focuses on productivity and measurable outputs (Burrows, 2012). Research-active academics are evermore evaluated in terms of their publications; the income they generate; and their 'impact' on the world. Much of this has become reduced to numerical detail, for example in citation rates and the impact factors of journals, h-index scores and so on.

> **Pause for thought**
>
> Do you know your h-index? This is a metric based on an author's most cited publications. If you want to find out your own one of the easiest ways is to sign up to Google Scholar. You will need to input your complete publication list for your h-index to be calculated.

Such a mathematical approach has overall, and unsurprisingly, contributed towards a targeted culture of research within HE. In the UK, this instrumental environment is exemplified by the way in which doctoral study is organised, with centres and partnerships established to maximise the efficiency of institutions and academics' specific expertise. PhD students and their supervisors are typically required to confirm and assess progress in the research and skill development through doctoral study, demonstrating to those tasked with auditing that they are industrious and productive. As will be explored in chapter 6, being a PhD student is now not just about producing a thesis for examination, it is about building a curriculum vitae that presents demonstrable and measureable evidence of productivity in job applications.

For PhD students, their supervisors and beyond, on the one hand a culture of targets and productivity can create a very driven environment in which to work, encouraging individuals to disseminate their work and generate income to sustain their academic area. If those interests happen to coincide with a rising popular and political interest in your discipline or field of study, then you may find that such an emphasis on demonstrable productivity results in an enormously fertile period of your career as it enables you to 'produce'.

On the other hand, such an emphasis on targets and productivity may mean you feel drawn, or pushed, into subjects and topics that appear more financially lucrative but which for you hold little intellectual interest. You may also encounter pressure to publish in specific journals, apply to particular funders, or work with particular peers and colleagues – with whom you may, or may not, personally collaborate with well. You may find yourself caught in power struggles between colleagues regarding research agendas and priorities, or pulled between competing institutional interests, or working within hierarchical structures that privilege the research interests of those more senior to you. And you may move from this into a more constructive environment, or vice versa into a more challenging one, owing to a huge number of factors beyond your control, such as:

- A new Head of Department or senior figure in your institution, or a change in institutional support;
- An event in the world that shifts your field, the policy agenda, or available research funding, for example a natural disaster;
- A technological development that significantly alters how you or others work;
- A national or international financial crisis.

Where you are in the ebb and flow of your early research career, what is important is having an informed, well-defined and articulated sense of purpose, vision and clarity about your own research interests, your research priorities and where you want to be in the future. Thus, it is sensible to expend energy in crafting your purpose and vision, and to revise it periodically as your career unfolds, your personal life changes and your priorities shift. What follows intends to help you do so, by giving you the opportunity and tools to consider where you are right now, and where you want to be in the future.

Cultivating credibility and providence

There are a multitude of different ways to create and establish your academic research credibility depending on how you have entered academia, your areas of research, the institution within which you work, and so on. What follows are some suggestions for issues to think about and address, in no particular order of importance.

Your disciplinary identity

A key issue to identify early on is how you wish to identify yourself in relation to academic discipline(s). This will influence where you apply for jobs, the types of jobs you apply for, where you publish, the research you conduct and with whom you work. Having a sense of breadth, longevity and tradition associated with a discipline can help you to feel part of a wider community of scholars engaged on a particular issue within the world, and it will also help others identify who you are and what your work is about. This is particularly important for research funding where reviewers will appreciate clarity over your position and subject area in relation to your field/discipline. However, it may also serve as a misnomer, pigeonholing you and inaccurately reflecting your inter-disciplinary or trans-disciplinary perspective.

> **Pause for thought**
>
> However your peers or your institution regard disciplines, how do *you* feel about aligning yourself to one or more disciplines? Do you want to bridge disciplines, brokering research and ideas *between* them? Do you want to be an academic who works beyond a discipline – using whatever theories and methods are available to you to make sense of a problem?
>
> Building on these reflections, what type of department would you want to be working in, and who do you want to be working with? Are you a single discipline academic, or someone who enjoys working with others from different disciplines?

How you feel about academic disciplines will frame your research activities, such as where you apply for funding, the journals in which you publish, and the audiences you engage with. You may find at points in your career that your personal regard for academic disciplines closely aligns with that of your colleagues, department or institution. At other times you may feel that they are at odds. This latter experience can be challenging as you can end up trying to fit your round peg into their square hole; hence the importance of recognising that that mismatch is part of the ebb and flow of your career and it will not last forever as the tides will inevitably change around you.

> **Author reflection**
>
> Although all my degrees are sociological, my academic working life has been spent employed in departments where sociology is not the main disciplinary focus. As a result, over the years I have fluctuated between trying to complement and conform to a department's research identity and vision, and wanting to retain my sociological identity.

You may or may not be strongly associated with one or more disciplines (or none) as a result of previous work, whether academic or not. For example, if you have entered academia following a period in commerce, you may find yourself as an early career academic working within the amorphous 'business studies', which melds together disciplines including but not isolated to management, accountancy, human resources, marketing, economics, sociology, psychology, politics, but with little attachment to any. If this sounds familiar, your task is to explore and investigate whether or not you want to (or are required to) affiliate to a particular theoretical and/or methodological disciplinary approach to business. This includes your epistemological perspective; that is, how you see the construction of knowledge and the status of 'fact'.

You may already have a clear sense of your disciplinary identity and where you 'fit', or at least where you want to 'fit' within academia. However not everyone has this clarity, and if you are feeling adrift or disconnected to academic disciplines and/or the way in which institutions organise their departments and academic areas of excellence, it is worth digging deeper to understand disciplinary foundations and your affinity to them. Philosophical foundations, that is, the values, beliefs and perspectives that underpin academic disciplines, are important to acknowledge as these have had, and continue to have, influence over the direction of the disciplines, and the associated methods and techniques employed to undertake research and produce original thinking. These philosophical origins are connected to epistemology and ontology, which warrant some consideration if you are seeking to find your disciplinary fit. Both are talked about frequently and readily in the social sciences, and broadly speaking, they are as follows:

- Epistemology is an understanding of the way in which knowledge is regarded, produced and used. Those academics that seek irrefutable 'facts' are usually called positivists, as they seek to organise the world into component parts in order to test, establish, deny and confirm factual information. Other academics, who are interested in understandings and perspectives of the world align themselves to interpretive paradigms.
- Ontology is the way in which people construct meaning and know the world around them. You are likely to be familiar with two well established ontological positions: objectivity and subjectivity. Objectivity is where the world is external to you and is something that can be observed beyond you. Subjectivity is where you create understanding from within, meaning that the way in which you perceive the world comes from you, rather than external, observable facts.

Though these are limited explanations of epistemology and ontology, they give you a sense of how important your view of the world is to your academic research and finding your disciplinary fit and kindred spirits within the academic community. If you are a committed positivist, you may feel very frustrated and unfulfilled working within a group of interpretivists, and vice versa.

> **Tip**
>
> From my own experience, and echoed by colleagues in conversation, it is not unheard of to pick up on a mismatch in epistemological positions even at the early stage of interviews for posts, when candidates and panels have revealed the values they place on different types of knowledge(s) and subsequent judgements they make about research 'worthiness' and societal 'need'. Attune yourself to these types of differences within your department to help you understand where colleagues are coming from when they make claims about the merits and worth of particular types of knowledge.

While some academics will have a very clear conceptualisation of their epistemological and ontological paradigm (that is, way of thinking), not everyone will. If you have, or have not been encouraged to engage with these underlying foundations, it is worth taking a moment to consider your own epistemological and ontological beliefs and values, and which disciplines and/or academic departments would be your best 'fit'.

> **Pause for thought**
>
> How well aligned are you at present to your lab, your group, your department or Faculty when it comes to a shared perspective of the world? Does it matter to you share a worldview or not?

Such a philosophical approach to your research will not be everyone's cup of tea, and you may of course resist this approach as you seek to use any disciplinary lens and method available to you to holistically examine a particular intellectual problem. For example, you may be focused on examining land management in Brazil, drawing on literatures and tools from civil engineering, policy studies, and history and so on – all of which are disciplines that have epistemological and ontological variation within them. However, with most qualifications partitioned into science or humanities/liberal arts (as per the US model of HE), the probability is that you will unlikely have been schooled in sufficient disciplines to be able to be an expert in all. Accepting the limits of your knowledge is part of recognising your strengths and understanding where you can develop in the future.

Finding a department that fits

Finding your academic disciplinary fit is not just about your own worldview, it is about working with others who have similar and differing perspectives. When you are starting out in your academic career you need to pay attention to the department in which you are working, or want to work in. This includes the research narrative and department working environment that has been fashioned over time; it will also include the research culture and the worldview of colleagues.

Every reader of this chapter will have a varying preference early in their career for working with others, and the extent to which they want to work with like-minded academics, or colleagues who will expand their understanding(s) and challenge them. When applying for jobs and when you are getting to know your new workforce, be mindful of your colleagues' approach(es) to research and the extent to which their paradigmatic worldviews align or contradict yours. You may want to work with them either way – whether they will complement and understand, or test and stretch, you.

> **Tip**
>
> Some academic departments and colleagues will be more transparent than others in terms of worldviews. If you work in an amorphous inter/trans-disciplinary field such as area studies, international development, liberal arts, classics, or business studies you may find

> yourself working with colleagues who have a wide variety of academic backgrounds: anthropology, history, psychology, economics, sociology, languages, media, management and marketing, for example. Take the time to find out more about their backgrounds – you may come to welcome and embrace your similarities and differences in time. They may also be helpful future guides in providing alternative perspectives and arguments based on a different way of understanding a problem.

Conversely, you may have entered academia with a tight alignment to a sole discipline. If you have been working on a research topic for a number of years it is unsurprising that your fledgling academic identity may have become closely entwined with that topic, both for yourself and to others (Huston, 2012). Depending on the topic and your field you may continue to work on a specific area for many years to come. Equally likely though is the chance that as your academic career develops your ideas evolve and opportunities present themselves that take you down a different path. Letting go of, or loosening, the disciplinary identity you hold dear is thus a significant milestone as you make the transition into the role of an early career academic.

Letting go is not just about your identity though, it is also about letting go of your research. A further challenge that you may encounter when you begin to publish, be it in academic or non-academic outlets, is that you relinquish control of what happens to your work, your claims, your arguments and your ideas once they are in the public domain. Once you start 'putting your work out there', whether that be through peer review or by disseminating your work via non-academic avenues, you are opening yourself up to critique, appraisal and to others using your work in ways you had not envisaged, and possibly not in ways you agree with. This willingness and capacity to share your work is, however, the bread-and-butter of the research-active academic, as "to be a researcher is to be someone who is systematically engaged in the production of knowledge that will be in some way, however limited, in the public sphere" (Dunne et al., 2005: 158). Those critiquing your work may have a contradictory worldview, work within a different discipline, and fail to comprehend or fundamentally agree with your work. Part of your role as a research active academic is to be able to justify your arguments and analysis, defend your methods and techniques where needed, and let go of the need to control your ideas once your work is in the public domain.

Positioning yourself

Given that part of your role as a research-active academic is to put your work into the public domain, it is important that you spend time locating yourself in relation to your peers. Hopefully you will have made some headway in this as you applied/apply for jobs, and as you learn to articulate your work within broader theoretical, empirical, historical and practical debates.

> **Tip**
>
> Questions to ask yourself regarding your own position within your field of research include:
>
> - How am I building on what has come before me, and where do I fit in with the history of this research topic? Can I explain that succinctly to others?
> - How am I similar or distinct from my contemporaries in my research? How do I differ to my supervisor (if appropriate)?
> - Do I want to be a 'big fish in a small pond or a small fish in a big pond?' (see chapter 1 and below).

Continuing the water metaphor, your relative fish size, that is - your position within/to your field, will depend on the dimensions of the existing pond(s) you have available to you, and the type of lily pad - your institution - that you shade yourself under. You may live in an enormous lake covered in lily pads, all competing for the same resources. In that large lake you have many fish buddies to spend time with, flitting from one to another as your interests change and you age. The lake has enough space for lily pads to grow and provide more shade for the ever-growing fish population. The lake is full of life; you may reproduce, creating more fish for the lake, establishing your legacy (and conversely, your competition for resources!)

In that large lake however, you may also become lost, easily overlooked by other fish, and struggle to make yourself distinctive when there are so many comparable fish around you. The lily pads may become so numerous that they stifle the life of the lake beneath them, as they compete for resources. And in a drought the inhabitants can be ill prepared for when the lake becomes a series of puddles, lacking connection. Or you may find yourself in a puddle without a lily pad. It's a scary thought.

In contrast, you may live in a very small pond with only a few lily pads for shade. You know every other living thing in that pond very well. You group together under the few lily pads that you have, fostering very close relationships. You know all your buddies by name, and when with your friends you make the best of that small pond. But when you have difficulties spending time together that pond can suddenly became very cramped and choked up. It can become quite incestuous as you only ever reproduce with the same small group of fish. And if one lily pad dies it can have a seismic impact on the health of the pond and every fish in it. You are thus dependent on getting on with those other fish and those few lily pads sticking around.

At the outset of your academic career you may feel as if you have little option over the pond in which you live. After all, your choices about your lily pad, that is where you work, are constrained by broader practical concerns about geography, income, job availability, research income, responsibilities external to work and so on. But such a passivity towards the pond in which you live belies the choices you *do* have and that can influence the trajectory of your career. You can, over time, grow or shrink in size and occupy different ponds depending on where you want to position yourself.

Author reflection

As an academic specialising in 'death studies', over the last ten years I have worked with peers from a range of different cultural and academic backgrounds. In death studies, there are colleagues from archaeology, history, anthropology, sociology, psychology, economics, epidemiology, psychiatry, management, marketing, English literature, geography, planning, and many more. We are a rather specialist group who share a common interest, reflected in the oft-overheard shorthand of being called 'Dr Death', or as we were known for a while in one department, 'the Death Squad'.

> While I value the shared interests with this group of colleagues, there are relatively few conferences, funding opportunities or journals in which to publish. In order to grow, in recent years I have sought to broaden out my research interests to extend into and contribute towards the Sociology of the Family literature and community. This is a much bigger and well-established interest group within Sociology, with different interests and worldviews around the world. Emerging from the early phase of my career this was a deliberate and considered move to grow the influence of my work and my academic reputation. I did it through submitting conference papers to particular themed events and journal papers to more general discipline journals where my work might find a larger audience. So far, it has yielded exciting and stimulating conversations with new colleagues who have, I think, enjoyed learning about families in relation to death, dying and bereavement.

Catching waves

There are many, many factors outside of your control that will shape your research and the environment in which you conduct it. There is a substantial political dimension to research, both in terms of the agendas, policies and funding priorities of the state, and the influence of the commercial market on academic research (see Caulfield and Ogbogu, 2015). Some readers of this book will embrace and respond to these influencers, others will resent and resist the ways in which research can be, and is, manipulated to conform to political priorities and funding, commercial trends and media sensationalism. Some may have never considered these contexts at all.

However you regard these influencing factors it is important to not ignore them, hoping that they will somehow, at some point, disappear. Rather, you need to be attuned to them so that you know when to 'catch a wave' and ride it out, and when to lie back and let it pass – so that you can be ready for the next one. In other words, you need to be aware of and, where appropriate, respond to the factors beyond your control that can shape your research and career.

Having established the importance of finding your niche throughout this chapter so far, it is important to note that there remains one key feature of being research-active that will not diminish, and that is publishing. The remainder of this chapter is therefore devoted to establishing your research credibility via publishing, recognising some of the broader political and economic contexts in which publishing takes place.

Publishing and the measurement of research

An often-cited phrase, a culture of 'publish or perish'[2] sums up the emphasis on publishing for (1) establishing your academic credentials and (2) in the US at least, securing tenure/a permanent job. This culture of publishing has, in the UK, been cemented by the periodic nationwide assessment of research – principally publications – which at the time of writing is called the Research Excellence Framework. A method of evaluating the quality of research of and ranking universities by subject area, the prize originally offered by the REF was research income, yet as state research funding has been progressively withdrawn, the reward of the REF is as much about potential income as it is prestige. One outcome of this recurrent evaluation of publications is that the strategising that takes place to secure a high(er) ranking can come to dominate agendas within departments and across institutions. 'Readiness exercises' are conducted to establish whether colleagues are 'REF-ready' or not. On the one hand, in a potentially constructive way this calculation of readiness can lead to colleagues deemed *not* ready obtaining time and support to complete their work and publications. On the other hand, it can lead to an intensification of pressure to perform and produce.

Institutions handle the evaluation of publications differently. Much will depend on their departmental make-up and size of staff. Some are highly democratic, seeking to ensure that all staff regardless of seniority have the opportunity to ready themselves and produce sufficient work to be 'REF ready'. Others select staff and focus on their potential – for example relinquishing them of teaching or administrative responsibilities so that they have the time and opportunity to do research and associated impact activities (see chapter 8). If you are one of those lucky few you may see your research career flourish; but of course, if not, there can be much resentment, frustration and sense of injustice. Unsurprisingly, such a divisive

---

2 The consequence of which is summarised neatly by Rawat and Meena (2014).

approach to managing research can potentially damage morale and create much acrimony between staff.[3]

> **Pause for thought**
>
> If you are based in the UK, what is your institution or department's research strategy and approach to the REF? Who has influence over its direction?

Such strategising of research shows why – beyond sheer aptitude for research – some individuals seem to progress faster in their research work and publishing than others. Not everyone is given equitable opportunity to do it, and not all decisions about who gets the opportunity are based on the ability of the individual academic. Moreover, as this chapter has already shown, the political and economic contexts in which research takes place means that at any point in your career you can find yourself riding a wave up or down of popularity and corresponding decisions about funding availability, publishing options and so on.

As an early career academic, it is important therefore to recognise that you are working in a politicised environment where decisions are made about the positioning of the department/institution, about establishing and maintaining expertise in specific areas, and about building subject and topic areas that are both responding to societal need, and are *seen to be* responding to societal need. Many of these decisions are made to ensure that the institution is financially viable into the future in research terms. Such is the political economy of academic research, where much energy is put into creating research themes, clusters and groups that can create a sense of identity and purpose internally, and can be presented externally as a coherent and articulated research strategy. Sometimes

---

3 At the time of writing, the grounds on which the REF 2021 will be conducted and practiced are currently being negotiated, with the likelihood that all research active staff will be submitted. If this is the case, then it is likely that there will be bargaining and trade-offs so that colleagues are able to contribute to the REF. There may also be issues of academic publishing 'stars' carrying other colleagues with less prestigious outputs. Time will tell as to what emerges. A good summary of concerns and lessons learned about the last REF exercise in 2014 can be found in Murphy (2017).

you and your work will be at the centre of these, sometimes you will be on the periphery. What is key to remember and manage is your own sense of direction and where you are going with your work, so that you are able to better address and work with, rather than resist, those fluctuating waves and navigational plans.

What gets ranked?

If you have an interest in how publications are ranked, it is recommended that you do some investigative work within your own subject area and/or national context. Senior colleagues in your institutions or librarians are likely to be able to surmise for you the current thinking of how publications are determined to be 'world-leading' or not, and the grounds on which these determinations are made (for example, via star ratings of journals). Beyond star ratings there are international rankings of journals that are used by institutions and individuals to determine which are 'the best' journals in which to publish. These rankings are created via a multitude of factors, the most commonly cited of which are citation rates[4] and impact factors.[5]

There are many issues with the value and merit of such metric information to determine journal quality (see Gasparyan et al., 2017). Principally, the important things to remember are that journals being ranked against each other are:

1. Not comparing like for like subject areas.
2. Using data that does not represent all papers in the journal – so one or two key high profile papers may skew the metric data for that journal any one year.

---

[4] Which are themselves problematic, see Remler (2016).
[5] Defined by Thomson Reuters (nd) as "all citations to the journal in the current JCR [journal citation reports] year to items published in the previous two years, divided by the total number of scholarly items . . . published in the journal in the previous two years. Though not a strict mathematical average, the Journal Impact Factor provides a functional approximation of the mean citation rate per citable item. A Journal Impact Factor of 1.0 means that, on average, the articles published one or two years ago have been cited one time. A Journal Impact Factor of 2.5 means that, on average, the articles published one or two years ago have been cited two and a half times. The citing works may be articles published in the same journal. However, most citing works are from different journals, proceedings, or books indexed in Web of Science".

126 *Establishing your niche*

3. Owned by publishers that have commercial interests in the position of their journals, and will market the journals and control access to papers accordingly (see below).
4. Influenced by how open access publishing (where articles are placed in an open access repository) impacts on the availability of papers online. While efforts have been made to circumvent this control of access by enabling pre-publication articles to be placed in publicly accessible repositories and by building in the payment of one-off fees for open access into research funding, the vast majority of peer-reviewed journal articles are still hidden behind publisher paywalls, meaning that you need to either pay for a paper individually or be affiliated to an organisation or institution that has a subscription to that journal. Some journals will provide open access to specific papers for a time-limited period in a bid to boost readership, circulation and citations.
5. Not complete – not all journals publish data on impact factors and so on, meaning that the rank orders of subject areas are partial.

Suffice to say, publishing is not an exact science and should not be treated as such. Journal rankings are not perfect, nor are determinations of what constitutes journal and publication quality. As a career academic you thus need to be mindful of the political and economic forces that shape and influence journal publishing, and recognise that this is the environment in which you are seeking to get your work 'out there'.

Getting going with publishing

In practical terms, it is important that you have a clear strategy for submission of your research to the journals in which you want to publish. There are a number of factors to consider here such as, for example:

- Prestige: which are the most prestigious journals in your subject area?
- Audience: who do you want to read your work? Are they individuals who work in the same discipline? Or specialist audiences?
- Scope: is your work most appropriate to national or international readerships?

Sometimes these factors are actually conflicting in that the audience you want to read your work – because they will use it, refer to it in their own work, and it actually might make a difference to their practice – is not itself associated with a prestigious journal. It is at these junctures that you are in a position where you need to decide your priorities – is it to publish in esteemed journals or in journals where you share interests with the audience?

Another key factor to consider is the frequency of your publishing activity. This will differ between disciplines, not least because of the culture of multi-author papers in some fields and sole/joint author papers in others. It will also differ between institutions and the extent to which an institution dictates the minimum number of papers to be published per year. The volume of papers you can therefore be working on at any one time and (hopefully) get published will therefore vary wildly depending on your area. Success may be 5 papers a year for one person and 1-2 for another.

> **Author reflection**
>
> As a social scientist, working outside a culture of multi-author papers, I have received four very useful pieces of advice from more senior colleagues about how to publish:
>
> 1. Produce a mixture of sole and joint authored papers, to establish your credibility as an individual but also work with others to maintain networks and cross-fertilise ideas.
> 2. Always have three papers on the go: one either submitted or at the point of submission, one worked-up draft and one budding idea for a paper, to ensure that you have a throughput of work and do not focus all your energies on one paper that may take years to get published if there are multiple revisions and re-submissions.
> 3. Aim to submit two journal articles a year, whatever the circumstances.
> 4. As you become more established and senior in your career, focus on quality over quantity. Prioritise work on papers that you feel enthused about, aiming for well-regarded journals, rather than adopting a scatter-gun approach focusing on papers that have little academic currency.

Establishing your niche

The types of papers you wish to publish will also depend on your subject area and discipline(s). You may focus entirely on empirical research papers, typically around 5,000-8,000 words long. However, there are a range of different types of publications to be found in different journals, and it is worthwhile exploring what specific journals invite in terms of contributions:

- Review papers;
- Research reports;
- Discussion pieces;
- Rapid response articles;
- Conference reviews.

Depending on your own views on quality and quantity, as well as how guided you are to produce work for the purpose of the REF or the extent to which publications form part of your institution's promotion criteria, it is important to understand what is likely to be included in any evaluation of your work, and why. Sometimes only empirical or original long papers will be regarded as research outputs.

> **Tip**
>
> Make a list of the journals you want to publish in over the next five years, and the reasons why. Have a copy of this to hand and keep a record of your achievements when you get that all-important acceptance email from a journal editor.

At the outset of your academic career there are also other ways to publish, beyond research articles.

Publishing for your teaching career

As noted in chapter 3, you can publish in relation to your teaching activities. Your discipline(s), their theoretical foundations and the methods employed, are continually developing and advancing through the sharing of new knowledge, experiences and perspectives. These types of publications do not need to remain in the domain of educationalists, or senior, more experienced academics; as an early career academic with fresh eyes, you too can contribute to this literature.

> **Author reflection**
>
> My most successful publication at the time of writing this book was with a former colleague and originated from a conversation we had about our respective research projects and frustrations with research ethics conventions in how to 'protect' participants in dissemination. This led us to co-write a paper, which I think we would both say was an enjoyable experience in terms of working together and getting our frustrations down on paper, and which has gone on to be successful in terms of being widely used by others. I have referred to this paper in job applications to demonstrate that I am engaged and interested in the craft of undertaking social research, and regularly draw on it in teaching research methods to both undergraduate and postgraduate students.

It can be helpful to think about what you could publish early on in your career to (1) orientate yourself to your field/discipline(s) and colleagues beyond your specific research problem and (2) demonstrate to students, colleagues, employers and/or prospective employers that you have experience and insight into the formation and conduct of your area.

> **Pause for thought**
>
> Is there an issue within your area or discipline, not necessarily attached to your specific research field that interests or irks you? Could you publish on it, with a view to it being useful to the development of your area and for students?

Book reviews

Although book reviews are not typically regarded as research outputs, they are a useful way to get access to (sometimes costly) newly published books.

130　Establishing your niche

If you find a book that has been recently published, or is due to be published, and you are willing to read it and offer an informed opinion and overview, then writing a review can be a useful way of accessing literature. Moreover, it can be a great way to start to write for publication, developing your written communication skills and ability to complement and offer constructive criticism at the same time. Book reviews are usually quite short and can be turned around relatively quickly; and book review editors are usually quite receptive (I have found) to requests for feedback from writers in the early stages of their career.

> **Tip**
>
> If you think that you could benefit from either getting access to books or your writing could be enhanced through writing a few reviews, it is worthwhile making yourself known to the book review editor of your chosen journal(s), either offering to review more generally or volunteering specifically to review a text.

Books and chapters

The worth of books and book chapters to you will depend on your discipline(s) and area, and your own personal goals. In my own field, sole-authored books have some research currency, although monographs and textbooks have less than that of a scholarly or theoretical tome.

> **Author experience**
>
> For me personally, a sole-authored book is something I aspire to (one day) as a more enduring legacy, compared to publications in journals. Similarly, I have enjoyed writing book chapters and being a part of a collection of chapters in an edited collection that has made a contribution to the development of a particular area/subject matter. Yet in REF terms, book chapters I have written have had very little value.

Establishing your niche 131

You need to understand what counts within your own field and what you wish to prioritise in your career. If you know, for example, that peer-reviewed publications are the number one priority but you want to write books then you need to be prepared to be able to justify your decision(s) to those tasked with supervising you and/or be prepared for slow(er) career progression as it will take you longer to build up a body of evidence of your academic prowess.

> **Tip**
>
> To get a sense of what is valued within your own discipline or field, have a look at job descriptions for current vacancies that are more senior to yours, or are in institutions where you would like to work. These will usually specify the type of publishing activity that employers are expecting at the different stages in an academic career. Some job adverts will specify a publications record 'commensurate with the stage of career'. If that is the case, look at the staff profiles of those colleagues currently employed at your (desired) level in the department where the vacancy is located. What do their publishing profiles look like?

Digging deep and dealing with rejection

However you choose to publish, and wherever you choose to publish, as your career unfolds you will learn and develop your ability to get papers into journals. This ability however is much more than simply writing well-informed and well-defended articles; it is an ability characterised by drive, tenacity, fortitude and resilience. Why? Because most of the effort and energy expended in the dissemination of research in academic journals is concealed from public view.

Conducting research takes time, but so does writing it up for publication and getting it published. Moreover, submitting a paper to a journal can be, for some people at least, extremely daunting – as you let go of your ideas and put them out for peer review. At worst, you have to be prepared for critique, condemnation, and outright rejection. At best, you can hope for constructive feedback and insights into how to develop the paper to its full potential, or even a straight acceptance (although this is rare). Moreover, peer review is a contentious process that can be critiqued in terms of bias, partiality and the fallibility of human-reviewers.[6]

Certainly, once you submit a journal paper, be prepared for a long journey ahead. The process of submission, review, revision, re-submission, and potentially more revision and re-submission can take a very long time. Once accepted, your paper may be placed online in some form of 'first view' but many take many more months (or years) before it is published in an issue of the journal, as the journal works through its backlog of papers. The slowness of academic publishing thus both upholds the integrity of the work produced, but presents considerable problems in terms of being up-to-date and responsive. You need to be mindful and organised for this time-lag early on in your career, especially if you are under pressure to publish to achieve tenure or pass probation.

> **Tip**
>
> Before submitting to a journal you can approach the editor to ask if they would be interested in your paper. You can also ask the editor, or editorial assistant if there is one, regarding the backlog of papers they are currently working with. Some journals will have a very quick turnaround and if your work is accepted you could find it published relatively quickly (within months ideally). Others may have a much longer lead-in time. If so, check to see if they have a method for disseminating accepted papers pre-publication, so that (1) your work is in the public domain and can be referenced and (2) you can reference it in tenure/job applications if appropriate.
>
> Once accepted, make sure you are aware of your institution's rules on submitting the accepted form of paper into their own repository. The same goes for research funders.

In terms of building up resilience, there is no doubt about it, being told that your work is not going to be published can be difficult news to receive.

---

6 In the UK, one of the most famous examples of the fallibility of peer review was the publication of research claiming that the MMR vaccine was connected to autism (see Henderson, 2010).

However, beyond its content it is important to be mindful that there are a number of reasons for why your paper may be rejected:

1. The paper does not fulfil the remit of the journal.
2. The journal is in high demand and can cherry pick what the editors regard to be as the highest quality papers.
3. The journal has a significant backlog and the editors are therefore selecting the highest quality papers only, to get back on track with turnaround times.
4. The editors are protecting the high ranking of their journal and are selecting papers that they speculate will achieve high citation/impact rates.
5. From the reviews received the editors can see that, from their perspective, too much revision is required, or that the suggested revisions are either unrealistic or would essentially be creating a different paper, thereby nullifying the first submission.

> **Tip**
>
> If you receive a request to revise your paper, from my own experience I would recommend completing them *as soon as you can* – so that you are working on the paper while it is still relatively fresh in your mind, and so that you can re-submit and move on to other tasks and/or papers. Having paper revisions hanging over you as a 'job to do' on, let's face it, work you have *already done* can hinder you from moving forward in your career. Paper revisions and the seduction of aiming for flawlessness can also become somewhat obsessive and all-consuming; better to submit the best piece of work you can, knowing that it – as with all academic work – can always be improved, and is instead contributing to the *continual development and evolution* of the literature and practice in your field.

In practical terms, to limit the possibility of receiving a rejection it is important to:

1. **Target, target, target.** Write your paper *for* that publication. Cross reference previous work in the journal, clearly articulate to readers *why*

your paper is in the journal and how it builds on the journal's previous publications.
2. **Do your homework.** Pick the right journals for your work! Make the effort to contact the editor or editorial assistant to check the fit of your work.

In other words, preparation is key. Do not expect that writing a decent paper alone is ample enough to get it published. You need to be mindful of the paper's 'fit' for the journal, the journal's turnaround times, where the journal is going in terms of its focus and content, the rankings of journals and the pressure(s) that these rankings create for publication, and so on. Importantly, you need to invest time (which is usually not accounted for in workload models and is one you have to carve out and protect) to write, but also to understand – before you 'click' to submit your paper – the context in which your paper is going to be received, reviewed, accepted or rejected, and ultimately read by the journal's readership. They are your peers and your job is to find your 'niche' within their group.

> **Tip**
>
> As you get more adept at publishing, and if you are in the UK, make sure you join the Authors' Licensing and Collecting Society (ALCS). They collect money you are entitled to every time someone uses or copies your work.

Finding your research niche has never been more important, in terms of your own identity, where you want to work, who you want to work with, where you want to publish and how to do so. At the start of your academic career it pays to have an understanding of the political economy within which your research agenda, experience and credibility will be established, unfold and evolve. Doing so will cultivate your resilience in the face of critique and rejection, your fortitude in keeping going, and make your experience of those successes even sweeter.

References

Burrows, R. (2012) 'Living with the h-index? Metric assemblages in the contemporary academy', *The Sociological Review*, 60 (2): 355–372.

Caulfield, T. and Ogbogu, U. (2015) 'The Commercialization of University-based Research: Balancing Risks and Benefits', *BMC Med Ethics*, 16: 70, available online at https://bmcmedethics.biomedcentral.com/articles/10.1186/s12910-015-0064-2 [accessed 08/12/17].

Dunne, M., Pryor, J. and Yates, P. (2005) *Becoming a Researcher: A Research Companion for the Social Sciences* (Maidenhead: Open University Press).

Gasparyan, A.Y., Nurmashev, B., Yessirkepov, M., Udovik, E.E., Baryshnikov, A.A. and Kitas, G.D. (2017) 'The Journal Impact Factor: Moving Toward an Alternative and Combined Scientometric Approach', *Journal of Korean Medical Science*, 32 (2): 173–179.

Gilbert, N. (ed.) (2006) *From Postgraduate to Social Scientist: A Guide to Key Skills* (London: Sage).

Henderson, M. (2010) 'Problems with Peer Review', *BMJ*, 340: c1409.

Huston, T. (2012) *Teaching What You Don't Know* (Cambridge, MA: Harvard University Press).

McLachlan, F. (2017) 'Being Critical: An Account of An Early Career Academic Working Within and Against Neoliberalism', *Sport, Education and Society*, 22 (1): 58–72.

Murphy, T. (2017) 'Revising the Research Excellence Framework: Ensuring Quality in REF2021, or New Challenges Ahead?', *Perspectives: Policy and Practice in Higher Education*, 21 (1): 34–39.

Rawat, S. and Meena, S. (2014) 'Publish or Perish: Where are We Heading?', *Journal of Research in Medical Sciences*, 19 (2): 87–89.

Remler, D. (2016) 'Are 90% of academic papers really never cited? Reviewing the literature on academic citations', LSE Impact Blog, available online at http://blogs.lse.ac.uk/impactofsocialsciences/2014/04/23/academic-papers-citation-rates-remler/ [accessed 29/11/17].

Thomson Reuters (nd) 'Journal Impact Factor', available online at http://ipsciencehelp.thomsonreuters.com/inCites2Live/indicatorsGroup/aboutHandbook/usingCitationIndicatorsWisely/jif.html [accessed 11/11/17].

Further reading

Becker, L. and Denicolo, P. (2012) *Publishing Journal Articles* (London: Sage).

Benson, P.J. and Silver, S.C. (2012) *What Editors Want: An Author's Guide to Scientific Journal Publishing* (Chicago: Chicago University Press).

Goodson, P. (2016) *Becoming an Academic Writer: 50 Exercises for Paced, Productive, and Powerful Writing*, 2nd edn (London: Sage).

Murray, R. (2013) *Writing for Academic Journals*, 3rd edn (Maidenhead: Open University Press).

Sword, H. (2012) *Stylish Academic Writing* (Cambridge, MA: Harvard University Press).

Sword, H. (2017) *Air & Light & Time & Space: How Successful Academics Write* (Cambridge, MA: Harvard University Press).

Thomson, P. (2012) *Writing for Peer Reviewed Journals: Strategies for Getting Published* (Abingdon: Routledge).

Useful journals

Higher Education Research and Development
Minerva
Studies in Higher Education

6 Building critical mass

Following the previous chapter, which focused on establishing your credentials early on in your research career, this chapter explores how to build a critical mass of colleagues and peers to work with, both within your institution and beyond. It is divided into three sections: research projects and leading teams, PhD supervision, and external networking. Each section examines ways in which you can meet and work with kindred spirits, as well as ways of working with individuals, teams and institutions who do not share your vision or goals. Recognising that much of who you work with can be outside of your control early on in your career, the chapter's emphasis is on what you *can* do to shape your career. It is framed by two questions: Who do I want to be working with, and on what, in 5-10 years' time? Why?

Why working with others matters

First and foremost, it is worthwhile spending some time reflecting on why working collaboration and with others matters more than ever within academia. Historically and culturally, and of course varying to some extent depending on your field, the profession of academia is predicated on a 'lone wolf' model. Or, at least, what constitutes success for an academic and how this is measured is typically based on individual outputs or an individual's contributions to said outputs.

The result of this focus on individual accomplishment has been an intensification of pressure and expectation on what any one individual can achieve (Gill and Donaghue, 2016). Driven by institutions who expect their academic workforce to be as productive as possible during their tenure, it has emphasised continued excellence and 'high achievement', pushing academics to adopt low-risk research strategies and along increasingly specialised routes (Back, 2016). Such an escalation in the importance of specialism has, to a degree, created artificial barriers between academics who are placed in competition with one another, rather than emphasising the importance of collaboration (see chapter 1). In turn, this can lead to defensive practice, with a reluctance to share ideas and work.

Of course, this is a rather cynical and pessimistic view and I have no doubt that there will be some readers of this chapter who feel that this perception of individualistic success is either not in evidence or, if it is, not necessarily a 'bad thing'. After all, such an emphasis on individual excellence and achievement can in the right conditions lead to great breakthroughs and major societal developments. However this chapter and, indeed, this whole book, advocates that such a focus on individual merit and success can serve to hinder academic and intellectual progress. It can create very narrow fields of expertise, devoid of input from wider technological, scientific, commercial, social, political, historical, cultural and economic forces and contexts that shape research and expertise. It overlooks the richness that can come from working with others, particularly those outside of your own specific interests and area. This can be key to:

- Expanding your horizons;
- Being intellectually creative and dynamic;
- Generating and responding to intellectual and practical problems and solutions;
- Sustaining your career over the long term.

The extent to which HE institutions are set up to accommodate and promote collaboration within the university and beyond will depend very much on the institution. However, regardless of the posturing and positioning of an institution and its organisation, as an early career academic you do have some liberty in determining how you will go about navigating barriers to working with others. While this chapter focuses specifically on three practical ways to work with others while building your own critical mass, there might also be specific organisations and populations with which you could make connections in the early part of your career. You do not necessarily need to work with these contacts immediately, but putting yourself on their radar and likewise getting them on yours, is a good start.

> **Pause for thought**
>
> Are there any individuals or organisations that you would relish the opportunity to work with in the future? Make a note – you may be able to include them in your research career using the three suggested areas within this chapter. If not, you will at least have taken the time to think beyond your desk space.

Research projects

If your job role entails research then you can be assured that your institution will expect you to seek funding to conduct that research. At the outset of your research career you are (hopefully) an asset to a department and your field owing to your fresh ideas, enthusiasm and (hopefully) boundless energy. Your eagerness to establish your research credentials and reputation will be hugely invigorating for your colleagues, who may have very different priorities, agendas and energy levels depending on where they are within their career trajectory and overall phase of life. You may find yourself dealing with many invitations to participate in projects. On the other hand, you may find that within your particular institution or department colleagues' priorities are so at odds with yours in terms of scope and areas of interest that you struggle to find common ground. You may find yourself pulled in many different directions as you try to 'establish your niche' within the department (see chapter 5). You may also find yourself in receipt of hostility, jealousy, scepticism and resentment if you are seen as an outsider, a challenger to the status quo, or someone who might reveal the inadequacy or weaknesses of individuals or an organisation.

> **Tip**
>
> If you are the recipient of such negativity at the start of your career it is worthwhile (1) doing some groundwork to establish why this might be the case in terms of the institution's history and (2) equipping yourself with the personal resources and skillset to maintain resilience in that environment.

Wherever you end up, at this stage in your career, it is important to have your own vision for research that you want to be engaged in and, crucially, who you want to be working with. This is to ensure that when you are buffeted by winds of change or the whims of colleagues, you have a clear sense of where your career is heading, and why. While I am not promoting that you take a wholly strategic and instrumental approach to undertaking research you do however need to be mindful of where you want to be in 5-10 years' time, what you want to be working on, and with whom.

> **Pause for thought**
>
> Write a project outline (1-2 pages) for your dream research project. Who would you want to work with on it? What would the aims and objectives of the project be? Why does this study matter to the world? What does it contribute? Keep this project in mind (and do not be afraid to modify it) as your research career evolves. This is your research vision. It is something for you to be aiming for, with your preceding efforts (for example, research funding bids and publications) channelling you towards this goal.

> **Tip**
>
> When it comes to developing your own vision for research, unless you have very clear reasons for not sharing your aims with others, I would always advocate creating your own network of 'trusted advisors' both inside and outside of your institution and with whom you share your outline ideas. While some academics can be fiercely protective of their domain, the most successful academics I have witnessed have been those who have been generous with their ideas and feedback to others. This willingness to share has resulted in, for them, an exchange and reciprocation of ideas, time, energy, and intellectual engagement.

One thing is for certain, applying for research funding takes time and energy, and the labour involved is largely invisible to others. Unless you are successful in your bid for funds, have line management responsibilities or you are involved in supporting colleagues via internal mechanisms (see below), or unless your institution or department has a (divisive and pressure-inducing) policy of 'name and shame', your immediate colleagues are unlikely to know how many bids you have submitted nor their value. Within the UK there are varying success rates for different funders, ranging from just over 10 per cent to just over 30 per cent (Matthews, 2016).[1] Thus, depending on your field you can expect that for every hour you spend crafting, revising, seeking feedback, editing, and developing your bid, very few projects will come to fruition.

Before you even submit your proposal to a funder it is highly likely that your institution will have its own internal mechanisms for assessing proposal quality. This approach to 'demand management' can be implemented to ensure that the bid has the best possible chance of success, or can result from a stipulation of the research funder to guarantee that there is a preliminary sifting of proposals and only 'the best' come to their attention. This effectively means that, on occasion, you may find yourself in a competitive process internally before your bid is even considered by others external to your organisation.

Tip

Make sure that you are familiar with your institution's procedures for reviewing and providing feedback on research proposals internally, so that you can make good use of colleagues' input and feedback during the crafting of a research proposal.

What constitutes a brilliant proposal will varying according to who reads it (which, after all, is one of the weaknesses of peer review); the social, political and economic priorities of the day; and where your institution wishes

---

1 These figures relate to the latest available at the time of writing, with the Economic and Social Research Council funding 12 per cent of bids (the lowest UK Research Council success rate), compared to 33 per cent by the Engineering and Physical Sciences Research Council.

to position itself. Reflecting on chapter 5, it is worthwhile knowing therefore how you 'fit' within your department and institution, and how your research area aligns itself with current funding priorities, so that at any given moment you are able to articulate this and respond to funding calls. It is also advisable to have to hand a brief synopsis of why your research area matters to a non-specialist in case it is called upon. This will be good practice for trying to convince academic audience(s) about the benefit and value of your proposed research.

> **Pause for thought**
>
> In a couple of sentences, can you articulate the relevance and importance of your research interest(s) to a non-academic audience? Why does anyone need your research? Why does it matter?

Being ready to respond to a funding call will be more straightforward for some topic areas and disciplines than others. Moreover, it will depend a great deal on an individual's existing working relationships with colleagues and networks – and the capacity of the individual to mobilise their colleagues and networks at short notice. In this way, academic areas where scholarship is an individual pursuit rather than a collaborative one (which you can broadly estimate by the number of authors on a journal paper) are at somewhat of a disadvantage when it comes to being responsive to funding calls, as the onus is on the individual to create and generate a proposal, rather than a team of people.

Thus as an early career academic, while you hold onto your long-term research vision, be prepared to be responsive to research funding as opportunities arise. As the start of this chapter advocated, it is worthwhile cultivating and nurturing your networks before you are in this position. These networks, both within your institution and externally, are vital in your ability to call on people at short notice to either contribute to a project proposal, or to provide feedback on a draft. Given their importance, they need periodic attention and nurturing, to ensure that relationships remain positive, constructive and fruitful.

> **Pause for thought**
>
> You have already thought about people you may want to work with in the future. What about people you are working with *now*? Do you have a contacts list or way of recording your network so that you can contact individuals or organisations for input at short notice? How are you looking after those relationships – do you see those people regularly? Do you need to periodically 'check in' with them to make sure that you are 'on their radar'?

As with expectations regarding income generation, there may too be expectations from your institution regarding the number of bids you submit, or the value of funding applied for. What is important to remember is that for the vast majority of academics, research funding is something of a lottery, where your own ideas (however brilliant) will be competing with others. Like a job interview, it is highly likely that you will not know with whom you are competing, nor their assets or their weaknesses. Moreover, as with job interviews, you may have a pretty good idea of the priorities of the research funder/institution, but you may not know the political and economic constraints and contexts within which decision-makers are working and how decisions regarding funding are made.

Given such uncertainty, you need to make sure that from the outset of your career you are setting yourself up for an experience of applying for funding that is characterised by learning and eventual success – rather than focusing on failure and disappointment.

> **Tip**
>
> Wherever possible, regard writing and submitting bids as an opportunity to develop ideas and work with others, rather than the 'be all and end all' of your career.

Importantly, you also need to ensure that you set yourself reasonable expectations about what you can and cannot do, and reflect this clearly and articulately to your institution in any planning or appraisal process in which you may take part. To be clear, this is not about shying away from commitments or readiness to submit research bids; far from it, it is about ensuring that you are a responsible colleague and employee, who does not burnout nor risk losing their job because they have promised too much and not delivered enough. As a very senior colleague once told me, it is best to limit expectations and set reasonable objectives and then *over-deliver*, than promise the earth and fail.

> **Tip**
>
> Make sure that you complete any appraisal or commitment of future research funding with an experienced and supportive colleague. You need to be attuned to the commitments you are placing on yourself if you declare, for example, that you will secure X amount of research funds in the forthcoming year. The subtleties of language in your aims, objectives and commitments to securing research funding really matter. You can aspire to submit X number of research bids in any given year, but you *cannot* guarantee raising X amount of funds nor be held accountable for the socio-economic and political contexts that shift the changing priorities and availability of research funders.

As you bid for funding you need to hold onto your research vision and remember that even writing proposals is a positive step towards fostering and building your critical mass. Indeed, you do not have to actually have a sizeable research team on a project; you will likely also have an advisory board in some form, which itself is a way of working with people from your network(s). As you plan, prepare and craft your research proposal(s) you also need to remember that while undertaking research first-hand can be extremely fulfilling and intellectually creative, unless your contract is based solely on research it may also be time consuming and pressure-inducing. Indeed, depending on your discipline you may not even be expected to conduct research yourself but instead build and recruit post-doctoral teams. Unless you cost in sufficient funding to 'buy you out' of teaching and administrative responsibilities (that is, through your research funding your institution can afford to pay someone else to cover for your duties while you do the research), you may find that actually being successful in attaining funding and committing to undertaking empirical work yourself serves as an additional burden on your working week. Moreover proposing to undertake research yourself may be viewed in a dim light by some funders and their reviewers, who understand the reality of balancing teaching and administrative duties with physical research. Thus in terms of your career development and depending on discipline, do not automatically shy away from regarding research funding as the possibility of recruiting *others* to undertake empirical research, enabling you to develop your leadership skills through research project management.

> **Pause for thought**
>
> How does the thought of leading a research project team leave you feeling? Excited and enthused about the potential, or dread and anxiety about the responsibility? Or even jealousy of others who get to do the empirical work, or resentment that you cannot? While I cannot wave a magic wand to help you address any gut reaction you may have to leading a research project, be sure to pay attention to your initial response and reflect on what this tells you about how prepared you are for the reality of this as your career advances. Is there anything you could be doing now to help you prepare for the prospect of a project leadership role?

PhD supervision

A second key way to build critical mass is to get involved in PhD supervision. As the next generation of academics, PhD students can be a fulfilling group to work with as (in an ideal world) you foster a stimulating and constructive working relationship that can hopefully extend beyond their doctoral studies. PhD students are a significant responsibility too however, so it is important to approach supervision as a developmental process, taking on increasing responsibility as your experience of supervision progresses.

Make no bones about it, building up your academic reputation and (inter)national esteem – both of which raise your profile as a potential PhD supervisor to keen students – can take time. Thus, in the early days of your academic career it is best not to rely on potential doctoral students to approach you, and instead to find ways of recruiting students or getting involved in PhD supervision. Ways to do so include:

1. Joining established PhD supervisory teams as the junior member. These teams do not necessarily have to be directly associated with your work. You may join the team not because of shared intellectual interests, for example, but because of your methodological insight and experience.
2. Applying for PhD funding for projects via internal and external funding competitions. Sometimes these sources will specifically allocate funds to early career academics to get their PhD supervision record off the ground. Keep an eye out for those as there will be a smaller pool of applicants bidding for that resource. Successful projects are then advertised and the student recruited much like a job interview – they are working on a project for which you have set the parameters. There may also be PhD studentships attached to centres and research areas within and across different institutions, with only specific 'priority' areas achieving funding. In this climate your field/disciplinary positioning can be critical as may need to you align yourself to an area of research in order to be considered eligible (see chapter 5).
3. Negotiating a PhD studentship as part of your academic position. If an institution wants to back you they need to provide you with the resources to succeed, and this includes people.
4. Approaching industry directly, which will often rely heavily on your external networks (see chapter 9), and can be extremely difficult without a track record of supervision or academic/industry success.

Tip

Ask whoever oversees PhD students in your department/institution how you can get involved in PhD student supervision, and whether there are any teams that you could join to develop your skills as a co- or secondary supervisor. Your case to do so is based on the importance of ensuring that there is a steady up-skilling of academics to take on PhD supervision.

You may find students approaching you to become a supervisor, and if so make sure to seek advice from more experienced colleagues before responding. Some potential students have done a lot of preparatory work and have deliberately sought you out; others may have simply fired off an email en masse to potential supervisors across the country/round the world in the hope that someone 'bites'. On other occasions you may find that your department has been approached by a student and a call goes out for interest in supervision. However a potential student arrives at your doorstep, make sure that you take time to reflect on their proposed ideas, their background, the commitment involved in taking them on, and – to reiterate – seek advice from more experienced supervisor colleagues regarding the approach that has been made.

> **Tip**
>
> If you are unclear as to the sources of PhD funding, investigate! Your institution may have an individual, team or department that are tasked with securing and organising PhD funding. Your professional association (see chapters 4 and 9) may have details as to sources of funding.

Types of supervisory teams/supervisors

There are many ways that a supervisor/supervisee relationship can develop. A fantastic source of insight into the varying relationship and expectations that a supervisor/doctoral student can have is Lee's (2008) paper on types of doctoral supervision. She outlines five different types of supervisory arrangements as follows:

Table 6.1

Functional	where the focus is on project management
Enculturation	where the emphasis is on socialising the student in their becoming part of an academic community
Critical thinking	where the importance is on the student questioning and analysing their work
Emancipation	where the supervisor(s) encourage the student to question and develop themselves
Quality relationship	where the stress is on enabling the student to feel enthused, inspired and nurtured

Depending on your topic area and interpersonal skills, along with – of course – the priorities and stipulations of the funder and/or institution, you are likely to gravitate more easily to 1–2 of these arrangements and supervisor roles than others. The role you take on will also, of course, depend on the number of PhD students you are supervising at any one time and your other commitments. Whichever model suits you, make sure you are upfront with the student about your priorities for supervising them, and where (if there are any gaps) they might seek alternate support or guidance. If you are a functional supervisor focused on the task at hand, for example, try to resist the impulse to promise the student a quality relationship when you know that it is highly likely you will not be able to fulfil that promise. Make sure, too, that you are aware of the supervision culture within your department, as there are risks associated with one-to-one supervision, such as isolation for the student and the supervisor (Grant, 2010).

> **Author reflection**
>
> Throughout my supervision of PhD students I have found that I have naturally committed to the enculturation model of supervision. I have felt strongly that my responsibility as a supervisor is to expose the student to 'the back stage' of academia. While prioritising the thesis I have encouraged them to engage with activities and commitments that will enable them to learn what being an academic constitutes, while at the same time developing their CV to ensure that they have transferable and attractive skills and attributes for future employers. Although not all students I have supervised have wanted to have a career in academia, we have typically focused on activities over their years of study that have kept their options open for future employment, whether in HE or not. This has included, for example, peer review publishing, reports, conference papers, conference/seminar organisation, teaching, public engagement activities, entering into research competitions and so on.

If there is training out there available to you on how to supervise or how to improve as a supervisor – use it! It may only be an afternoon seminar, or it may be a comprehensive term-long course on supervising; whatever the case, gaining insight into the obligations and practice of PhD supervision is vital. As Lee shows, there is much more to doctoral supervision than simply supporting a student in writing a decent thesis. As you supervise a student you will simultaneously be supporting their intellectual endeavours, while also being mindful of their (and your) time management; building and maintaining a good working relationship with the student; the economic implications of their study (if there are any); their career prospects; how their work complements the endeavours of (for example) your lab; and institutional requirements such as upgrade processes, ethical approval and so on. It is a considerable responsibility and one that requires a mature, informed supervisor that will provide the student with time and guidance over a sustained period of time. Training will not magically tell you how to do this, but it will provide you with important information regarding institutional expectations and requirements, and the opportunities and pitfalls of working with doctoral students.

What happens if it goes wrong?

As your academic career progresses you are likely to hear horror stories regarding PhD supervision: of very poor supervisory practice, with few meetings and input from the supervisor; of supervisors who disagreed about how to conduct the study and put the student in the middle of their disagreement; of extremely challenging students with very high or low expectations of what is required; of students who seem to be incapable of managing their time; or of students who are simply not up to completing a PhD. Whatever the issue, relationships between PhD students and supervisors do break down (see Gunnarsson et al., 2013), with appeals and litigation an important issue within institutions (Phillips and Pugh, 2010). As a result, most institutions will have appointed administrators (academic and non-academic) to oversee PhD supervision within departments/faculties and across the institution. Their role is to provide support and guidance to students, and training to supervisors. Institutions are also likely to have an extensive set of regulations regarding PhD supervision and the expectations of students and supervisors, plus clear procedures of viva examinations and appeals. These are all in place to provide structure and guidance over a multi-year period of study.

> **Tip**
>
> Make sure you are clear about your institution's expectations regarding PhD supervision. When you become a supervisor, make sure the student is aware of these too.

Let's be frank about this, PhD supervision does not always work out. There may be gaps on supervision teams for a reason – because of personality clashes between colleagues and/or the student, or because of the specificities of the project. Indeed, you may join a team and feel that *you* knowingly or unknowingly contribute towards a problem, for example because you have a very different approach to deadlines and feedback to the lead supervisor, or you find that you and the student have insurmountable intellectual disagreement(s) about a specific issue.

Whatever the challenge, it is important to address it – ideally informally at first. Seek guidance from more experienced colleagues or those tasked with overseeing PhD studies. Do not fall into the trap of believing that flagging up an issue is tantamount to failure or giving up. It is a better use of everybody's time if issues are brought to light and addressed, rather than heads becoming stuck in the sand with the hope that the problems will disappear.

If you have concerns about PhD supervision, you need to be sensitive to the situation in hand. Academics typically work with PhD students much more closely than undergraduates, and relationships between PhD students and their supervisors really, really matter to the students' success. Where you may be teaching 100–200 students in a lecture theatre, you may be working very closely with a PhD student and/or another supervisor on their project – getting to know them both personally and professionally. As a consequence, tact and diplomacy are imperative when raising concerns. Important points to remember when you are highlighting issues include the following:

- Make sure you are aware of your institution's regulations regarding handling issues with PhD students. These will usually be stipulated in a Code of Practice, or comparable regulatory document. There is likely to be a 'chain of command' for how to deal with problems as and when they arise.

- A very basic recommendation is: do not commit anything to email that you would not be willing to say in person (as mentioned in chapter 4). There are mechanisms (for example, Freedom of Information Requests) through which the content of emails can be requested and solicited.
- Whether you like it or not, as a supervisor you are an important part of the student's career and their future, not least because you may be called upon for a reference in the future. Do not exploit this position nor do the student a disservice.
- There are likely to be experienced PhD supervisors within your institution who have a wealth of anecdotes and experiences of working with students. As with a lot of the challenges you may face in your academic career, you do not need to reinvent the wheel. Can you find one of those experienced colleagues and ask them how they have dealt with issues previously? Indeed, is there a precedent within your institution as to how to deal with problems?
- Make sure that the colleague tasked with overseeing the support for PhD students in your department or Faculty is aware of your concerns. If they are the problem, then find a trusted colleague or approach your line manger to seek guidance on how to handle the issue.

Overall, PhD supervision should ideally be a satisfying experience for both the supervisor and student and I hope that, at least early on, you do not encounter issues that require intervention from others. Do remember not to shy away from challenges however, as the likelihood is that over time they will escalate rather than disappear.

Building your external networks

Much of the literature on the research component of the academic's role are focused on publications and research funding, evidenced by the number of texts on how to create successful research bids and how to write for publication. There are, however, a range of complementary activities that you could, and arguably should, be undertaking to build up your 'portfolio' of research experience, and to inform your own research ideas. Uniting these activities is the importance of networking early on in your career; that is, meeting others beyond your institution, your specific field, and your previous networks. It is about 'putting yourself out there'. There are a number of tried and tested ways of doing this.

Conferences and seminars

These are undoubtedly one of the best ways to extend your networks. By meeting face to face with peers and colleagues, you get the opportunity to find out more about them beyond their publications and, ideally, to meet some kindred spirits. Be warned through, networking this way is a long-term game – you are likely to need to attend the same conference(s) repeatedly, year on year, to build up relationships and build a memorable reputation with colleagues.

Conferences and seminars can be an expensive endeavour too, both in terms of finances and time. In an ideal world, you will have attracted research funding that has included conference and travel fees, but if you are not yet in that position then you need to think creatively about how to raise funds to attend. Some institutions will have resources available that are either automatically allocated to individuals/groups, others will require 'bidding' for funding. Some conferences are free to attend, or have bursaries for early career academics. Some conferences will have early career sessions built in to them, or have special study days beforehand or afterwards, with funding attached. Moreover, attendance at a conference is not just about the financial cost of registration; if attending a conference involves travel you need to be budgeting in both the cost of that and the time it will take you to do so. A two- or three-day conference can quickly become a week's work when it involves a long-haul flight and train journey at the other end. So, while attending conferences and seminars can be appealing in terms of both their content and networking potential, and the opportunity to visit different parts of the world, you do need to be mindful of the commitment you are taking on.

There are a number of ways to make the best use of your time (and money!) when it comes to attending conferences and seminars. First and foremost, make sure you are targeting conferences and have a clear rationale for attending. Is it to present your work to a specific audience? Is it to meet others working within your discipline(s)? Is it to meet international colleagues? There will always be more conferences, more places to visit, and more people to meet – so make sure that you submit abstracts for presentations at conferences where your paper will be attended and where you have a clear sense of what you want to gain from it.

> **Author reflection**
>
> Very early on in my academic career I went to a conference in Florida with the aim of meeting US colleagues working in the same area. The networking during the breaks was, overall, a success. However, because of the number of parallel sessions and, perhaps because of my paper's topic, only five people showed up to my talk – two of whom I knew already and were from the UK! I cannot say that presenting at that conference was worth the airfare, but it did mean that at least I could add an international conference presentation to my CV.

Other ways to make the most of conferences and seminars include:

- Going through the abstracts and timetable beforehand and contacting colleagues to arrange a meeting, so that you have some allocated time with them.
- If publishers or journal editors will be attending, making contact beforehand to arrange a meeting to discuss publication plans.
- Planning out which papers you will be attending beforehand, while giving yourself time to network during breaks.

Journal editing and peer reviewing

It may be bold to envisage that you will be editing a high profile academic journal early in your career, but that should not prevent you from aspiring to this and working towards it through gaining editorial experience. A key way to gain editorial experience is to review papers and/or join journal editorial boards. In terms of peer reviewing, at the start of your career when you likely do not yet have a high enough profile to be called upon to review specific topics, you need to be pro-active in putting yourself forward to review.

> **Tip**
>
> If you want to peer review for a particular journal make contact with the editors to volunteer to do so, specifying the areas you can review in.

When papers do come to you for review, make sure you are realistic in terms of how many you can review at any one time (invitations to review will keep on coming!), how long a paper make take to review, and your competency in reviewing in the specialist area. If you are in any doubt about your ability to review a paper both in terms of knowledge and workload, then do not agonise unnecessarily. While journal editors rely on colleagues to provide peer-insight and feedback on the merit and quality of submitted papers, they also rely on the understanding that colleagues will do reviews in a timely manner and in areas in which they are knowledgeable. If you have a reservation about your capacity to review a paper then do not do it, and be secure in the knowledge that you are not the first to do so: academics turn down invitations to review all the time.

In terms of joining editorial boards each journal will have its own method of recruiting new members, and will have a different way of organising their boards. Some will have a single board, others will have two, divided into a national and an international board. Others will have an editorial board and as associate editorial board. The historical reasons for such divisions may or may not be transparent, but the reasons for having such organisations of boards include: expanding the pool of reliable paper reviewers; promotion; attracting highly experienced and/or 'big names' to the board; providing avenues for new members to join; and so on.

Some journals will have a formal process for appointing editorial boards, with a clear term of office. Others will be more informal and will be more interested in the disciplinary/specialist mix of the board, with editors approaching individuals to fill a perceived 'gap'. The best way to approach journal editorial boards therefore is to identify the journal(s) you would like to be associated with and review for, and then investigate how they compose their board and on what terms. Identifying a journal to work with and review for depends on your priorities at that time, for example, whether you want to raise or cement your profile and credibility in a specific topic area or discipline, or whether you want to network internationally with specific colleagues.

Tip

You may have a long-term aim to edit a specific journal, so investigate joining the editorial board of that journal in order to build up a history and reputation for supporting its ethos and endeavours.

Sabbaticals

As with many of the opportunities listed in this book, the availability of sabbaticals and secondments will depend on your institution and the type of employment contract you have. They are, however, a worthwhile opportunity to look out for as they can provide you with time and space to focus on specific projects and/or work with others.

Sabbaticals are typically one term/semester long, or 6-12 months, and provide 'leave' from teaching and administrative duties to focus on research. Year-long unpaid sabbaticals may also be an option open to you, if you can afford it. Sometimes those with a sabbatical use the opportunity to travel abroad, securing a 'visiting' title at an institution that may or may not come with expectations regarding contributions towards the institution itself, in the form of seminars, supervisory support and teaching. Others may stay on 'home turf' and focus on a specific project or publication.

Whatever you do on a sabbatical, you need to be mindful of (1) how sabbaticals are allocated amongst academic staff within your institution and (2) expectations regarding 'outputs' from a sabbatical period. In some institutions, sabbaticals happen automatically every few years, or as a result of taking on a significant administrative role. You may be able to negotiate a sabbatical with your line manager in agreement for taking on a particular duty. In other institutions, they may have to be applied for and are awarded competitively.

> **Tip**
>
> Find out your institution's policy on offering sabbaticals to its academic staff. Does it stipulate specific expectations regarding entitlement for early career academics?

However sabbaticals are administered, it is worthwhile – if you are entitled to one – to plan for, and apply for if needed, a sabbatical period to enable you to refresh, recharge and focus. If you are on a contract that combines teaching and research especially, as seen in earlier chapters of this book, the immediate needs of teaching can be demanding in terms of teaching to be prepared, assessments to be marked, and issues to be addressed. Such immediate demands can result in the loss of research time, but also take their toll intellectually, emotionally and physically. With academic years increasingly rolling into one another with little time to recover in-between, a sabbatical period can therefore serve as a much-needed opportunity to (re)gain perspective, insight and energy.

Secondments

Secondments are similar to sabbaticals in that they provide time away from everyday institutional activities. They are different however in that they typically require working within a different organisation for a period of time. They are an excellent way of exposing yourself to other workplace cultures, for networking, to work collaboratively with others, and to develop your research projects, ideas and outputs. Not all institutions will offer these, and depending on your specific area of work they may or may not be applicable to you at the start of your career. However, if the idea of working with another organisation, team or individual, or experiencing another sector appeals to you, then they are an invaluable way of expanding your horizons, learning new skills and, importantly, being able to gain some perspective on HE.

In terms of setting up a secondment, opportunities will depend on your field, existing networks, and the relationships your institution has with industry/external parties. For example, there may be pre-existing 'knowledge-exchange' arrangements where academics and non-academics swap positions for a brief period of time, or for academics to enter into organisations with a specific aim of building partnerships. Alternatively, secondments (like mine, see below) may arise out of existing individual relationships and from which you can capitalise. For my secondment, I literally sent an email asking if it might be a possibility as part of my sabbatical, and the conversation went from there.

> **Tip**
>
> If your institution supports secondments, what opportunities are there for working in other sectors or organisations? From your existing networks are there any organisations in which you would relish the opportunity to work for a period of time? Such opportunities may not fall into lap – you may need to be very pro-active to make them work. Don't be afraid to do so if they appeal to you!

Author reflection

I have just finished a six-month sabbatical at the time of writing, during which time I also undertook a secondment with a government department. Throughout the six months I learned several unexpected lessons. First and foremost, while I enjoyed being able to focus on research outputs and being liberated from the immediate demands of students and administrative roles, I did (in hindsight) become rather isolated as I worked at home and/or on my own for the majority of the time. This was a mixed blessing as it meant I could be more productive, but it also meant that I became a ruminator. I missed talking through concerns and reflecting on funding changes in HE with colleagues – which were dominating the news agenda at the time. If I were to have a sabbatical or secondment again, I would make sure I planned in time with others to compensate for the periods of lone working.

Having bestowed the opportunities and positive potential of sabbaticals and secondments, it is important to recognise that they come with their own set of challenges. Not least is the change in pace that you may experience, moving from a fast-paced dynamic setting to a more isolated day-to-day working practice, or vice versa. You may find that you were *more* productive the more commitments you had in your diary – although, of course, being constantly productive and responsive can lead to intellectual and emotional exhaustion. It is therefore important to go into a period of 'leave' from your institution being mindful of some of the issues you may face, such as changes in the rhythm of the working week and subsequently having to 're-learn' time management. Unless you are working with a team or in another institution (for example, as a visiting scholar noted above) a sabbatical or secondment can be similar to the model of doctoral study, with substantial periods of working in isolation. Other issues include managing lone-working and potential seclusion; keeping in touch with colleagues and any commitments that cannot be 'dropped'; and how to support PhD students.

In sum, as this chapter has shown, there are a multitude of ways to expand and extend your research networks early on in your career but you need to be informed as to the time and energy that is needed to build up your critical mass. It is important to not neglect these activities if you want to have a long-standing and fruitful career – while publications and funding success are part of your academic 'currency', it is colleagues and your networks that will sustain you intellectually and emotionally over the years. Invest in them, nurture them, tend to them as you would friendships and, in time, you should reap the rewards.

References

Back, L. (2016) *Academic Diary: or Why Higher Education Still Matters* (London: Goldsmiths Press).

Gill, R. and Donaghue, N. (2016) 'Resilience, apps and reluctant individualism: technologies of self in the neoliberal academy', *Women's Studies International Forum*, 54: 91-99.

Grant, B.M. (2010) 'Negotiating the Layered Relations of Supervision', in Walker, M. and Thomson, P. (eds) *The Routledge Doctoral Supervisor's Companion: Supporting Effective Research in Education and the Social Sciences* (Abingdon: Routledge), pp. 88-105.

Gunnarsson, R., Jonasson, G. and Billhult, A. (2013) 'The Experience of Disagreement between Students and Supervisors in PhD Education: A Qualitative Study', *BMC Medical Education*, 13: 134.

Lee, A. (2008) 'How are Doctoral Students Supervised? Concepts of Doctoral Research Supervision', *Studies in Higher Education*, 33 (3): 267-281.

Matthews, D. (2016) 'UK Grant Success Rates Prompt Worldwide Comparisons', *Times Higher Education*, 6 October, available online at www.timeshighereducation.com/news/uk-grant-success-rates-prompt-worldwide-comparisons [accessed 10/12/17].

Phillips, E and Pugh, D.S. (2010) *How to Get a PhD: A Handbook for Students and Their Supervisors*, 5th edn (Maidenhead: Open University Press)

Further reading

Aldridge, J. and Derrington, A. (2012) *The Research Funding Toolkit: How to Plan and Write Successful Grant Applications* (London: Sage).

Crawley, G.M. and O'Sullivan, E. (2015) *The Grant Writer's Handbook: How to Write a Research Proposal and Succeed* (London: Imperial College Press).

Denicolo, P. and Becker, L. (2012) *Developing Research Proposals* (London: Sage).

Denscombe, M. (2012) *Research Proposals: A Practical Guide* (Maidenhead: Open University Press).

Halse, C. (2011) ''Becoming a Supervisor: The Impact of Doctoral Supervision on Supervisors' Learning', *Studies in Higher Education*, 36 (5): 557-570.

Kamler, B. and Thomson, P. (2014) *Helping Doctoral Students Write: Pedagogies for Supervision* (Abingdon: Routledge).

Lee, A. (2011) *Successful Research Supervision: Advising Students Doing Research* (Abingdon: Routledge).

Locke, L., Spirduso, W., and Silverman, S. (2013) *Proposals that Work: A Guide for Planning Dissertations and Grant Proposals*, 6th edn (London: Sage).

Nicholson, D.J. (2017) *Academic Conferences as Neoliberal Commodities* (Basingstoke: Palgrave Macmillan).
Peelo, M. (2010) *Understanding Supervision and the PhD* (London: Continuum).
Taylor, S., Kiley, M. and Humphrey, R. (2017) *A Handbook for Doctoral Supervisors, 2nd edn* (Abingdon: Routledge).
Trew, R.J. (2017) *Get Funded: An Insider's Guide to Building an Academic Research Program* (Cambridge: Cambridge University Press).
Wisker, G. (2012) *The Good Supervisor, 2nd edn* (Basingstoke: Palgrave Macmillan).

Useful journals

International Journal of Doctoral Studies
Studies in Graduate and Postdoctoral Education
Studies in Higher Education
Teaching in Higher Education

7 Beyond the ivory towers

Expanding upon the previous chapter, this chapter examines the growing impetus to generate 'impact' with research activities and how to work with others outside of academia. Exploring what this may look like, the chapter considers the potential of working with other sectors through undertaking engagement activities that disseminate your research to populations and publics that you may not typically reach, and as hinted at in the previous chapter, the importance of fostering relationships beyond the academy. The chapter is grounded in the principle that HE is no longer an ivory tower and that academia is simply another professional workforce that can, and arguably has a responsibility to, engage with other workforces to ensure fruitful sharing of knowledge, information, and ideas.

Moving into 'the real world'

To begin, and connected to developments outlined in chapter 1, there is a growing pressure and expectation that academics no longer confine their research to the appraisal of their academic peers and that their work will have a real-world application. Simply publishing high quality papers in peer reviewed journals is not enough, you must demonstrate beyond your publications the need for and value of the research and how it has contributed to something beyond your own intellectual curiosity. You may have heard of this emphasis on real-world application and getting academic research 'out there' in terms of 'knowledge mobilisation' and 'knowledge transfer'.

Such a move towards identifying, establishing and subsequently demonstrating the 'real world' impact of academia has significant ramifications throughout almost all aspects of an academic career. It has, for example, substantial implications for the way in which research is conducted and disseminated, challenging some of the conventions and standards of what constitutes normal research practice. For example, as I have argued with a colleague elsewhere (see Tilley and Woodthorpe, 2011), it raises questions about the presumed importance of anonymising participants and locations in much of the social sciences – but which, by doing so, creates issues when you need to be able to demonstrate that you have engaged in and are providing ideas and solutions for 'the real world'.

Moreover, working in 'the real world' means that emphasis for those in the early phase of their career is on creating evidence of engagement with others, and impact with organisations and individuals beyond academia from the outset. And it means that making an impact and showing engagement with different 'publics' matters more and more in terms of job and promotion prospects. So, what do we mean when we talk about impact and public engagement? Each will be dealt with in turn here.

Impact

There are many, many debates being had about what impact looks like and how it can, if at all, be measured (see Gunn and Mintrom, 2017; Wilkinson, 2017). These debates are not dissimilar to the concerns outlined in chapter 1 in relation to the rise of league tables, metrics and the quantification of outputs and success in HE. In the context of academic research, there are some very reasonable concerns about how 'impact' can be allocated to one individual's work, or whether impact is about a long-term contribution to the field and resulting developments, which are much harder to determine and measure in social and economic terms (Watermeyer, 2014).

It is not the purpose of this chapter or this section specifically to replicate these arguments. For now what I want to propose is that at the outset of your career it pays to envisage what type of impact you want to have in the world, and what drives that desire. In other words, what type of academic do you want to be, and why? For many (I would go so far as to say most) people coming into academia, whether relatively young or after many years in another profession, they are likely to be profoundly influenced and driven by the desire to change something. Obviously, what constitutes a change will vary depending on your field and topic area. For some it may have global reach, for others it may be highly localised and specialist. It may be about making a product or a process more efficient, cost effective, less risky or less harmful to the environment. It may be about seeking social equality or targeting corporate crime. Whatever it is, wanting to make a difference is at the heart of wanting to effect a change.

It is important to note however, that this desire for change is rarely driven by a single or shared motivation. An intention to make change through the advancement of knowledge and intellect, practice and process, can be founded on very different reasons. These reasons may be very obvious or they may be completely concealed from public view. For some, for example, a desire to effect change may be borne out of the potential for growth; for human development; and for societal, economic, technological or environmental progress. Alternatively, a motivation may be borne out of disillusionment and frustration, and perceived failings in current practice. It may even be compelled by anger or adherence to an ideological set of principles regarding justice, equality, the value of education, or it may simply be driven out of curiosity and an interest in learning; or borne out serendipity and opportunity, with academia regarded as a stepping stone or career phase within a lifetime of exploration and adventure.

Whatever the motivation behind your desire to be an academic and to effect some change (or 'impact') on the world, be mindful that your colleagues may not share your motivations nor make obvious their own. Indeed, unless they have actively reflected on their career choice(s) and paths, they may not even clearly know or be able to articulate those motivations.

> **Pause for thought**
>
> Why did you become an academic? What is driving that?

So how does what drives you relate to impact? Well, what 'impact' you want to have on the world will be intrinsically connected to your desire to be an academic and what motivates you. As Krznaric (2012) notes, the role of 'flow' in your work is about finding a synergy between your beliefs and desires, and the outcomes or products of your work. 'Impact' is one of those outcomes.

Understanding what impact means to you

In the early phase of your career it pays to expend energy exploring what impact in the short and longer term would look and feel like to you. As with much of this book, this is about establishing your own principles and goals, before you begin to embody and personify your employing institution's aims and objectives. This is not to say that your own goals cannot be aligned to your institution's; rather, it is about being mindful of your institution's aims and how important your own principles are to you. Do you want your desires and motivations for impact to remain distinct from the institution? Are you comfortable blending yours with those of your employers? It is within this context that you need to establish what an impact as a result of your academic contributions would look like, to you and to others.

> **Pause for thought**
>
> What kind of impact would I like to make on the world? Why? How?

When you have an idea of what impact would look like to you, the question arises of how that might be made possible. 'Pathways to impact' is now a well-established phrase in the UK thanks to the Research Councils UK (RCUK, nd), which emphasises the centrality of building in 'impactful' activities into the research process. These activities can encompass a range of actions that may take place to (1) engage with others and (2) make a difference through your research. There are, of course, very easily demonstrable ways in which impact can be made, for example:

- The production of a new engine component for motor vehicles;
- The implementation of a new technique for filming in slow motion;
- Changes in government policy.

There are also more subtle 'impacts' of your work that could include:

- Changes in communication strategies in an organisation;
- Development of new workplace practice;
- Newly engaged audiences.

Of course, as noted earlier, some 'impactful' activities will be much easier to both identify and quantify than others. It may be that you work in a field where it could be extremely difficult to demonstrate individual influence on societal, technological, or economic change. If that is the case, then it is worthwhile speaking with more experienced colleagues as to how, if at all, they have done it; what works and what does not; and how you might be able to influence using your work.

> **Tip**
>
> Learn from other's successes... and their mistakes. You are more likely to hear or come across stories of great achievements in making an impact, but do not be indifferent to accounts of experiences that were less than amazing. You can learn as much from efforts to make an impact that did not pan out as planned as you can from trying to replicate success stories.

As with the political nature of research funding, how activities that can help with impact are supported, regarded, recognised, enabled and utilised will depend on your institution and job type. For some institutions, research impact is core to their mission, and this may be clearly set out in job descriptions and promotion criteria. For others, it may be regarded as more of a 'bolt on' activity, although the likelihood of this 'bolt on' approach is diminishing as impact becomes increasingly important in terms of how successful an institution is in conducting effective and influential research (via the REF in the UK, see chapter 5). It pays to find out your institution's expectations and the provision of support for impact activities, so that you have a reasonable understanding of how much is expected of you as an individual and the methods through which you can garner support. This is particularly important as you expend energy to create, maintain and sustain external networks (see later in this chapter) that will enable you to undertake impactful activities.

> **Tip**
>
> Find out what support is available to you within your institution with regard to undertaking impact activities. Is there a specialist team, or body of knowledge and experience, to draw upon? How is impact regarded within your institution (or the one you want to work in)? Is it, for example, built into seeking research funds, promotions criteria and so on?

One of the most constructive but potentially detrimental outcomes of moves towards academic knowledge mobilisation and having an 'impact' has been the instrumentalism that has crept into the academic's research remit (Watermayer and Olssen, 2016). Research bids, by and large, no longer rely solely on exploratory methods with little planned for dissemination and how to influence others. Rather, activities that are anticipated to lead to impact are now typically woven into research funding proposals, with academics required to commit to actions that will identify and 'engage' with public audiences, to demonstrate the merit of the research, move the world on in some way, and create an 'impact'. Such instrumentalism means that at the outset of projects there have to be clear expectations and obligations set regarding if, when and how the research will have an impact – potentially hindering more risky projects where impact cannot be clearly defined or predicted, or limiting academics to topics and techniques where impact can be more-or-less guaranteed.

Public engagement

Essentially, public engagement is the activity that takes place to support, embed and cement potential impact into the world beyond academia. Along with impact, over the last decade it has grown in prominence and importance in research bids, as academics are encouraged and supported to work with and alongside non-academics. Becoming ever more formalised in the UK through the evaluation of research in the REF, the extent to which public engagement has been institutionalised varies between universities:

> It is observable as a smorgasbord or patchwork of different, sometimes unrelated activities, initiatives and programmes with various intentions and unequal status and presence across UK universities. It may have the appearance of 'corporate' social responsibility perhaps even educational philanthropy and public goodwill, yet be motivated by an altogether more self-serving agenda.
>
> (Watermayer and Lewis, 2017: 2)

If impact is the outcome of the research, public engagement is typically what happens during the research process, and includes the mechanisms and methods through which non-academics will participate in the research or contribute to it in some way via feedback and validation exercises, or writing, for example, recommendations for practice or processes stemming from the research findings. Examples of public engagement can include:

- Working with public(s) to establish research problems;
- Validation exercises such as stakeholder roundtables;
- Promoting work through non-conventional channels such as public exhibitions, talks, and activities.

> **Pause for thought**
>
> What does public engagement in your field look like? Are there any success stories you can learn from?

Key to the success of public engagement is, first and foremost, identifying who the 'public(s)' is/are with whom you wish to engage. While it may be as simple as 'the general public' this can be a hard and heterogeneous group to work with, difficult to access with any real meaning, and problematic to qualify and accommodate owing to their diversity. Often more productive is identifying a sub-set of 'the public', organised by (for example) occupational group, age, gender, location, socio-economic status, belief, and so on. These groups may or may not have political leverage and power, they may be extremely influential (such as policy makers) or disenfranchised and/or marginalised by the state (for example, people who are homeless). They may be employed within large corporations, they may be volunteers or simply people affected by a particular issue. What is important is to be able to identify who your public audiences are, why you might engage with them, and how you might do so.

To be sure, there are benefits and risks associated with public engagement. Bringing alternative perspectives, real-world experiences and fresh eyes into projects can be a tremendous source of enrichment – both for you, your research and for your public(s). It can be a very rewarding experience to work closely with different groups of people or individuals, to build shared goals and see them (hopefully) come to fruition. Yet, it also pays to be mindful of the amount of time it can take to establish relationships with the public(s) you want to work with and – critically – to demonstrate an empathetic understanding of where they are coming from and why they are working with you. You cannot simply assume that because you are an academic trying to pursue a noble intellectual goal that this will be recognised, wanted or admired by others. It is therefore important to walk in the shoes of those you are working with (or want to work with), to understand their perspective, motives, drivers, fears, aspirations and objectives.

> **Pause for thought**
>
> Who are the public(s) you would like to work with over the next five years? Why would they want to work with you? What can you offer them?

Building up your own networks

Although there exists an instrumentalism that accompanies a lot of the push towards impact and public engagement, there are tremendous benefits to be had in working with others in terms of intellectual potential, the richness and applicability of research to 'the real world', the methods used and so on. Yet with ever more demands on your time, it pays to have a reasonably clear idea of the people and public(s) you wish to work with beyond academia, and to then have a short to medium term 'game plan' for how you will build up relationships with them.

If you struggle to find the time to do this, or reject the idea of being so strategic, it is important to recognise that a fundamental part of this is about establishing and cementing your reputation as an academic who has something to contribute beyond academia. It is not just about what you can get out of other people. If you have completed a PhD, it is about establishing yourself beyond your supervisor(s); if you have moved into academia from another sector, it is about establishing and consolidating your academic, scholarly identity.

As noted in the previous two chapters a key component of establishing your research identity is about your networks; be they pre-existing or your own. One of the most frequent queries I have heard from early career academics (and one I asked myself regularly) is: how do I build up networks outside of academia? While there are tried-and-tested ways of getting to know academic colleagues (seen in the last chapter – via conference attendance, journal editing/peer reviewing, sabbaticals and secondments) there is no quick-win, one-size-fits-all solution for building relationships with non-academic audiences, nor is there any escaping from the fact that networks need time, energy, enthusiasm, perseverance, and cultivation. Networks of people will not present themselves to you, unless in the form of email lists (where there is a high likelihood of being overlooked, see below), and any networks that you build up over time will require nurturing to ensure that they grow, evolve and expand as your work develops and individuals leave and join organisations. It is worthwhile therefore thinking of your networks as a garden, ripe for production but requiring consistent refinement and input to ensure yield; and, importantly, *you get out what you put in*. You are, unfortunately, not going to have a garden (network) akin to the Palace of Versailles with minimal effort on your part.

Penetrating networks

There are thousands, if not millions, of pre-existing networks within academia. If you look at your disciplinary association alone you are likely to find sub-set interest groups. Finding and getting involved in networks of people beyond academia might not be as straightforward however. For example, if you are interested in working with civil servants on particular policy areas, they are often not named on government websites. Commercial organisations similarly might not provide publicly accessible contact details below their senior management team. Local organisations or community groups may not have an active list of people involved. So how might you locate and access groups of people? Below are some suggestions for how to start to build up, or infiltrate, networks.

Networking sites

There are many available networking sites online that are readily accessible and a useful way to create and sustain an online presence. LinkedIn is one of the best examples and provides an online platform to showcase your interests and skills, and 'connect' to others – both who are suggested to you by algorithms generated via your email and social media contact lists and histories, and through you actively searching for specific individuals or job types. It is a useful way to identify individuals, but you need to be prepared to update it semi-regularly to make sure it reflects your everyday work.

Email lists

As noted above, email lists are plentiful within academia, and many can be found via the National Academic Mailing List Service or 'JiscMail'. These email lists can be an extremely useful way of keeping up-to-date with the field, for identifying some of the most prominent, or at least active, people in the field, and to ask questions yourself. You have to carefully manage list subscriptions however, as you may find your email inbox overloaded with list messages and replies. When you want to make yourself known and post a question or response, you can be overlooked within a quagmire of messages. Conversely, you may find that a list is inactive and provides little sustenance or opportunity to network.

Outside academia, there may be comparable lists within your areas of interest, and it is worth searching online or asking colleagues. Alternatively, there may be pre-existing dissemination lists or newsletter lists for large organisations, in order to receive updates on activities and so on.

> **Tip**
>
> Sign up to as many newsletters and lists as possible and then unsubscribe as and when you learn what the typical content of their email notifications and exchanges are, and how relevant they are to you and your work. Inbox management is key to dealing with email overload!

Social media

Of course, there will be many groups on social media sites that you can join to become part of the conversation. Alternatively, you can set up your own social media handles, pages and links to other individuals and organisations, to become part of a network of online commentators. If you go down this route make sure you regularly update and participate in conversations if you want to stay relevant and not just be a 'lurker' (see Carrigan, 2016 for more helpful hints about how to use social media as an academic).

Signing up for webinars

Some organisations now regularly offer the opportunity to be involved in seminars via webinars where you participate remotely. Some will charge you to do so, others will provide this option for free. These are a good way to stay on top of issues and hear key stakeholders speak on topics of interest. It is also a useful way to get your name into discussions on topics where you can provide insight and input.

Job adverts

While you may not be actively seeking another job, publicly advertised job vacancies provide a useful gateway into learning about job roles in other sectors, ones that are unoccupied, and contacts for said roles. You may want to hold back from contacting a named individual as a point of information during a recruitment period, but once the vacancy has closed you could make contact with them to see if you share mutual interests in relation to your own work. Key to this approach is thinking creatively about how to find out who does what within an organisation, and the methods through which you can find out more about them.

Writing for other audiences

It may be that the groups of people you want to work with have trade journals or similar publications/online activities that will always require 'copy' (see chapter 4). These are a fruitful way of placing yourself and your work before a potential public or audience, as long as you write for *them* rather than for yourself. In other words, this means putting yourself in their shoes as a reader and not as an academic: What would they want to know? Why? How can you explain without making assumptions about prior knowledge? If this sounds like a viable option to you contact the editor, publisher(s) or appointed contacts to propose a contribution.

Author reflection

Early in my academic career I was guilty of writing from my own perspective for trade journals, meaning that many of my pieces were focused on identifying problems and describing them, rather than suggesting solutions. Although the pieces went through editors and were accepted, if I were to do them again I would spend much more time on addressing the 'so what' question of my work and make an active effort to propose solutions or ways forward rather than simply posing the questions for others to 'solve'.

Consultancy

Another useful way to build up networks is to take on consultancy projects. The availability of opportunities in consultancy will be contingent on your discipline/field and the position of your institution as to what they regard as consultancy and how much you are permitted to take on as additional work. In terms of how consultancies are arranged, sometimes an organisation will approach you directly (through existing contacts or via an online search – make sure your staff profile and/or webpage is up-to-date!) or you may come across organisations that periodically put a call out for consultants so that they have a pool of individuals with specific areas of knowledge/backgrounds to call on as and when they need them.

> **Tip**
>
> Find out what your institution's position is on consultancy and what support is available internally. If there are specific organisations that you would like to work with, do some investigative work into their research/development opportunities, and/or make enquiries as to whether they work with consultants and, if they do, how they recruit.

How much to take on?

Reminiscent of chapter 4 where prioritising was considered in relation to teaching (or, as I named it, when to say 'no'), conversely the challenge here is when to say 'yes' to attending external events, responding to opportunities and taking on additional responsibilities and commitments such as those listed above. Very few of these activities will have currency when it comes to appraisals of your work, or applications for jobs. They are typically regarded as enjoyable 'extras' that accompany the somewhat intransigent mission of a research-active academic: to publish and bring in research funds.

> **Tip**
>
> If you are unsure of how much kudos your current or prospective institution gives to public engagement and networking activities do some investigation. Are colleagues working on/promoting their work via networking activities? Are research centres/institutes undertaking comparable engagement activities?

The question at the outset of your academic career is the extent to which you build public engagement and collaboration with others outside academia into your everyday work, so that it becomes a habitual rather than a concerted effort. If you choose to do so, your next challenge is to weave these activities into your overall research 'narrative' – that is, the story you create about your work and/or the way you describe yourself to colleagues, your line manager, your appraiser, the peer reviewers, the shortlisters or to the interview panel. Rather than working with others outside of academia being then seen as a 'bolt-on' activity or an after-thought, a collaborative way of working becomes your ethos and part of your academic biography.

As with learning when to say no, when seeking opportunities and responding to requests which will come your way as your reputation and willingness to engage beyond academia becomes more widely known, your task early on in your career is to make informed decisions about when to say yes. In order to do so, more experienced colleagues are of most help – but it is usually better to approach colleagues who have experience of working in the sphere of public engagement. This is because, in my view, they are more likely to be accustomed to the variety of ways in which early career academics can generate and share their work, beyond the conventions of publishing and research funding, and are also more likely to be thinking about the risks and benefits of taking on additional research-related activities.

Author reflection

Since my first full-time job in academia over ten years ago I have undertaken most of the activities listed above, with varying success. One thing is clear: the 'payoff' from public engagement activities has taken years to become apparent (if it has at all), and there are rarely any instant successes. As noted earlier, this kind of work is therefore a long-term endeavour requiring commitment, and you need to be attuned to opportunities as and when they arise.

To reiterate, engaging with individuals and groups beyond academia needs to be regarded as an investment. You may not see the benefits of working with others outside of academia for a considerable length of time and your efforts may not necessarily lead to the impact or influence that you envisaged at the outset. You are, after all, but one small cog in the giant machine of HE and its aligned organisations and sectors. But such uncertainty about the worth of such endeavours should not be a barrier to making the effort in the first place; indeed, if you were to be governed solely by such instrumental approaches to academia you would be flying in the face of the key and underpinning principle within the academy: discovery.

The challenge therefore is to persevere, while being mindful of the need to strategise and embed engagement activities within your work so that they all contribute towards a common goal. At the same time, do not be so focused on end goals that you miss out on opportunities as they present themselves, or to be responsive to working with non-academics as and when they need input and insight from academics. They can be a source of great fulfilment and inspiration.

References

Carrigan, M. (2016) *Social Media for Academics* (London: Sage).
Gunn, A. and Mintrom, M. (2017) 'Evaluating the Non-academic Impact of Academic Research: Design Considerations', *Journal of Higher Education Policy and Management*, 39 (1): 20-30.
Krznaric, R. (2012) *How to Find Fulfilling Work* (London: Macmillan).
Research Councils UK (nd) 'Pathways to Impact', available online at www.rcuk.ac.uk/innovation/impacts/ [accessed 10/12/17].
Tilley, E. and Woodthorpe, K. (2011) 'Is it the End for Anonymity as We Know It? A Critical Examination of the Ethical Principle of Anonymity in the Context of 21st Century Demands on the Qualitative Researcher', *Qualitative Research*, 11 (2): 197-212.
Watermeyer, R. (2014) 'Issues in the Articulation of 'Impact': The Responses of UK Academics to 'Impact' as a New Measure of Research Assessment', *Studies in Higher Education*, 39 (92): 359-377.
Watermayer, R. and Lewis, J. (2017) 'Institutionalizing Public Engagement through Research in UK Universities: Perceptions, Predictions and Paradoxes Concerning the State of the Art', *Studies in Higher Education*, DOI: 10.1080/03075079.2016.1272566.
Watermayer, R. and Olssen, M. (2016) ''Excellence' and Exclusion: The Individual Costs of Institutional Competitiveness', *Minerva*, 54: 201-218.
Wilkinson, C. (2017) 'Evidencing Impact: A Case Study of UK Academic Perspectives on Evidencing Research Impact', *Studies in Higher Education*, DOI: 10.1080/03075079.2017.1339028.

Further reading

Bastow, S., Dunleavy, P. and Tinkler, J. (2014) *The Impact of the Social Sciences* (London: Sage).
Bennett, D.J. (2011) *Successful Science Communication: Telling It Like It Is* (Cambridge: Cambridge University Press).

Bowater, L. (2012) *Science Communication: A Practical Guide for Scientists* (Oxford: Wiley-Blackwell).
Daly, I. and Brophy Haney, A. (eds) (2014) *53 Interesting Ways to Communicate your Research* (Newmarket: The Professional and Higher Partnership).
Denicolo, P. (ed.) (2013) *Achieving Impact in Research* (London: Sage).
Holliman, R. (ed) (2009) *Practising Science Communication in the Information Age: Theorising Professional Practices* (Oxford: Oxford University Press).
Mollett, A., Brumley, C. Gilson, C. and Williams, S. (2017) *Communicating your Research with Social Media* (London: Sage).
Reed, M.S. (2016) *The Research Impact Handbook* (Kinnoir: Fast Track Impact).
Watermeyer, R. (2015) 'Lost in the 'Third Space': The Impact of Public Engagement in Higher Education on Academic Identity, Research Practice and Career progression', *European Journal of Higher Education*, 5 (3): 331-347.
Watermeyer, R. and Hedgecoe, A. (2016) 'Selling 'Impact': Peer Reviewer Projections of What is Needed and What Counts in REF Impact Case Studies. A Retrospective Analysis', *Journal of Education Policy*, 31 (5): 651-665.

Useful journals

Journal of Education Policy
Journal of Higher Education Policy and Management
Perspectives: Policy and Practice in Higher Education
Reflective Practice
Studies in Higher Education

Section 3
Administration, management and leadership

This section explores the final potential remit of the early academic's role, that of administration and management. Such activities can take place within HE institutions or outside, and may or may not involve opportunities for leadership. Some administrative roles are extremely functional in terms of acting as a gatekeeper or disseminator of information, others can be highly demanding and require considerable guidance and direction from you. These chapters will help you to ascertain the difference, the opportunities and risks associated with different tasks and duties, and how you can make the most of this part of your role.

The final chapter of this section, and the book overall, aims to bring together the themes and ideas presented throughout, to enable you to consolidate your learning and reflections, and to consider where you want to go with your academic career. There are no right answers here, but key to this final chapter is remembering that your academic career is *part* of your life and while you will have duties and obligations to your employer/institution, you also have a responsibility to yourself to make the best of your academic life, in terms of how it fits in with your other interests and concerns.

8 Getting stuck in

Opening Section 3, this chapter is the first of two that specifically explore administration and management roles and qualities that accompany an academic career. Arguably, it is only in recent years that administration and management have been acknowledged as a legitimate and sizeable part of the academic's role. Within institutions themselves, part of this has been a recognition of the internal administrative responsibilities that academic staff can shoulder as a result of the (ever increasing) evaluation and documentation associated with teaching and research (see chapters 1 and 4). At the same time, leaders of institutions and those tasked with implementing objectives, goals and initiatives want to ensure that these tasks are being carried out by competent and reliable colleagues, who get the job done. This has led to varying structures and methods for dispersing administrative and management responsibilities around the organisation.

Administrative and management responsibilities are the principle focus of this chapter, which specifically examines the structure and organisation of universities, their governance, and methods in which you can get involved as an early career academic. It will outline the tangible and identifiable ways in which you can 'get stuck in' through taking on university administrative roles, serving as a precursor to considering the further development of your soft skills through taking on external roles in chapter 9.

Thinking ahead

It is probable that the more senior you become within your academic career, the more likely it is that you will be asked to take on administrative and management roles. Similarly by taking on administrative and management roles, you will find yourself becoming more senior, or at least having more of a say (and ideally being influential with it!) over directions, priorities, processes, strategies and so on. In the early phase of your career you may gravitate to some administrative roles far more easily than others, for example in leading research teams, or roles that involve working with students. Some of the skills required in the available roles, which are explored later in this chapter, will resonate with your existing skillset. However, as in common with the rest of this book's theme of thinking ahead, it pays to have an idea of the types of skills that you wish to develop, and the opportunities for administration, management and leadership that you may want to explore in the future.

> **Pause for thought**
>
> Before you read on about the administrative activities involved in academic careers, spend a few moments evaluating your existing skillset and strengths, how these may align with particular administrative tasks, and where your weaker areas requiring development in the future may lie. For example, are you a highly organised person who prefers to plan ahead or do you prefer to focus on the 'here and now' tasks in hand? Do you enjoy instructing others or would you prefer to be instructed? Examples of the types of skills you have/need to develop may include:
>
> Time management
> Team-working
> Project management
> Strategy creation and implementation
> Presentational skills
>
> How do these skills relate to your existing ability to do the following, or the type of administrative and leadership activities you want to do in the future?
>
> Chairing meetings
> Going through reports in fine detail
> Mobilising groups of people into action

> Budgeting and resource allocation
> Strategic planning
> Networking
> Writing reports
> Receiving instruction
> Implementing strategies
> Negotiating
> Problem-solving

A highly focused reflection like this will help you to identify your existing strengths and potential areas for development. It may also enable you to reflect on how you could get involved within your institution, and at what level. Getting 'stuck in' inevitably comes with time and energy implications, and at the outset of your career it is worthwhile considering:

- What activities will play to your strengths when you have extensive demands on your time;
- What activities will detract from your other commitments and potentially create much work and subsequent stress;
- What activities you would like/be willing to take on to learn.

Moreover, what strengths do you want to have or establish? Understanding these will (hopefully) equip you with a clear(er) idea of your existing and potential capabilities and capacities for when your line manager or equivalent comes calling, asking you to take on an administrative role.

Governance and administration in universities

There are an endless number of ways in which a university can be structured, organised and governed, as "in practice, governance [in HE] today is messy and contested territory where the boundaries between levels are blurred and where power and authority between different actors in the system are in the flux" (Middlehurst, 2013: 276). Some institutions are 'flatter', with governance and decision-making processes shared across and between different constituent parts of the organisation, while others are very hierarchical with a clear 'chain of command' from the top to the bottom (see Martin, 2017). In both models there are likely to be very senior committees composed of senior management, representatives from parts of the university and students; as well as bodies that include non-academic and non-university representatives from the local community, alumni and beyond. How these structures operate will be dictated by University regulations, statutes, codes of practice, and so on.

> **Tip**
>
> Your institution should have a description or pictorial representation of its governance structure publicly available. Have a look at it to see how the 'chain of command' is organised, how committees feed into one another, and how decisions are made.

The autonomy of universities has been fiercely protected over the years but there have been several waves of change over the last five decades (Shattock, 2017). A key factor in how your institution is structured will be the distinctive relationship(s) between academics, the professional services/administration, and senior management and executive team(s) (Carpenter-Hubin and Snover, 2013). Typically, academics are those operating in departments/faculties and are either teaching or research active. Professional services/administration may include academics, but their role is usually to provide supporting services to the university, to enable each department or faculty to function and perform. Examples of professional services include payroll and human resources, teaching and staff development, e-learning, and research support. Senior management and executive team(s) include the Vice-Chancellor and their deputies, and associated senior staff such as the Finance Director, Director of Human Resources, Estates Director and University Secretary/Registrar. It is likely that some of those in these most senior of positions, particularly those that oversee teaching and research, retain an academic identity and were once 'practising' academics (and may be again).

In recent years, changes in university funding and the intensification of a competitive market in HE has "... put greater stress on the marketing function [of the university] and reinforces the role of senior management" (Shattock, 2017: 11). At the same time, Shattock notes, the risk of market failure has magnified a sense of insecurity amongst academic staff. This, coupled with the introduction of a league table culture (see chapter 1), has meant that:

> A new era of competition, national and global, has been born, again strengthening the role of the executive vis-à-vis the governing body on the one hand and the academic staff on the other.
>
> (Shattock, 2017: 12)

While the gulf between executive and academic staff may have grown,[1] the boundaries between academics and professional services is not as clear. What this means at the start of your career is that you may find that many activities within an institution have moved from the academic's remit into professional services, creating a workforce of specialists that support university activities. For example, student admissions, research support, and development of teaching may have once fallen within the academic job role, but it is now just as likely that much of this will have been siphoned off to specialist units and teams. Alternatively, you may still be tasked with admin but be supported or even directed by specialist units and teams – which may in turn increase administrative demands on your time. Certainly, the boundaries between academics and 'the administration' have become less straightforward as the diversification of universities and accompanying moves towards a devolved management of university strategy and operations have made it increasingly difficult to ascertain who is responsible for what (Whitchurch, 2006).

On one hand, a division between different components of the organisations has been beneficial for institutions and the academic, as responsibilities are handed to teams that build up expertise in (for example) marketing and student recruitment over a sustained period of time. Moreover, those teams can devote 100 per cent of their resources and time to focusing on their specified issue, sharing experience and expertise across the institution. On the other hand, the split of specialist services from academics can result in fragmentation between the different priorities of an institution and a disjuncture between those tasked with the 'frontline' of teaching, research and departmental administration, and those tasked with organising and overseeing strategy, such as recruitment and admissions. Such detachment can inevitably lead to

---

1 Exemplified in the UK in 2017 in debates about Vice Chancellors' salaries.

tension between the different component groups within the university where, unless careful attention is paid to effective communication and engagement on both sides, difficulties regarding competing priorities and functions can arise.

For example, using the case of recruitment and admissions, academics may feel dismayed that they are losing control over the type of student that the institution attracts and recruits, having to teach whichever student cohort is deemed a priority. They may feel disenfranchised from having an input into strategic decisions about the goals and teaching vision of the institution, cut off from wider strategies regarding the student body and sustainability as they deal with the consequences of admissions decisions that are out of their hands. Yet they may feel relieved of that burden of responsibility; grateful that specialists in student recruitment are able to focus on and plan ahead for school-level policy change and the consequences for HE provision, and so on.

On the other hand, for professional services staff academics may appear out of touch with the realities of creating attractive educational propositions for students, or obstructive and difficult in the pursuit of an institution that is highly efficient and financially secure (see chapter 1). Academics may simultaneously appear idealistic in their concerns regarding student competencies and blind to the fruitful potential and consequences of targeted admissions strategies. At the same time, professional services staff may be welcoming of academics who recognise their efforts and contribute their knowledge and first-hand experience of working with the students that they have recruited.

Thus, there are a number of consequences for the split between academics and administrative staff, for both sides, including:

- Relinquishing of autonomy and influence;
- Diminishing skillset;
- Freeing up of time and resources;
- Ability to focus and build up expertise;
- Sharing of expertise across an institution.

The extent to which tensions exist will depend on the organisation of the institution, and its culture of communication and collegiality (see Tight, 2014). Not only that, it will depend on relatively unassuming factors such as the layout of the institution, including where departments and teams are located; the accessibility of different groups within the university

Getting stuck in 183

(and member of staff's willingness to travel to those groups); and the availability of appropriate meeting space.

Another considerable source of tensions between university workforce(s) is divergence in the underlying principles of the university's mission, and the use/measurement of success indicators. Reflecting chapter 1 and the marketisation of HE, there may be fundamentally opposing/differing priorities within a workforce, for example when it comes to what constitutes success in:

- Student learning;
- Equality of access;
- Justice/fair treatment;
- Financial sustainability;
- Profitability;
- Opportunity for all;
- Promotion prospects.

It is the task and responsibility of those in leadership and management positions across the different constituent groups of a university to communicate these priorities in a coherent way that enables different teams and individuals to identify and engage with them, while also recognising and supporting existing shared idea(l)s of the purpose of HE and academia (Kligyte and Barrie, 2014). A question for you as you move forward in your career is whether you want to be in those types of management positions, brokering between groups.

> **Pause for thought**
>
> In chapter 1 it was suggested that you should locate your university's mission statement. You may also wish to identify your university's top-level corporate/teaching/research strategies. Do they resonate with you? Do you want to have an influence over these in the future?

Administration and management early in your career

If you are working in a well-functioning department, those allocated with workload management should be looking across the department to: (1) identify staff members with capacity to take on administrative roles,

(2) be acquainted with the stage they are at in their career and suggest the types of roles that will help to collate evidence to enable them to progress, and (3) subsequently match staff to roles.

Such attention is to ensure that the distribution of administrative loads across the academic workforce is fair and transparent, and builds the capacity and skillsets of staff members at different stages of their career. Beyond the intrinsic benefits of building experience across a staff group a key reason for this, for early career academics, is that probation and promotion criteria will include the need for confirmation of management, administration and leadership experience, and some of the roles available internally are tried-and-tested methods of creating demonstrable evidence.

In most institutions there are administrative roles allocated to academics within a department or faculty, founded on the understanding that these roles need to be administered and driven by academic staff 'on the front line' of teaching and research. These often revolve on a specified cycle (for example, every three years) so that the opportunities and burdens associated with respective roles are shared around the department whereby:

- The time and energy required for some roles is time-limited;
- The opportunities afforded to some roles in building a career are equally given to all;
- New energy and thinking can be brought in as administrative post holders (can) become institutionalised and stagnate.

It is likely that at some early stage in your career you will be asked by your line manager, or those tasked with workload management, to take on an administrative role (or even multiple roles). Alternatively, a call may go around for expressions of interest for a role. The method of recruitment to administrative roles will depend on your department's culture, the urgency of the need to fill the role, and the number of roles available. This is not to say that you have to sit back and wait for that call or to be personally approached. You can certainly be pro-active and pre-emptive in how you take on administrative roles, by:

- Identifying the type of role you wish to do;
- Finding out what the role is like by speaking with the current role holder and/or shadowing them for a period of time;
- Expressing an interest in a particular role to your line manager or those tasked with workloads.

Similarly, you can find out whether there are incentives attached to roles, be they financial, scholarly and practical. For example, some roles may come with a guaranteed sabbatical attached, or a pay rise, or an allocation of hours within the workload model that means you are effectively 'bought out' from other tasks such as teaching.

Thus, as with the governance of an institution, how the administration of a department or Faculty is organised via administrative roles and responsibilities is endless in possibilities. Common examples of roles available include:

- Head of Department/Department Chair: manages the running of the department; acts as line manager to colleagues; oversees department-wide strategies and priorities; supervises operational issues associated with the department.
- Directors of Learning and/or Teaching, and Research: tasked with organising strategies and oversight; responsible for liaising with senior management and supporting colleagues; facilitates teaching and research activities; fosters the development of staff in relevant areas.
- Programme Leaders/Heads of Year Groups/Directors of Studies: oversee the day-to-day running of courses; student-facing and highly visible in the department, often seen as the 'face' of the teaching staff by students; heavily involved in student problem-solving; oversees curriculum management and organisation of teaching staff.

Other roles can include:

- Exams and assessments officer;
- Admissions officer;
- Dissertation officer/supervisor;
- Widening Participation officer;
- Equal Opportunities officer;
- Ethics officer;
- Marketing officer;
- Exceptional circumstances officer/chair;
- Public engagement/Impact officer.

Within this gamut of administrative roles there will be differing expectations with regard to the autonomy of the role and/or the extent to which the post holder is expected to work with other parts of the institution. Sometimes, for example, a role may simply equate to being an identified individual within a department, to act as a gatekeeper or liaison between the department and professional services or other committees within the university. In other roles, there may be enormous scope to develop practice and strategy, with either significant engagement from others or, conversely, very little oversight. Some roles will be extremely visible to other colleagues and parts of the university, others not so much.

Imagine the roles as existing on two intersecting spectrums, of visibility and engagement:

Table 8.1

High visibility	High visibility
Low engagement with/from others	High engagement with/from others
Low visibility	Low visibility
Low engagement with/from others	High engagement with/from others

The extent to which particular administrative roles are visible will depend on the constitutional requirement for that role within a department, how that role feeds into committee structures, and whether there are comparable roles across the institution. A good example of this is the Programme Leader/Heads of Year Groups/Director of Studies role which is typically high visibility and involves high engagement with/from others. Those tasked with this role will find they sit on several committees that deal with student and curriculum issues, both within their department and potentially beyond. It is highly likely that every department or faculty across the university will have a comparable role, although the finer details of the role's remit and everyday working practices may differ slightly between departments. As a key lynchpin role liaising between students and staff, Programme Leaders/Heads of Year Groups/Director of Studies are highly visible, need to be very accessible and responsive, and are expected to work closely with colleagues and students to ensure the smooth operation of the courses on offer.

In contrast, a department may be split into nominal disciplinary or research groups that have little formal status within the university, each requiring a nominated lead. These groups and their nominated lead may not have comparable counterparts in other departments, might not be accountable to any committee, and are organised mainly to provide a sense of coherence and belonging across the academic staff. Those tasked with acting as a group lead may find that they have relatively low visibility beyond their immediate colleagues, but are highly engaged with others in trying to build and sustain a sense of identity and collegiality.

> **Tip**
>
> Identify the existing administrative roles in your department, and the cycle of recruitment attached to those roles. Will any become vacant soon? Is there a likelihood that you may be being lined up for one, or is there one you would like to take on?

Across the two spectrums of visibility and engagement exists a third factor: autonomy. Some administrative roles come with considerable independence owing to, for example, lack of accountability, low visibility, and so on. Others will come with significant constraints on activities owing to restrictions from institutional governance, regulation and compliance. The extent to which an administrative role is autonomous will shape the type of influence and impact an individual can make within it. Sometimes an administrative role comes with responsibility but very little autonomy or power to make changes; or equally, a great deal of opportunity to make change but with very little recognition.

Thus, when you are considering what type of administrative role you would like to take on early in your career, or are approached with a request to take one on, you need to have a clear understanding of the expectations that accompany that role and the potential (or lack of potential) there is for impact and influence – and how that aligns with your own skillset, capabilities and career stage. Are you yearning to 'stick your head above the parapet' and influence the future of your department and beyond? Or, for now, would you prefer to focus your energies and attention on other facets of your life and career? Certainly, when taking on an administrative role you need to be mindful of the demands of that role bearing in mind your present workload and personal life commitments.

> **Author reflection**
>
> My available energy and enthusiasm for administrative responsibilities has reflected my stage of career, work goals and personal life responsibilities. In the early stages of my career while I was single, renting accommodation, and had fewer responsibilities, I had a lot of energy for significant administrative roles, often holding two or more at once, as I 'threw myself' into my job (risking burnout in the process, as I described in chapter 1).
>
> As my research career has evolved and I have more responsibilities outside of work, I have found that the hours available to engage in such a variety of tasks is increasingly difficult – and I cannot rely on working in the evenings and at weekends to 'absorb' the demands on administrative duties. Nor, importantly, do I want to.
>
> I recognise however that this is a particular phase of my career and life, and anticipate that as I move further into 'mid-career' and my life beyond work continues to evolve my priorities will shift again as I pursue and take on other administrative roles that will test and expand my skillset.

Ways to influence

As noted, some administrative and management roles come with high visibility and autonomy, others not so much. Whether or not you are in a specific role there are a considerable number of ways in which you can exert influence within a university, some of which are more formal, perceptible and recognised than others.

Committees

One conventional way of influencing is to take on a visible administrative role that means that you will attend documented (that is, minuted) committees where you can air your views (with mixed success!). There are practicalities when it comes to committees however, including which to sit on (if you have a choice), which to volunteer for (if there are any), when to attend and when to send apologies.

It is likely that the structure of governance within your university means that there will be a large number of committees at different levels that feed into one another to form a chain of command and documented decision-making. Some of these committees will accompany, and be a requirement of, particular administrative posts, whereas others you may wish to volunteer to be a part of, or become elected to, as a member of the academic staff.

When it comes to deciding if you want to participate in particular committees, you need to think carefully about the time commitment involved, expectations regarding contributions to that committee, and – if you decide to go for it – how you will get involved. For example, if your university has a Senate or Council, there may be periodic elections of academic staff to act as representatives. If you want to go for election, you need to be prepared to campaign to encourage colleagues to vote for you. In other cases, you may find that an administrative role that you take on is accompanied by membership of multiple committees, all of which are non-negotiable (and may even have sub-committees that need staffing too!).

> **Tip**
>
> Do not be deterred by your junior status when it comes to volunteering or putting yourself forward for election to committees. It is likely that even the most senior decision-making bodies/committees are required to have representatives of staff from all levels and groups and there is no reason this could/should not be you.

Beware of the paperwork involved in some committees. When taking on admin roles it is important to be clued up on the through-put of paperwork. Some committees will be very 'paper-lite' in that there is little to read and it is more of a discussion forum. Other committees will involve reams and reams of paperwork that require considerable attention outside of the committee itself.

As part of your initiation into university governance and committee attendance, it pays to be mindful about expectations regarding attendance. Some committees will be held infrequently with relatively low levels of expectation of attendance; others may be more frequent and also have relatively low levels of expectation of attendance owing to their regularity, and vice versa. It is up to you how you manage your attendance at committees, but make sure that you have a very clear idea of:

- What is expected of your contribution from your line manager and colleagues;
- The extent to which you are required to prepare beforehand and have prior knowledge of the agenda items under discussion;
- How you are expected to 'report back' from committees to others, and
- How much committees will shape yours and others' working practice.

> **Tip**
>
> If you are not going to attend a minuted committee, you always need to give apologies.

Mentoring

If you have not been allocated a mentor at the start of your academic career, you can request one. These are supportive roles provided by colleagues that are intended to enable you to navigate a particular career stage or milestone. They are a really useful way to learn the ropes, find out about a department culture, and to help with decision-making, prioritising and so on. At a later stage of your career you may be asked to perform the role of mentor. You may feel yourself gravitating or retreating from these roles, but in my experience they are a very fulfilling and rewarding part of the job in terms of supporting and enabling colleagues to feel positive and constructive about their role, status and work.

> **Tip**
>
> What is your institution's policy on providing mentoring support, and supporting mentors?

Champions

Periodically you may find that a call goes out for someone to lead on an initiative or champion a particular cause within your department or faculty. These are usually time-limited causes that may not attract much visibility or receive recognition from others. Occasionally, if the cause is very high-profile then you may find that they involve leading on an exciting initiative that provides much intellectual and emotional satisfaction. As a rule, do not automatically shy away from such opportunities as they may act as a stepping-stone or 'bridge' to another exciting career development of which you are not yet aware.

> **Pause for thought**
>
> If you could champion any cause, what would it be? Equality in access to education? Disability rights? Research ethics?
> It is worth having a sense of what you feel passionate about in HE, so that if an opportunity presents itself to get involved you can go for it with confidence.

Development opportunities

There may also be development opportunities and/or funding made available to you and others, for example in introducing teaching or research improvements. These can act as important openings to try out a new method of teaching or to introduce something innovative within your work, for example in leading a public engagement event (see chapter 7). Such development opportunities will appeal to you at different times depending on the call, your workload, commitments and priorities inside and outside of work, and how you can see them fitting in with your existing career trajectory. Sometimes they can have a huge payoff in terms of contributing to your teaching or research, raising your profile internally and externally, or providing evidence for innovation and improvement for the institution. At other times they can be a considerable distraction, energy-sapping and, if unsuccessful, rather deflating without appropriate and supportive processes of evaluation and reflection.

> **Tip**
>
> Make sure that if, or when, you decide to take on development opportunities, you have weighed up the time and energy required to achieve the prospective benefits so that your decision is well informed.

Being available

Another, much less formal, way of influencing is by making yourself accessible and visible within your department. Some of the most successful academics I have known have been those that have been willing to 'walk the corridors', call into each other's offices and readily meet with colleagues for a coffee or catch up. These encounters are not minuted, nor are they accounted for in workload models, but by being present in the department you can foster a sense of collegiality, trust and reciprocity. It is one of the best ways to hear about openings and opportunities in the department, and by making yourself available to others you are sending a strong signal that you are an active and valuable part of the staff and department. These spontaneous opportunities can be more challenging for part-time colleagues or those who work primarily away from the day-to-day hub of the department, who may not be as readily available to socialise.

> **Tip**
>
> Make time and plans to meet over coffee periodically if you cannot be readily and unexpectedly available to chat with colleagues.

A significant contextual feature of taking on administrative roles and responsibilities is your personal resilience, and how you respond to pressure and change. Administrative responsibilities can be extremely stressful, particularly at the outset of your academic career when you have little experiential knowledge to draw upon, and you can find yourself in demand, tested, exposed, and worn out by the demands of a role. Moreover, you may find that the (sometimes relentless) change in governance, regulation, procedures and priorities mean that you are repeatedly tasked with putting policies into practice, with little time for strategies to be embedded before they change again – as is one consequence of the marketisation of HE and the need for institutions to 'stay competitive' via what they teach and research (see chapter 1). Thus, be aware of the mental and emotional exhaustion that can accompany administrative roles, as you can find yourself in a cycle of responding and implementing with little time for reflection and consolidation. Indeed, as one very wise professional services member of staff told me, they found that their everyday work became considerably less stressful when they realised and started to accept that "the only constant is change". In this ever-changing environment make sure you are taking care of yourself (see chapter 2), and nurturing your resilience to the winds of change.

What's your institution?

As outlined in chapter 1, the HE sector is dealing with and responding to significant societal, economic and technological changes that are re-shaping funding streams, resource allocation, public perceptions of education, the utility of academic knowledge and insight, and the role of academics. Institutions are having to accommodate these changes, with senior management strategising to ensure sustainability, competitiveness, support for the workforce, high quality education and so on. Some institutions will flex and respond faster than others owing to their size, adaptability, vision, capacity of the workforce, and beyond.

Within this continuum of flexibility you may work in an institution that wishes to capitalise on opportunities, staying one step ahead of 'the competition'. That may be a permanent feature, leading to a buoyant and responsive outlook; or it may be a temporary period of drive and innovation. Indeed, it may be an act of necessity to ensure the viability of the organisation. In that institution, you may be empowered (or compelled) to regularly review the content of your courses; re-prioritise research areas; or move departments as they shift and merge. You may be tasked with an administrative role that means you have significant responsibility for some of these activities, or you may find yourself on the periphery of decision-making and feel thoroughly marginalised. Similarly, you may find colleagues embracing this call to action and responsivity, or you may find that they are disenfranchised and worn out. You may find considerable job insecurity, or you may find great opportunities to get involved in strategizing and leading change.

Alternatively, you may be working in an institution that is somewhat slower, some might say sluggish, in responding to external contextual changes; an institution that lacks the ability to adapt or is led by a senior management team that is resting on its laurels, believing that the reputation and prestige attached to the institution is sufficient to weather the storm. Here you may encounter barriers to change, but also a more sustained vision and identity. You may find yourself frustrated by the lack of innovation and risk-taking within a conservative institution, surrounded by colleagues who have stagnated and are 'sitting it out' or who, conversely, are willing to take the time and effort to appraise change once implemented, to ensure that future change is based on consolidation and reviewing of evidence.

> **Tip**
>
> Make it your business to determine the type of institution in which you work, explore the organisation of its governance by talking to colleagues, your line manager and by examining minutes of meetings and so on. This will provide insight into institutional expectations regarding change and adaptation, and your potential for influence within this.

Whether you are in a slowing burning or fast responding university, as an early career academic it is important to hold your nerve when you observe change, discussion of change, or resistance to change. There will be many, many, many institutional decisions at all levels of the hierarchy that are beyond your influence or control, some of which you will agree with and others that may leave you feeling confused, concerned or conflicted. Within this, it is key to embrace learning how and when to respond, when to challenge, and when to wait to see what emerges. Holding your nerve means developing your own resilience, and this needs to be a priority to ensure that you can sustain an academic career in the medium to long term (see chapter 10).

> **Pause for thought**
>
> If you have an appraisal/review process within your institution use it as an opportunity to reflect on how you will manage the differing, and often competing, teaching, research and admin demands on your time. Which one or two take priority for the forthcoming 12 months? And what of beyond that 12 months?

A key part of developing a career in academia, and as often repeated in this book, is recognising that at different points in your career you will have different demands on your time and different priorities. For example, sometimes you will be required, or want, to focus more on teaching – to ensure that your materials are up-to-date and that you are a capable member of the teaching staff, to ensure that students receive a good learning experience and so on. At other times research will take priority as opportunities arise, publications are accepted and funding bids are successful. At those times you may find that the time available to improve your teaching is simply not available and you have to accept that for that period you are aiming simply to do a 'good enough' job. At other times, for example when you are actively seeking a promotion or job opportunity elsewhere, you may need to develop your administrative skills to be able to demonstrate competence and influence. Sometimes those administrative responsibilities come at great cost to other parts of your job as you find yourself in endless meetings, with significant paperwork to read and give feedback on, or produce yourself.

Unless you are superhuman or willing to sacrifice evenings and weekends, there will be many occasions where you will need to make choices about which facet of the academic role takes priority. Importantly, you need to be clear as to how long this current priority will be in place; otherwise you may find your research untouched for years, or your teaching stagnating, or your energy for administrative roles and responsibilities draining away.

Importantly, you need to regard your academic career as a long-term investment, where dividends will pay off in some areas and yet at other times seem futile. It is a marathon, not a sprint. Above all else, your priority needs to remain your own goals, and ensuring that you have the resilience and capacity to evolve, grow, and adapt as your individual career and the sector you are working in develops and changes.

References

Carpenter-Hubin, J. and Snover, L. (2013) 'Key Leadership Positions and Performance Expectations', in Schloss, P.J. and Cragg. K.M. (eds) (2013) *Organization and Administration in Higher Education* (Abingdon: Routledge), pp. 27-49.

Kligyte, G. and Barrie, S. (2014) 'Collegiality: leading us into fantasy – the paradoxical resilience of collegiality in academic leadership', *Higher Education Research and Development*, 33 (1): 157-169.

Martin, B.R. (2017) 'What's happening to our universities?', *Prometheus: Critical Studies in Innovation*, 34 (1): 7-24.

Middlehurst, R. 92013) 'Changing Internal Governance: Are Leadership Roles and Management Structures in United Kingdom Universities Fit for the Future?', *Higher Education Quarterly*, 67 (3): 275-294.

Shattock, M. (2017) 'University Governance in Flux. The Impact of External and Internal Pressures on the Distribution of Authority within British Universities: A Synoptic View', Working paper No. 13 (London: Centre for Global Higher Research).

Tight, M. (2014) 'Collegiality and Managerialism: A False Dichotomy? Evidence from the Higher Education Literature', *Tertiary Education and Management*, 20 (4): 294-306.

Whitchurch, C. (2006) 'Who Do they Think they Are? The Changing Identities of Professional Administrators and Managers in UK Higher Education', *Journal of Higher Education Policy and Management*, 28 (92): 159-171.

Further reading

Bolman, L.G. and Gallos, J.V. (2011) *Reframing Academic Leadership* (San Francisco: Jossey Bass).

Collini, S. (2012) *What Are Universities For?* (London: Penguin).

Côté, J.E. and Allahar, A.L. (2011) *Lowering Higher Education: The Rise of Corporate Universities and the Fall of Liberal Education* (Toronto: University of Toronto Press).

Fitzgerald, T. (2014) *Women Leaders in Higher Education: Shattering the Myths* (Abingdon: Routledge).

Schloss, P.J. and Cragg. K.M. (eds) (2013) *Organization and Administration in Higher Education* (Abingdon: Routledge).

Shattock, M. (2006) *Managing Good Governance in Higher Education* (Maidenhead: Open University Press).

Soto Antony, J., Cauce, A. M. and Shalala, D.E. (eds) (2017) *Challenges in Higher Education Leadership* (Abingdon: Routledge).

Sugden, R., Valania, M. and Wilson, J.R. (eds) (2014) *Leadership and Cooperation in Academia: Reflecting on the Roles and Responsibilities of University Faculty and Management* (Cheltenham: Edward Elgar Publishing).

Useful journals

Higher Education Quarterly
Journal of Education Policy
Journal of Higher Education Policy and Management
International Journal for Academic Development
Perspectives: Policy and Practice in Higher Education

9 Leadership beyond your institution

While the previous chapter considered administration and management within HE institutions, this chapter examines opportunities and challenges in taking on leadership tasks and positions of influence beyond your university. It reflects on the pros and cons of assuming commitments outside of your 'everyday work' and, critically, considers some of the skills and insights you might be able to provide as an academic in sectors and organisations outside of the academy. It is the closest this book comes to discussing employment for academics outside of HE, although it is important to note that that is not the main goal of this chapter – if that is of interest to you, please see the further reading section at the end of this chapter.

Relevance

You will have opportunities to take on leadership roles outside of your institution at different points in your academic career depending on current departmental and institutional demands; the external economic and political environment that shapes the structure and funding of institutions and organisations, both inside and outside of HE; and your own seniority. Although at first glance it may appear that leadership and opportunities to influence are confined to the realm of colleagues in more senior positions or with more experience, it is important to realise that often junior or early career academics are actively sought by external organisations, academic-related or not, owing to their fresh perspectives and insights.

Early on in your career, it may seem that you have little opportunity for leadership or influence, but is that really the case? Examples of opportunities for leadership as a junior member of the academy can include

Leadership beyond your institution

identifying areas for improvement in an organisation or sector, mobilising a task force team to consult and suggest change, and then implementing that change. These areas may not be revolutionary but may make a significant difference to everyday work pressures and demands for yourself and your colleagues.

Moreover, there is considerable overlap in leadership activities in academic-related organisations and beyond, and the remit of public engagement-related research activities outlined in chapter 7. What unites them is finding academic application both inside and outside of HE. This has never been more important – a focus on 'brick-making', where making incremental contributions to scholarship has become a measureable end in itself, has stopped academics from identifying, naming and addressing the holistic backdrops and stories in which their work is located, and presenting practical solutions to their public(s) (Hoffman, 2016). Such a 'theory fetish' (Hambrick, 2007, cited in Hoffman, 2016) has, arguably, divorced academics from the real-world in which they work, leading to a crisis of relevance.

While public engagement activities are typically focused on research-related activities, the opportunities for leadership described in this chapter are those which might not fall under a specific research remit. They may not be direct contributors to the 'knowledge economy' in which you work (see chapter 1). They may be associated more generally with your field or discipline, or with taking on tangential responsibilities in organisations outside of HE that want to utilise your experience(s), skills and knowledge. Principally, the aim of this chapter is therefore to demonstrate that there is a wealth of opportunities open to you to influence, lead and make a difference in academic-related roles and organisations, and beyond. Its overall goal is to help you find your relevance to the world beyond academia.

Finding your relevance

In common with many chapters in this book, it is worthwhile first establishing your (pre)existing assumptions and expectations, in this case regarding your relevance to society as a whole. This is, in part, connected to the motivators exercise that you were tasked with in chapter 7, when you were encouraged to consider the driving forces that compelled your initial entry into HE as an academic.

Thinking about relevance, it is important to recognise the prejudices and assumptions that you may already carry about academia and the potential knowledge contribution of academics. For example, you may think that:

- Academic knowledge is a social 'good' that complements other forms of knowledge and is needed to provide objective insight and reflection on processes, structures and so on.
- Academic knowledge is an intellectual pursuit in its own right that warrants worth and value.
- Academics who create that knowledge are therefore needed as an alternative viewpoint.

Or, you may feel quite differently, for example:

- Academic knowledge and its importance is diminishing in a highly competitive knowledge economy.
- Academics who create that knowledge are surplus to societal requirements and their contributions are just that, 'academic' (that is, speculative).

Alternatively, you may find the following resonates with you:

- Academic knowledge is one of many sources of knowledge available and it is the responsibility of academics to ensure that society makes best use of that knowledge.

Or

- The commercial contexts in which academic knowledge is now produced and accessed means that 'click-baiting' is becoming increasingly important (Holmwood, 2017). Academics produce work that will generate online interest and downloads as quantifiable displays of the numbers of people reading their work and therefore indicative of its relative influence.

Pause for thought

However you regard academia at the moment there must be a reason why you are working in this sector, so take a few moments to

1. Note your underlying assumptions about the purpose and role of academic knowledge, and those who produce it.

2. Review these alongside the personal motivators that you reflected on in chapter 7.
3. Note if there are any similarities or differences between the two and how these shape your vision of the work of academics more broadly and their relevance to society.

For some readers of this chapter it may be patently obvious what your relevance is to society; for others however, this may be a series of very challenging questions having spent several years on fixed-term contracts, facing many setbacks in your applications for tenure-track positions. It may be hard too, if you have had several paper and funding rejections. However straightforward or difficult you find this task, the main purpose is to think beyond your immediate situation and, importantly, beyond your immediate academic outputs and products. This is more about recognising your own preconceptions and prejudices regarding the sector that will at some point (if not already) shape and influence how you navigate your career and decisions within it.

How you regard the relevance of academics, and your own relative relevance to society, will shape how you see leadership opportunities and your ability to influence and affect change. If you regard the relevance of academics as on the wane, then you may have accompanying limited expectations regarding the opportunities open to you. Conversely, if you regard academic knowledge and academic's work in an optimistic light, you are likely to see more opportunities for making a difference, both inside and outside academia.

Tip

Although there is a plethora of discussion by academics regarding their relevance, the HE sector has never been so large, so full of posts and opportunities, and so global. So, if you are feeling dispirited by the above 'pause for thought' exercise, try to remember that you are embarking on your academic career at a time of considerable expansion. There may be much concern regarding commercialisation, control, productivity and relevance, but there is also much potential for having an impact and influence in a well-established contributor to the world's knowledge economy.

Opportunities for leadership and influence in academic-related organisations

There are many ways to get involved in academic-related organisations, such as professional associations, funding organisations, governing bodies and so on. Some organisations will advertise vacancies, others will approach individuals depending on disciplinary or career-stage-related gaps on their respective boards. Most of these positions will be unpaid, although you may be able to claim back travel expenses. Examples of opportunities for involvement include:

Governing boards

Most academic funders and regulators have governing committees that are intended to represent the interests of the body and academic community that they serve. Recruitment methods for such panels vary, but sometimes they will deliberately request and seek more junior members of academic staff to ensure that their contributors reflect the composition of the HE workforce. Sometimes such boards are understood as panels that will serve over a particular period of time and for a particular piece of work, for example as part of the Research Excellence Framework or the Teaching Excellence Framework in the UK.

Professional associations

Similarly, professional associations will likely have a multitude of opportunities to get involved at different levels. Some roles will require leadership skills that can be developed 'on the job' (or not – any calls for expressions of interest should specify expectations regarding leadership experience), others will be more 'light touch' in terms of the leadership and commitment needed/expected. Beyond developing your experience and skillset, getting involved in the running of professional associations is a great way to expand your networks (see chapter 4) and to evidence your commitment to the development and success of your field and/or discipline.

Other universities

Most universities will have some form of senior governing committee or board that requires individuals from outside of the organisation (see chapter 8). They will have their own mechanisms for recruitment. If you go down this route this could be a very useful way of observing how other institutions operate.

Student unions

Along with voluntary positions that may or may not be open to you, SU's will typically have a board of trustees that govern their activities. Becoming a trustee comes with a particular set of responsibilities (see later in this chapter) and being part of an SU team can be hugely satisfying in terms of supporting their activities, strategies and so on, which often complement the work of the university – although sometimes they may be at odds! It is unlikely that the SU where you work will recruit from their own institution owing to possible conflicts of interest, but SU's in other institutions may be very interested in your potential contribution.

> **Pause for thought**
>
> Can you identify any professional associations or other organisations that you would like to be involved in? Is now the time to get involved?

The benefits of participating in academic-related organisations is that it is likely that colleagues, interview panels, and promotion committees will have heard of or experienced equivalent roles themselves. Such roles therefore have a 'currency' within the academic job market, and can be drawn on without excessive explanation to evidence leadership activities and ambitions. They can be used in job applications and promotion cases as confirmation of management and leadership experience, while at the same time enabling you to develop those skills.

> **Author reflection**
>
> I learned a huge amount regarding negotiation when I was involved in my professional association's annual conference organising team. It was a mammoth task for the (employed) administrators and the

> (voluntary) academic team in negotiating between competing interests and academic areas, trying to deliver a financially viable conference while also meeting the needs and wishes of the academic community. I also learned a lot about listening and letting others find their own solutions – to begin with I was often quick to try and find a resolution when in fact it turned out that letting others have the time to reflect meant that they would come up with their own suggestions, which they were always more pleased with than any solution (I or others) imposed on them!

Such involvement in academic-related organisations can be refreshing too, in that it can foster a sense of relevance and purpose in supporting the wider academic community that is not contingent on your research outputs or effectiveness as a teacher within your own institution. Although your research and teaching credentials may act as a gateway into some of these roles, it is unlikely that once you are in them your peers will be expecting a blow-by-blow update on your career development and progress (unlike your institution).

Leadership beyond the academy

With a more inscrutable 'currency' are leadership roles beyond HE and academia. While they are less easily defined and categorised compared to their counterparts within academic-related organisations, arguably some of the most exciting opportunities to influence can come with assuming responsibilities such as these. Similar to the types of impact activities that you may take on as part of a research remit, these activities are about having an influence on the world beyond academia.

Advisory boards and steering committees

Many organisations, institutions, charities and centres have permanent or temporary project-based boards that require staffing to guide their work. Such strategic input can be both exciting and stretching in terms of contributing to the success or failure of an initiative, stratagem or policy. They are a great way to meet peers from different sectors as often you will find that these boards and committees are deliberately organised to bring in expertise and insight from varying parts of their community.

Most boards and committees of this type will be invitation only, so opportunities will be contingent on your networks. This does not mean that you cannot volunteer yourself for such opportunities when you meet peers and colleagues, even if there is not an opening currently available. People usually like having ready volunteers to call on, and having shown an interest and willingness to participate is a huge bonus when they have to decide who to approach.

Trustee boards

Becoming a trustee of a charity comes with a particular set of responsibilities regarding financial conduct and governance. Much of these will depend on the size and reach of the charity. Often trustees will be recruited because of a particular skillset lacking on the board, and you may find that as an academic your educational and research experience will be in demand.

When going for a trustee position, make sure you have a clear idea of what their expected commitment is, how often meetings are held, at what time of day and so on. It is important to make sure that you have the capacity to take on the role, not just for yourself and your own employment but for the charity too.

Royal societies

Many of the UK Royal Societies have opportunities for getting involved as members or fellows, where you act as something of an ambassador for the field in engaging with the public. Involvement with a Royal Society may encompass your broader interests in a particular area. Sometimes these societies oversee qualifications, which you could potentially become involved in as an educator.

Fellowships

Similarly, there may be opportunities for fellowships in other national organisations, institutes and centres. For example, in the UK, the National Institute for Clinical Excellence (NICE) has schemes for fellows and scholars that may be open to you if you are working in an associated field. These are intended to serve as (typically unpaid) opportunities to enhance leadership and thinking in a particular area, and may come with considerable mentoring and development support.

Getting involved

Networking and being visible, both online and off, are key to being on the radars of others outside of HE. This can include contributing towards their public and specialist events, attending their training, responding to their blogs and social media feeds and so on. Other ways to enhance your visibility are by creating your own personal webpage and connecting this to your social media activities, and writing your own blog (see Carrigan, 2016). Essentially, you have to be your own best advocate.

> **Tip**
>
> Find a mid-career academic whose strategies for demonstrable leadership outside of their own institution are obvious, either through their institutional webpage or their own personal webpage. What have they been particularly successful at in terms of their academic journey to date? What would you want to emulate (or avoid)?

What appeals to you when exploring such options will depend on your existing commitments and whether you want something to intersect with your everyday work, or whether you are seeking a period of time away from your everyday work to focus on a different area of activity. Some opportunities will be paid, or provide expenses, others will not. Some will require a particular level of seniority or experience before you are eligible to get involved, others will be deliberately targeted at early career/more junior potential participants. Some will require applications or elections, or you may be invited directly.

> **Tip**
>
> Whatever the shape and format of the role, and how you could be recruited, make it part of your periodic review of your work, commitments and interests to consider external opportunities, so that you are aware of current and future opportunities to expand your horizons.

Importantly, when you take on commitments and responsibilities outside of your day-to-day role you need to make sure you are consolidating them within the narrative of your career. If you recall back to chapter 1 when you were asked to reflect on the type of academic you wanted to be and why (a superstar or a good citizen?) the key here is to consider how these additional activities contribute towards this goal. Underlying this is the importance of being authentic (see chapter 10) and achieving 'flow' (Krznaric, 2012) between your values and beliefs, and employment activities. That is, you need to make sure you are consciously and deliberately aligning your goals and career objectives.

> **Tip**
>
> Make sure you keep a record of all these commitments, however brief or unsuccessful. Make note of opportunities you went for and did not get – these are opportunities for you to reflect on your career trajectory and journey in the future, and can contribute to your goal-setting. For example, so you were unsuccessful in getting elected to that governing body – what does that tell you about your own campaigning for the post, your networks, or the priorities of your peers when voting? How in touch with your peers are you? Can you do or learn more in the future, in case you wish to go for this type of role again?

Your skills and insights

In terms of what you can offer the example organisations listed in this chapter, this will vary enormously depending on your field, your experience and ability to communicate. You may be in demand because you have expertise in a very specific area that is wanted/required for an organisation; or because of your wide-ranging experience in various positions and roles; or because you are particularly good at public speaking and engaging audiences. These can broadly speaking be grouped together under 'hard' and 'soft' skills. When it comes to reflecting on what you have to offer, likely you will be engaged in doing so via applications and responses to invitations. But, as always, it pays to be prepared in advance.

Hard skills and soft skills

Hard skills are typically thought of as abilities and skills that are relatively straightforward to measure and quantify, while soft skills are more difficult to identify and appraise. Both hard and soft skills can be learnt, fostered, nurtured and developed, although soft skills cannot be acquired 'by rote' in the same way as hard skills because they require emotional engagement and intelligence. Examples of both skills include:

Table 9.1

Hard skills	Soft skills
Statistical proficiency	Teamwork/collaborative ability
Language ability	Leadership characteristics
Typing/data entry	Empathy
Specialist knowledge/expertise	Time Management

As an early career academic, you are likely to possess a relatively sophisticated combination of both hard and soft skills that will be of interest to organisations and, hopefully, be in demand. But the extent to which you are able to narrate, mould and shape these so that you can participate, contribute, influence and lead will depend on your ability in being able to make these skills transferable. Key to your ability to do so will be your emotional intelligence, which is defined by *Psychology Today* (nd) as:

> . . . the ability to identify and manage your own emotions and the emotions of others. It is generally said to include three skills: emotional awareness; the ability to harness emotions and apply them to tasks like thinking and problem solving; and the ability to manage emotions, which includes regulating your own emotions and cheering up or calming down other people.

Emotional intelligence is a key skill in being able to work effectively with a wide variety of students, colleagues and peers. This is no different when working with organisations and individuals beyond your institution and outside HE, as all will carry with them expectations of charisma, relatability, cordiality, vitality, and so on. Your task as an early career academic is to be able to identify and develop your aptitude for emotional intelligence so that you can effectively translate or even convert your knowledge/skillset into something of use for others. It is, going back to the opening section of this chapter, about *you* developing your ability to make yourself relevant to and for others through your ability to engage, collaborate, and find constructive solutions, influence change and so on – rather than expecting others to do so.

> **Pause for thought**
>
> What are the skills and assets that you might bring to a role in supporting an activity, board, organisation, institution, charity? Are they hard or soft skills? Are there others that you could develop?

There is likely to be training available to you in emotional intelligence (or psychological understandings of work and intelligence, see chapter 10) as part of your institution's support programmes. If not, there are many readily available tools online that can provide more detail on what constitutes emotional intelligence, how to foster and nurture it, and how to utilise it effectively.

Taking a 'wide' view

Overall, taking on varied roles and responsibilities within academic-related organisations and those beyond the academy are all opportunities for expanding your horizons and becoming engaged in what Krznaric (2012) has called 'wide achievement'. Rather than focusing on 'high achievement' within a narrow field, it involves accumulating a range of transferable skills, experiences, assets and insights from working with and within different sectors, organisations, and individuals. It is about developing your leadership skills over the lifetime of your career, finding opportunities for those skills to emerge and evolve at different times. Moreover, you do not need to be a senior academic before you begin to take on these opportunities:

> Learning to be a successful leader . . . isn't the same as learning to drive an automobile, where you use a set of taught techniques. It's finding your own way to lead via some basic attributes: integrity, commitment to the work, knowing and believing in yourself, and the ability

to communicate your enthusiasm and develop good working relationships with other people.

(Holgate, 2012)

> **Pause for thought**
>
> What opportunities exist for wide achievement for you? For your skillset? For your areas of knowledge and experience? What other sectors or organisations would you like to work in?

The benefit of taking a 'wide' approach is that it will expand your horizons and provide you with a greater variety of experiences than participating solely in academic leadership opportunities. Many universities are now enacting 'talent management' programmes to try and identify leadership talent and provide opportunities for skill development, experience and growth. However, these are often limited to the HE sector, which as chapter 1 has shown, has its own particular set of pressures, constraints, issues and challenges. Thus, participating in opportunities beyond university administration and management will enable you to situate HE within the broader context of social, political and economic change, to observe and learn about common pressures and strains, and where HE differs in your location/country and beyond.

Pacing yourself

Taking on such opportunities comes with a caveat – do not take on too much at any one time! As the foreword of this book observes, the autonomy associated with an early career academic post can be seductive for its flexibility and lack of boundaries. Such freedom can be hugely emancipating and allow you to explore openings inside and outside of HE as they arise. But it can also be detrimental in that without due care and attention you can easily overload yourself and find you have very little 'give' in your working week. As chapter 4 noted in terms of the cycle of the academic year and the way in which opportunities in teaching will often (usually) open up again in the future, so too will opportunities for leadership inside and outside of HE. Your task therefore is to determine *when* to take on opportunities, so that you are pacing yourself both in terms of the number of responsibilities and commitments you have at any one time, and the energy you can give them.

> **Tip**
>
> As your academic career 'widens' make sure you always schedule in free time into your diary. Some commitments in your everyday working week will inevitably take longer than planned; urgent requests come from students and colleagues; and invitations to review, participate and engage will arise. Without sufficient 'give' in your schedule you will find yourself working 60-hour weeks, sacrificing much needed recovery time outside of work. While it can be flattering to be in demand when asked to take on some of these 'wider' roles, if you take on too much you will run the risk of exhaustion.
>
> Remember, you need to prioritise and practice self-care (see chapter 2) to ensure that you do not burnout and can sustain a career over many years.

Importantly, do not be afraid to withdraw from roles if you find that you cannot provide the time and intellectual engagement required. It can sometimes be better to step back from activities rather than give them limited time and potentially impact the organisation and in turn your reputation as an academic who does not pull their weight.

In deciding what to take on and when make use of colleagues, mentors and coaches as sounding boards. At the same time, make sure you possess the skills being sought in job vacancies, for passing probation or seeking promotion, and that you are mindful of these when exploring your options so that you can align your activities if needed, and provide appropriate evidence. Taking on additional work should be something that provides fulfilment, enrichment and interest, not serve as a burden on your life.

References

Carrigan, M. (2016) *Social Media for Academics* (London: Sage).
Hoffman, A.J. (2016) 'Reflections: Academia's Emerging Crisis of Relevance and the Consequent Role of the Engaged Scholar', *Journal of Change Management*, 16 (2): 77-96.

Holgate, S.A. (2012) 'Enhance your Career with Leadership Skills', *Science*, 23 March, available online at www.sciencemag.org/careers/2012/03/enhance-your-career-leadership-skills [accessed 01/10/17].

Holmwood, J. (2017) 'Academic Click-Baiting and the Neo-Liberal University', *Discover Society*, 4 October, available online at https://discoversociety.org/2017/10/04/academic-click-baiting-and-the-neo-liberal-university/ [accessed 10/10/17].

Krznaric, R. (2012) *How to Find Fulfilling Work* (London: Macmillan).

Psychology Today (nd) 'Emotional Intelligence', available online at www.psychologytoday.com/basics/emotional-intelligence [accessed 12/10/17].

Further reading

Aschwanden, C. (2007) 'Transferable Skills and Portable Careers', *Science*, 20 April, available online at www.sciencemag.org/careers/features/2007/04/transferable-skills-and-portable-careers [accessed 30/11/17].

Charity Commission for England and Wales (2015) 'The Essential Trustee: What you Need to Know, What you Need to Do', available online at www.gov.uk/government/publications/the-essential-trustee-what-you-need-to-know-cc3/the-essential-trustee-what-you-need-to-know-what-you-need-to-do [accessed 30/11/17].

Daniels, J. and Thistlethwaite, P. (2016) *Becoming a Scholar in the Digital Era: Transforming Scholarly Practice for the Public Good* (Bristol: Policy Press).

Fitch, P. and Van Brunt, B. (2016) *A Guide to Leadership and Management in Higher Education* (Abingdon: Routledge).

Forbes (2007) 'How to Set up an Advisory Board', available online at www.forbes.com/2007/05/02/advisory-board-nfib-ent-mange-cx_mc_0503nextleveladvisory.html#28ded172782e [accessed 11/12/17].

Grint, K. (2010) *Leadership: A Very Short Introduction* (Oxford: Oxford University Press).

Jobs.ac.uk (nd) 'Tips for the Transition from Academia to Industry', available online at www.jobs.ac.uk/careers-advice/working-in-industry/2481/tips-for-the-transition-from-academia-to-industry [accessed 03/12/17].

Northouse, P.G. (2016) *Leadership: Theory and Practice*, 7th edn (London: Sage).

Veletsianos, G. (2015) *Social Media for Academics* (Abingdon: Routledge).

Useful journals

International Journal for Academic Development

Journal of Higher Education Policy and Management

10 Your journey ahead

This final chapter seeks to provide you with the opportunity to reflect on your priorities, enabling you to set yourself achievable and manageable goals. By this point you may or may not have read the rest of this book, and completed the various pause for thought tasks. If you have done so, hopefully you will have built up a picture of what drives you, what type of tasks you want to take on, the impact you want to have now and in the future, and so on. Building on these, this chapter aims to encourage you to consolidate your learning and determine what you want out of an academic career, so that it is fulfilling and satisfying for *you*.

Why you?

As an academic, you will be asked to complete many, many documents for your employers over the years accounting for your hours, for your efforts and the objectives set for you/you set. Often these will be shaped by institutional goals and objectives, and considerations as to priorities and the importance attached to specific tasks will be made according to the HE climate at the time. Given this, the goal in this chapter is to, as much as possible, 'future-proof' your career by establishing your own aims and what you want out of the journey ahead, rather than you being solely reliant on the winds of change to direct your career. Its objective is to get you into the habit of building in reflection points and opportunities, so that as your career evolves you have a clear sense of where you are going, and why.

Taking on extra activities that require reflection, insight and energy may feel onerous and burdensome when you have a million jobs to do. If that is the case try to remember that the reason for doing so is because your academic career is about *your* efforts, *your* goals, *your* ambitions – not just your employer's. It pays to be mindful of where you have come from, where you are going, and where you want to be - and to keep on top of these ambitions as your career unfolds. You are not solely on this earth to respond to the needs, whims and wishes of your employer. Importantly, you need to hold yourself to account, and take ownership for your future, rather than letting it be dictated to you by others - who may or may not have your best interests at heart.

What are your interests and where have they come from?

You have been encouraged throughout this book to think about the origins of your goals, your style of teaching and added authentic 'extra', your approach to research, and your administrative strengths. Bringing all these together, a good place to start this chapter is thinking about your ideal academic role, the balance between the different demands of the role, and where you want to be in 5-10 years' time.

Key to this exercise is removing the rose-tinted spectacles of what a model career might look like based on (potentially outdated) ideals of what it means to be an academic, and addressing the reality of the academic's role and duties, as outlined in this book.

> ### Pause for thought
> - What would be my ideal balance between teaching, research and admin/leadership, now and in the future?
> - Imagining your ideal role in 5-10 years' time, what would your teaching load, research work and admin activities look like? What would the balance look like between teaching, research and admin?
> - What does the promotional criteria for my institution and/or job adverts for the role I am aiming for state regarding teaching experience and teaching activities? What do I need to be taking on/developing at this point in my career?

Once you have established where you want to be in 5-10 years' time, your next objective is to break down your goals to be able to ascertain what it is you need to do to get to that ideal role. When thinking about your own goals, make sure you are thinking beyond the objectives that you may be setting for yourself as part of your employment and/or a formal appraisal process. Your goals are about distinct tasks, such as publishing in a particular journal or working with a particular person, but they are also about the type of academic, and person, *you* want to be. Do you want to:

- Be an academic superstar? Or a good departmental citizen?
- Lead others? Or collaborate within teams?
- Be driven by achievements and success (remembering how 'success' in academic is measured)? Or,
- Prioritise a good work/life balance, accepting the potential career costs that might accompany that balance?

The decisions you make about the type of academic you want to be and the career you want will change as life unfolds and, sometimes, be out of your hands. Sometimes your decisions will involve personal or professional sacrifice and compromise. Having young children may prevent you from travelling the world to international conferences; an intense period of publication or grant writing may mean giving up Sunday league football. When you make those decisions, just remember chapter 2 and the importance of self-care – you cannot expect colleagues or your line manager to be looking out for you, and it is unlikely that anyone is ever going to tell you that you are doing too much. In the academic working environment where there are typically no set working hours, your job description might be quite expansive, and there is always the potential/risk to do more (more writing, more reading, more teaching preparation, more work on that report) and feel accompanying guilt if you do not. Your work-life balance is thus down to you. You need to be your own boss.

A good place to start with breaking down your goals into manageable and discrete tasks is to create a matrix that identifies key areas of activity, and tasks that you could complete to help you get to your goals over a period of time. For example:

Table 10.1

Year	Teaching	Research funding	Publications	External commitments	Leadership
1	Take on a well-established course	Co-applicant on bid(s)	Publication(s) in specialist/generalist journals	Attend international conference in specialist area	Take on minimal admin role
2	Modify the above course following student feedback	Seek funding for and take on lead supervision of a PhD student	Co-edited book on specialist area – establishing leadership in field	Contribute to or take on organisation of specialist group	Take on more substantial admin role
3	Create a new course, new assessment pattern	Principal applicant on bid	Reports written for commerce, policy or third sector	Organise national conference	Seek election to university-wide committees
4	Oversee curriculum development across the degrees	Leading research centre/lab bid	Sole-authored book on specialist area	Join journal editorial board or become journal or book series editor	Lead initiatives, shadow Head of Department

Of course, a career is not mapped out so easily and some of the above tasks may be more straightforward than others. However, having a sense of progression and career development will help you to feel in control of your academic journey and the tasks you want to undertake to help you on your way.

> **Tip**
>
> Make sure you are documenting your work (even if it never sees the light of day), so that you have a record of your efforts, achievements and lessons learned.

Goal reviewing

There are multiple ways of reminding yourself of your goals - which you may find yourself having to endorse and teach to students - such as 'personal development plans'. Certainly, there is an enormous literature available to you regarding methods to set and review your own goals. As food for thought, here are just a few that may be useful to you:

An on-going weekly diary

Every week/month write a brief summary of what you are doing and where you want to be in 12 months' time. As the anniversary comes around, review what you were doing a year ago, and continue adding to that summary - over time you will have a clear picture of what you are doing at any one point, the cycles of the year, and how your goals are evolving over time.

This is a particularly good method for capturing the rhythm of the academic year and how demands fluctuate according to where you are in the cycle. There will be peak times in the academic year when teaching has to be the focus and other commitments have to take a temporary backseat, for example. Using an ongoing diary like this will enable you to effectively identify key pressure points, so you can better plan and utilise your time.

Mind-mapping

Mind-mapping, or brainstorming, your goals is an alternative and attractive visual way of organising your thoughts and ambitions. Such a visual aid can really help you to see how you can be pulled in different directions depending on where you are and where you want to be.

Although most advice regarding mind mapping is future-orientated, a very useful exercise is to explore what you have done and achieved already, and the major hurdles and milestones that you have navigated. Looking backwards like this can help you to understand your motivations, stressors, approaches to career development and so on.

> **Tip**
>
> At the start of your academic career, a mind map may include reflections on:
>
> - Previous qualifications and subjects studied – what motivated you to do these? What guidance did you draw on? Any regrets? Any valuable lessons?
> - Previous work experience – how did you find these jobs? How were you recruited? Why were you recruited? What was the experience like working in that organisation? What were colleagues like? Any major setbacks? Any fantastic experiences? What helped you when you were there?
> - Life changing experiences – have you had any experiences of travelling, birth, bereavement, moving home, separation, health and so on? What were they? How did you feel/do you feel now about them? What did you learn from these experiences? Who did you spend time with?
> - Everyday life – do you have interests and hobbies beyond work? What motivates you to do them? What do you value about them? What annoys you about them?

Mentoring and coaching

Mentioned already in chapter 8, building up a fruitful relationship with a mentor can be an excellent way to set and review your goals. Importantly, a mentoring relationship needs to work for both the mentee and mentor, so make sure to invest the time and energy it takes to establish a good working relationship with someone.

A coach can help you set small, manageable goals in work and beyond, and at the commencement of every coaching session can hold you to account and review your progress on them. With a focus on the immediate term, with the right coach you can work through challenges, issues, successes and reflections to learn, consolidate and develop. It is different to mentoring in that your coach may not have worked in the same sector, and it is usually focused around skills and life holistically, rather than specific questions regarding your career.

> **Pause for thought**
>
> What is your employing institution's policy on mentoring and coaching? Are there any resources allocated or available for a coach external to the institution?

Training and support opportunities

The rule here is simple – take advantage of the training and support open to you! Most institutions have a rolling programme of events for staff development, some of which will be applicable to you, others not. Make the most of them, as you will learn new skills, perspectives and information on, for example, interviewing skills/chairing interview panels; writing press releases; counselling skills; equality legislation; leadership; and so on. Not only could all of these be added to your CV as evidence of learning, they might lead you down new, unexplored (or not even considered) avenues. You might discover a new-found passion for advocating for gender equality in the workplace, or working with a press office, or in providing pastoral support for students.

There may also be specific support open to you with regard to research, such as writing retreats, proposal planning, funding guides; or for teaching, for example in how to achieve professional accreditation, to supervise doctoral students, or to teach large lecture classes. While this plethora of opportunities are open to you, they might not be well advertised or you might be working in an institution where there is a culture of 'waiting until I am required to attend a training course'. Why wait though? Better to be prepared, up-skilled, and primed ready for opportunities – or that next brilliant job – when they arise, so have a look around online, contact HR or an equivalent staff development team, and ask to participate.

Psychological resources

It is likely that your institution offers training and guidance on personality and psychology, and approaches to work. These can be valuable resources to help understand some of the 'softer' skills involved in the academic role, including methods and approaches to organisation and working practices; communication styles; conflict resolution; stress management; and so on. Very well-established personality tests such as Myers Briggs can be useful tools to help you to make sense of your own likes/dislikes, strengths/weaknesses and areas for improvement, and to help you to recognise diversity within the workforce and that not everyone will see the world similarly. Such tools can be particularly useful when you are struggling to communicate with colleagues, or if you find that you have contrasting expectations regarding the importance of evidence, detail, thinking and action.

> **Tip**
>
> Your preference for these types of personality testing will depend very much on you. Do not force yourself to overly engage with these resources if they do not help you make sense of what you observe around you. Correspondingly, if they help you understand yourself and others, then make as much use out of them as possible – remembering that they are always imperfect tools, of course.

Short courses

Both within and outside of your institution there may be courses that you are able to take that can contribute in terms of career development. You may find that you are eligible for a considerable discount for courses run internally, and it is not unheard of for academics to take advantage of their institutional discount to study for an MBA (or parts thereof). You may be required to undertake a teaching qualification early on in your career, and if that is the case then be mindful of what you might want to do with regard to studying for your career development post-certificate. Are there any advanced teaching courses available? Or courses on curriculum design and assessment strategies? Or are you more interested in skills development, for example communication strategies, counselling skills, leadership skills, management techniques and so on?

External sources and opportunities

There may also be external opportunities open to you depending on your field, administrative responsibilities, affiliations, gender and so on. For example, as part of the strategy to empower women in academia there is a highly successful training programme in the UK called Aurora, which may be open to you. Alternatively, The Staff and Educational Development Association (SEDA) provide a range of courses for those interested in education and teaching.

> **Tip**
>
> Find out what short courses or training your institution provides or supports. Are there internal competitions for which members of staff are selected for programmes? Is there funding for going on external courses? Check with your line manager or HR if need be.

Staying up-to-date

When reviewing and revising your goals it is also worth ensuring that you are up-to-date with current and future policy, organisational changes, funding streams, issues in HE and so on. There are many sites available online that provide insight, commentary, and opinion. Some of the best I have come across are:

- Wonkhe.com – a really good opinion and commentary site for the UK.
- jobs.ac.uk – arguably the best website for UK academic vacancies, it also has a good section on career advice.
- vitae.ac.uk – has some great advice for UK-based researchers.
- Researchprofessional.com – provides updates on international policy and practice news.
- timeshighereducation.com – UK equivalent to the US-based Chronicle of Higher Education, providing insight, news and opinion.

- Insidehighered.com – US-based source of opinion, commentary policy and practice, includes international issues.
- The Guardian – a UK newspaper and online news source, that provides a decent commentary on UK-based HE matters.

Ultimately, it is up to you how much you engage with the resources available, how much you reflect and review, and how you balance these activities alongside the commitments for which you are being evaluated/measured as part of your employment. One thing is for sure though, you are working in a well-established sector that employs a lot of people, is highly political (and politicised) and has ingrained expectations regarding employment rights and opportunities. Make the best of working in such a sector, where training is provided and there are multiple media outlets specifically focused on the sector.

> **Tip**
>
> Take the time to find useful and supportive resources through searching online, asking colleagues and via your staff development team. Find the ones that resonate with you and sign up for newsletters or briefings, to make sure that you are up-to-date with opportunities and discussion.
>
> And, periodically, if you find yourself deleting the newsletters and briefings because they are not relevant, then make sure you unsubscribe – there are enough pressures within your working life without additional emails adding to them.

Keeping a record

In the league table culture of HE (outlined in chapter 1), success is often measured across an institution via admissions, progression, graduation, grades and so on. This evaluation of the quality of the institution will happen with or without your participation – so make sure that you are documenting your activities so that you have an accurate account of what you have been doing – whether or not this results in 'success' that your institution can identify, claim and measure.

Certainly, as you move forward in your career you will inevitably struggle to recall the early years beyond a memory of hard work, long working days and weeks of stress. I remember on many occasions telling colleagues I felt like a duck, calm on the surface but paddling madly under the water to keep going. I hope that your early career is not as frantic nor as draining, but there is no getting away from the need for the energy required in building momentum in your research, nor the animation needed to walk into a classroom with enthusiasm and passion, nor the focus needed to work through and create the administrative paperwork that can accompany the operation of an academic department.

While you work on these everyday tasks, make sure that you keep a record of what you are doing. This is beyond the workload models that set out courses taught, funded research and PhD students supervised; this is also about keeping a record of unsuccessful bids, of papers that are submitted but then rejected, of the number of undergraduate dissertation students you successfully supervise. It is all the things that do not get recorded on workload models but make up your working day, and it is the things that (1) you will learn from and (2) will be asked to reflect on in appraisals and future job interviews.

The idea here is simple: if you have successfully piloted an initiative in your department, record it. If you have submitted a paper that was rejected (while you are hopefully working on it for a different journal), record it. If you've reviewed a paper for a journal, record it. If you supported a colleague through their probation via informal mentoring, record it. Basically, make sure you build a picture of the tasks you have completed, so that you can review and account for your time, periodically take stock, and, most importantly, learn from your experiences.

Author reflection

It's pretty basic, but I keep a document for every year called 'Stuff I've Done'. I periodically update it with (usually very rushed) notes about things I have organised, contributed to, tried and so on. Things included on it are, for example, reviewing for journals and research funders, PhD transfer panels, supervising postgraduate students and working with the Students' Union sabbatical student officers on projects.

These working documents contain more detail than my CV (which I also periodically update, regardless of whether I'm job hunting or not) and means that I have a running record of most of things I have done over the last few years. I've had to call on it many times to complete documents about workloads, achievements and the like.

Part of a keeping a record of your own activities is to ensure that you have accurate information to hand, and so that you can be your own cheerleader. In the competitive and increasingly insecure environment of academia, it is vital that you continuously collate evidence of your successes and achievements, both for yourself and to evidence your abilities should you need to, or want to, apply for positions elsewhere. It is not rocket science, but there are a couple of ways to ensure that you mark achievements (whether these be ones that are officially 'recognised' by your institution, or count as a success to you personally).

Celebrating accomplishments

Get into the habit of revelling in both your minor and major successes. It can be very easy to dismiss, overlook or forget an achievement, particularly those that might not make it onto your CV (nomination for an award, election to a committee, an excellent student evaluation). So, early on in your career, make sure you do something to mark such moments so that (1) you are helping buoy yourself up and (2) you are keeping a record of all the things, however small or seemingly insignificant, in which you have succeeded.

Keeping plaudits

Over the years you will receive masses of feedback and evaluation of your work, be it in teaching or research or administration and leadership. The fixation with evaluation is endemic within HE. Within all this you will have moments of disheartenment, but also moments of great joy, fulfilment and satisfaction. Make sure you keep a record of those better moments!

> **Tip**
>
> When you receive an email containing a compliment, acknowledgement of achievement, or similarly positive affirmations, save it! A senior colleague once told me how they had an inbox folder called 'plaudits' and they would save emails to that. I do similarly now – it is nice to know they are there, and they can be drawn upon as qualitative evidence of your successes, recognition and societal contribution.

Some principles to live by

Bringing together some of the key sentiments and strands within this book, what follows in this final section are some suggestions for sustaining your academic career as it progresses. Not all will resonate with you, and not all will work for you. They are, however, a selection of principles that are intended to provide you with the tools that will enable you to have a successful, fulfilling and emotionally satisfying career in HE.

Slow down

The pace of the academic year and planning for the following year means that at many points you are likely to find yourself on a treadmill where outputs are scrutinised, evaluated and work prioritised accordingly. As I write, there is discussion of another REF-readiness exercise in my own institution, where research outputs will be selected, evaluated and feedback given on where improvements are needed. At the same time, there is discussion of the re-structuring of degrees. It is all 'go'.

Such a constant state of evaluation, refinement and improvement, be it in research or teaching, means that you can find yourself in the position of facing relentless pressure on your time. Arguably a result of the corporatisation of universities, Berg and Seeber (2016) advocate for a deliberate, mindful and conscious 'slowing down' of academia to allow curiosity and intellectual endeavours to flourish. They note, "The push towards the easily quantifiable and marketable rushes into 'findings,' and is at odds with the spirit of open inquiry and social critique' (p. 14). At the heart of their call in *The Slow Professor* is the potential to be found in resisting the pervasive time pressures placed on academics owing to the corporate imperatives that have become embedded within university management, and the benefits to be derived from slowing down and engaging with research, teaching, collaboration and risk-taking. At the outset of your academic career this may appear a foolhardy approach given the pressures you may face to secure a post, but it certainly pays to be mindful of the need to pace yourself to avoid burnout, and the long-term sustainability of the relentless pursuit of productivity.

Prioritise

One of the best ways to manage the never-ending time pressures and being pulled in many different directions is to refine and develop your ability to prioritise. This is about becoming your best advocate, so that you can make informed decisions about when to take up opportunities and when to let them pass by (and how to negotiate both ways!). There are many ways to hone your prioritising skills, not least making use of a mentor or colleague as a sounding board, discussing workload with your line manager, and planning ahead – all of which have been detailed in this book. There is no magic wand when it comes to prioritising however, and it is your own first-hand experience that will help you determine how you do it best.

What you do need to be mindful of when determining the relative significance, worth and importance of (what appear to be) pressing tasks is that an ongoing pressure to produce, perform and respond is difficult, if not impossible, to sustain for most people (Berg and Seeber, 2016). If you are in an overloaded period of work then you need to make sure you have built in recovery time to follow.

Be your own best advocate

As noted above, you need to get into the habit of being your own best advocate – that is, to act in your own best interests when it comes to managing your commitments inside and outside of work. Acting in such a way is not about being self-interested nor lacking collegiality, rather it is about taking responsibility for your career and its development and life outside of work, so that you do not burnout from overwork, exhaustion and stress. Taking such responsibility can be empowering in that you have a sense of control over your own destiny, rather than being subject to the tides of change that will inevitably surround you.

Author reflection

I recently had one of these empowering moments when I was asked by an organisation to write a commentary on a news piece. I said yes but then afterwards realised that it coincided with the start of the new teaching semester and I did not have the time nor the 'brain space' to engage with the topic. Rather than struggle on and churn out something half-heartedly that may have not accurately reflected my thinking or writing ability, and putting aside my own fear of letting

> others down, I went back to the organisation to say that on reflection I was unable to take on the piece of work at this time, and suggested another colleague who might instead be able to take it on. It was a leap of faith on my part as I have always tried to honour my commitments, but it was also liberating and a relief – it was one less task to think about. And I was very pleased to receive an understanding response in return. I will remember that sense of relief in future when I determine whether or not to take on a task!

Be authentic, find fulfilment

Do not try to pretend to be something you are not. Imposter syndrome was discussed in chapter 3, and in terms of a principle to live by – do not turn yourself into an actual impostor! If you are not a passionate champion for a particular cause, do not pretend you to be; if you are interested in having an influence over HE, do not pretend that you do not care. Over time the disconnection between your motivations and actions will become apparent to others as you struggle to maintain the façade (see chapter 9). As noted in chapter 7, take the time to reflect on what motivated you to join academia in the first place, own that motivation, and live by it.

What is more try to seek activities and goals that align with those motivations. As Reed (2017) notes, the most productive researchers are those that feel the most fulfilled; and the most fulfilled are those whose motivations and activities are aligned. As your career grows, Reed argues, make sure you have a clear sense of who you are and where you want to go – this will keep your drive, curiosity and personal ambition alive.

Aim for good enough

There are important moments in your early career when you need to aim high and produce your 'best' work. For most of the time however, producing work that is *good enough* in your given circumstances is usually sufficient (Reed, 2017). This may mean less time spent agonising over a paper or report on student numbers; it may mean less time spent on lecture preparation (which Huston, 2012, does not believe is a bad thing, see chapter 3). It may also mean being less precious about your time – you are unlikely to get many commitment-free days that give you the space and time to (for example) write, so do not expend time and energy waiting for those days to emerge. You either create them, or you build writing into your everyday practices and you learn to write in chunks of time. Setting lower expectations of yourself will not be known or perceptible to anyone else, but the pay-off for you and the relinquishment of the internal pressure you place yourself under will be immense. This also involves, as discussed in chapter 5, letting go – of your work, your ideas, and your possession over your outputs, be they in research, teaching or administration and management. You are but one cog in an enormous HE machine, and even if you one day win the Nobel Prize, that will not have come without accepting that not everything you produce is earth shattering.

Sustain a sense of self

It is important that in an environment and working culture where "the notion of students as customers combined with greater reliance on technology has led to the increased blurring of work and life" (Berg and Seeber, 2016: 7) you have a clear distinction between yourself as an academic and your life outside of your academic identity.

The importance of this is to ensure that your self-esteem and sense of worth is not completely tied to your academic achievements which, as this book has shown, can be buffeted and shaped by all sorts of social, economic and political whims, changes and impetuses.

> **Author reflection**
>
> I say this from experience as early in my career my sense of achievement was often tied into my academic employment and the measures with which academic success is measured. Now into my 'mid-career' phase, I am ever more mindful of ensuring that my sense of identity and worth comes from more than just my academic outputs.

Take risks where you can: nurture curiosity

I noted in chapter 1 that academics are becoming increasingly risk averse in the current climate of job insecurity and the dominance of league table measurements as indicators of success. But a career without risk may be one that is incredibly dull, leading to stagnation, inertia and detachment. It may lead to what Back (2016) describes as "intellectual mortification" where:

> On the one hand, it is important to do things that are going to help young researchers make that transition into their first academic jobs. At the same time, they have to keep their intellectual passions alive and curiosities awake.
>
> (Back, 2016, p. 174)

Thus, it pays to take risks where you feasibly can to sustain your curiosities, as long as those risks are well informed and in keeping with your own values and beliefs (that is, you are being authentic to yourself). Such risks push you to act outside of your comfort zone, and may or may not pay off in terms of the benefit you receive in return. They may include writing for varied audiences, making presentations to organisations, working with particular colleagues, engaging with different publics and so on – all of which may come to nothing, or instead be a turning point in your career. As noted in chapter 6, the most productive and satisfied colleagues I have worked with have not been focused on the net benefit for themselves when taking risks; rather they have entered into activities with a generosity of spirit and reciprocity that has enabled them to ride waves of stress, pressure and disappointment, and to focus on their potential.

> **Author reflection**
>
> Writing this book has been a risk for me. It has taken time away from other duties and commitments, and is unlikely to contribute to any institutional measurements regarding teaching or research outputs. At varying times it has been both enjoyable and difficult to write owing to my own fluctuating enchantment/disillusionment with HE, but the vast majority of the time it has been a very cathartic experience to get these words on paper and to feel that, in some small way, I might support someone else's academic career by provoking ideas and actions, or even just a sense of solidarity. It is a risk that has been worth taking.

Find kindred spirits

As detailed in chapter 7, there are a multitude of reasons for which individuals enter academia, and you cannot assume that what drives you drives other people. Whether or not you share beliefs, values and aspirations with colleagues, you will certainly benefit from building good working relationships with kindred spirits – that is, those people who you feel comfortable having a coffee with and discussing the latest developments in the department, or across the university, or even across the sector. They will assist you with rationalising developments and changes around you, hopefully providing an alternative perspective in times of need and, if you have a tendency to ruminate, help you to disengage from your inner monologue long enough to see that there are different ways to view problems. Nurture those relationships with kindred spirits, they are worth it.

Manage your attitude and approach to stress and change

An entry-level academic post can be a very stressful position to be in as you have little currency with which to negotiate; you have yet to build up your repositories and legacies of teaching materials, publishing successes, grant income and so on. However, compared to many other professions it is clearly structured, with a multitude of opportunities for career development and career enhancement. It is therefore down to you how much you engage with those opportunities, and the extent to which you embrace stressors as challenges to be learnt from, rather than barriers and burdens to be tolerated. As Grant with Sherrington (2006) note, there has been much airtime given to the issues of pressure and stress within academia. However, they also recognise that a little stress is not necessarily a bad thing:

> Stress can have its positive aspects. A life that was entirely free of stress might also be free of any stimulating challenges. Enervation is not a desirable outcome. Some of the most stressful jobs are those that are repetitive and monotonous and often badly paid. Young academics today face more pressures than earlier generations, but they also receive more systematic support and training to prepare them for those challenges, whether it takes the form of teaching

certificates, mentoring, short courses or induction training. It was not so long ago that being an academic was a craft where you learnt norms and skills from an older generation, with much dependent on the talents of your mentor in conveying to you what the craft entailed . . . The academic profession today is more systematically organized, so that less is open to chance and, in principle at least, it should be more open to diversity.

(Grant with Sherrington, 2006: 184)

In other words, periodic stress is ok, as long as it does not turn into chronic stress, fatigue, and burnout. The challenge is recognising signs of overload in yourself and finding the energy to act on these, rather than sink beneath them.

View it as a long game

As you embark on your academic journey make it a conscious habit to embrace challenges, note their impact, learn, and move on. This is particularly important given the number of setbacks you will likely encounter as you progress, and their potential for disillusionment and disenchantment. Not getting shortlisted or promoted, having papers and research bids rejected, receiving negative student feedback, and getting turned down for opportunities can all take their toll on your well-being. Make it part of your job to foster your resilience and robustness in the face of these potential knock-backs, revel in your achievements, and enjoy the journey. An academic career is a long game with relatively few moments of instant gratification. Nurture yourself, your sense of curiosity and your sense of fulfilment to ensure that you can keep going until the rewards and achievements come your way.

> **Tip**
>
> Keep any notes you have generated while reading this book and commit to reviewing them in a year's time. Will they still resonate with you then? How will your perspective and priorities have evolved over 12 months?

This is your life

I have thoroughly enjoyed writing this book, and I hope that you have found it useful. My final point is that, above all else (and something that I hope this book has endorsed throughout), remember that this is *your* life. Your employment certainly matters – after all, you have a responsibility towards the institution paying your salary and have committed to exchanging your labour for financial recompense. Such is the nature of capitalism. However, in the early phase of your career try hard to remember that:

1. Everything is leading to something else – you just might not know it yet.
2. There is always opportunity to learn. Indeed, it is highly likely that you will receive many rejections in your early career: for jobs, for bids, for papers, by students. The key is to regard these as learning opportunities, acquire experiential knowledge from them and apply that newly acquired first-hand knowledge in the future. They are life lessons.
3. You only live once. This is not to say act recklessly or hedonistically, but you need to think carefully about academic commitments and priorities, to ensure that you can continue in a sustainable way and not burn out.
4. Enjoy the journey. Easier said than done, but with mechanisms in place to reflect, consolidate, support and be supported, you are at least in a stronger position to weather the storms along the way.

Good luck!

References

Back, L. (2016) *Academic Diary: Or Why Higher Education Still Matters* (London: Goldsmiths Press).
Berg, M. and Seeber, B.K. (2016) *The Slow Professor: Challenging the Culture of Speed in the Academy* (Toronto: University of Toronto Press).
Grant, W. with Sherrington, P. (2006) *Managing your Academic Career* (Basingstoke: Palgrave Macmillan).
Huston, T. (2012) *Teaching What You Don't Know* (Cambridge, MA: Harvard University Press).
Reed, M.S. (2017) *The Productive Researcher* (Kinnoir: Fast Track Impact).

Further reading

Gawande, A. (2011) *The Checklist Manifesto: How to Get Things Right* (London: Profile).

Haviland, D., Ortiz, A.M. and Henriques, L. (2017) *Shaping your Career: A Guide for Early Career Faculty* (Sterling, VA: Stylus Publishing).

Hay, I. (2017) *How to be an Academic Superhero: Establishing and Sustaining a Successful Career in the Social Sciences, Arts and Humanities* (Cheltenham: Edward Elgar Publishing).

Hume, K. (2010) *Surviving your Academic Job Hunt: Advice for Humanities PhDs* (Basingstoke: Palgrave Macmillan).

Kelsky, K. (2015) *The Professor Is In: The Essential Guide to Turning Your PhD Into a Job* (London: Three Rivers Press).

McAlpine, L. and Amundsen, C. (2016) *Post-PhD Career: intentions, Decision-making and Life Aspirations* (Basingstoke: Palgrave Pivot).

Wright, G. (2017) *Academia Obscura: The Hidden Silly Side of Higher Education* (London: Unbound).

Useful journals

Compass: Journal of Learning and Teaching

Higher Education Quarterly

Higher Education Review

International Journal for Academic Development

Studies of Higher Education

Index

Academic news sources 95, 221
Accomplishments 224
Administration 183
Advisory Boards 204
Advocacy 226
Appraisals 101, 142, 143, 195
Authenticity 227
Autonomy
    Individual 85, 86, 182, 187, 210
    Institutional 4, 180

Boundaries 33, 44, 45, 102, 181, 210
Bureaucracy 13, 14, 85
Burnout 48, 63, 211, 226

Champions 191
Coaching 89, 218
Collaboration 64, 84, 136, 137
Collegiality 7, 82, 83, 99, 102, 103, 136
Commercialism 4, 5, 9, 16, 17, 32, 81
Committees 188
Conferences 151
Confidence 72, 90
Consultancy 169
Continuing Professional Development
    76, 191
Corporatisation 5
Credibility 90, 91, 114

Deep Learning 31, 65
Demand Management 140
Diaries 217
Disability 55
Distance learning 61
Documentation 101, 110, 207, 217,
    222

Email 34, 35, 45, 103, 167
Emotional intelligence 208
Epistemology 116, 117, 118
Ethnicity 90
Evaluation 7, 81, 82
Expertise 38, 64
External examining 93

Family 14
Fellowships 205
Fixed term contracts 15, 16
Flow 161, 207
Further Education 53

Gender 14, 90
Goals 20, 21, 111, 139, 207, 214, 216
Google Scholar 113
Governance 179, 189
Governing Boards 202
Guilt 35

H Index 113
Hot topics 12, 17, 112

Identity
　Academic 12, 15, 39, 111, 171, 215
　Disciplinary 114, 115, 116, 118, 119
　Institutions 9, 193
Impact 16, 160
Imposter Syndrome 66, 67, 68
Indicators 6, 183
Influence 188
Instrumentalism 5, 6, 139, 164
International Students 56, 57, 58

Job Security 15
Journal editing 152, 153
Journal citation rates 125
Journal impact factor 125

Kindred Spirits 117, 151, 230
Knowledge mobilisation 159, 164
Knowledge transfer 159

Leadership 178, 183, 198, 201, 204
League Tables 6, 8
Letting go 119

Market failure 3
Marketisation 2, 9
Mature students 52, 53, 54
Mentoring 46, 190, 218
Metricsation 6, 7, 125
Mind Mapping 217
Mistakes 73, 163
Motivations 161

Neoliberalism 2, 11
Negotiation 100, 101, 102, 103, 104
Networks 139, 141, 150, 166, 206
New Millennials 27, 28

Ontology 116
Open Access
　Learning 62
　Publishing 126

Pacing yourself 210
Part time students 52, 54
Performance management 11, 15
Personal tutoring 44
PhD students and supervision 113, 144, 149
Plaudits 224
Postgraduate 61
Pressure 123
Prioritising 195, 226
Probation 14, 75, 79, 110, 132, 184
Productivity 112, 113
Professional associations 77, 78, 93, 202, 221
Professional services 180
Promotion 14, 214
Psychological resources 220
Public Engagement 164
Publishing 74, 123, 127, 128, 130
Publishers 126

Quantification 6, 7, 9, 11, 12, 32, 40, 82, 83, 84, 113

Rejection 131, 132, 133, 134
Relevance 198, 199, 200, 201
Research Excellence Framework 123, 124
Research funding 39, 140, 141, 142
Research projects 138
Resilience 132, 192
Reviewing
　Books 129
　Journal papers 152
　Textbook proposals 95

Risk 7, 84, 100, 101, 137, 165, 228, 229
Royal Societies 205

Sabbaticals 154
Schools 16, 32, 37, 42
Secondments 155
Self-care 47, 48
Skillset 46, 47, 178, 207, 208
Slowing down 225
Social Media 168
Specialisms 7, 62, 63, 64, 68, 69, 121, 122
Speed 29
Stock answers 72, 73
Stress 230
Student
 Consumers 2, 3, 35, 36, 43
 Evaluations 86, 87, 88, 89, 90
 Expectations 34, 65, 66
 Support 58, 59
Students' Unions 203

Teaching Excellence Framework 83, 84, 92
Teaching
 Observations 75, 83
 Repository 70, 71
 Qualification 92
Team teaching 74
Time management 69, 211
Training 219
Trustee 205

Value
 Disciplinary 16, 17
 For money 5, 11, 32, 36, 81
Visibility 186, 187

Webinars 168
Wide achievement 209
Workload 69, 96, 97, 98, 99, 102, 103

Zero hour contracts 15, 16